EMU
Explained

REUTERS 🌐

EMU
Explained

Markets and Monetary Union

EDITED BY

RUTH PITCHFORD *&* ADAM COX

**KOGAN
PAGE**

First published in 1997
Reprinted 1997 (twice)

Kogan Page Limited
120 Pentonville Road
London N1 9JN

© Reuters Limited, 1997

British Library Cataloguing in Publication Data
A CIP record for this book is available from the British Library.
ISBN 0 7494 2377 3

Typeset by Saxon Graphics Ltd, Derby
Printed in England by Clays Ltd, St Ives plc

Contents

Foreword

by Andre Villeneuve, Executive Director, Reuters

Will European Economic and Monetary Union happen? Who will participate? How will monetary union impact the financial markets?

These questions have been the theme of an internal study by Reuters for nearly two years. Like many other aspects of EMU, these subjects have lacked open, objective debate. This book is an attempt to synthesise a broad cross-section of expert views, pulled together by some of our 1800 journalists.

It is a common error to view EMU as a purely European matter. Many in the U.S. started by ignoring developments, slowly yielding to a scepticism that EMU could actually work. These experts argued that monetary union based on the U.S. dollar took many years to evolve, and is supported by labour mobility and fiscal transfer mechanisms that are hardly developed in Europe. Since the Madrid Summit of European Union leaders in 1995, many U.S. observers have come to believe that EMU will happen anyway.

Reuters has tried to identify some of the threats and opportunities of EMU as regards the development of the financial markets, particularly in Europe. Unsurprisingly, most observers have highlighted the potential threats to the foreign exchange markets. Will the loss of trades between EMU currencies be totally replaced by trading in other mature or developing country currencies? Maybe not. Maybe factors other than EMU itself have been driving consolidation in foreign exchange trading. But EMU might present significant opportunities as a catalyst for the European equities and fixed income markets, which have a long way to go to match their U.S. counterparts.

In theory, denomination of many instruments in a common currency should provide good growth prospects for debt markets. The European government bond market is comparable in size to the U.S. market. Some Europeans have long envied the seignorage which the U.S. Treasury market has gained because of its depth and liquidity. Will the European sovereign debt markets seriously challenge the U.S. or Japanese sovereign debt markets? Will an active corporate bond market develop? Will we see active trading in mortgage-backed securities? Will municipal or regional borrowers find it easier to fund their debt?

Even if these developments eventually come about, we have tried to explore some of the barriers. How critical is the power and credibility of the U.S. Treasury to the U.S. sovereign debt market, and will EMU develop an equivalent? The U.S. is blessed with eight government sponsored enterprises such as Fannie Mae and Freddy Mac which play a significant role in the credit markets. Does Europe require such agencies? Will European central banks be able to coordinate sovereign debt issue size and timing along the benchmark yield curve?

Are foreign exchange reserves held by central banks in U.S. dollars likely to be transferred to euros, and will this threaten the dollar? Or will the euro take several years to establish its credibility, particularly in Asia where dollar holdings are so significant and growing? Certainly, Asian observers feel that the European institutions concerned with the EMU have done little to project EMU in Asia, or anywhere outside Europe.

Will an Asian market develop in euros? After all, Asian domestic bond markets are relatively narrow. A credible EMU might attract Asian investors as an alternative to the U.S. dollar or their often limited domestic markets. If investors are interested, why not borrowers? Why only Asia, and not other areas outside the union?

We have tried to explore which of the European financial centres might be winners or losers from EMU and its associated trends. As the markets become increasingly virtual, it is harder to see how geographical location matters for several types of activity. However, there is a strong belief that competitive barriers to cosy domestic franchises are breaking down, and a trend to centralise certain types of trading activity. At the same time the increasing emphasis on credit research and the need to sell ever more complex and tailored solutions to institutional clients with different needs may put a premium on local presence for certain activities. Pension fund reform alone provides substantial local opportunities in all European financial centres.

Some have attributed great importance to settlement system access by countries outside the EMU. We have explored the issues surrounding the debate over TARGET, the cross-border settlement system for the euro.

There is some disagreement as to whether access to TARGET can be defined as an essential matter of monetary policy or merely protectionism. However, many observers agree that any form of artificial protectionism tends to rebound on the countries imposing such protection, and favour more liberal financial environments.

Even as recently as one year ago it was difficult to get serious market input on financial market trends resulting from EMU. Now it is hard to find a financial institution of any significance which is not actively planning its trading operations on the assumption that EMU is likely to happen, on time and with at least a core group of six to eight countries.

Of course EMU is only one of many events that are impacting the organisation of financial markets. Others include technological change, consolidation in banking, the role of emerging markets. We have included a section on the impact of EMU on technology, which coincides uncomfortably with the millennium challenge. In the longer run, many believe the major shift in pension fund reform and general approach to public funding is likely to prove a much more powerful booster to the financial services industry than EMU itself.

We hope the reader will find some enlightenment on these and other EMU issues. We at Reuters have substantially boosted our news coverage of EMU matters. We have also started a series of regular polls to track market feedback on key EMU issues.

We are proud to be able to include contributions from Wim Duisenberg, president elect of the European Monetary Institute and governor of the Dutch central bank, and Christopher Taylor, one of the leading academics in the field.

Preface

by Dr W.F. Duisenberg

Within two years from now, on 1 January 1999, Economic and Monetary Union will be a fact. Early in 1998 the European Council will have decided which member states will qualify to participate in the monetary union right from the start and which will be joining at a later stage. As regards the preparation of EMU, the conceptual phase appears to have been concluded in most areas. Now the emphasis is shifting to the technical preparations, which sometimes have long lead times. In most member states preparations for EMU are well underway. In my opinion, the publication of this book is an example of excellent timing.

At this moment member states are making strong efforts, notably in the sphere of public finances, to meet the convergence criteria on time. However, the criteria should not only be met on time, but also – and this is the essence of monetary union – on a lasting basis. The assessment in early 1998 of which member states fulfil the necessary conditions for the adoption of a single currency should therefore incorporate an explicit judgement on the sustainability of the convergence achieved by the potential candidates for entering monetary union.

In this context a crucial role will be played by the stability pact, which aims to ensure that fiscal discipline will be maintained also after the start of EMU. The pact, while binding on all member states, differs in terms of the obligations it imposes on EMU member states on the one hand and on countries which do not participate in EMU on the other hand. Apart from a European Council resolution, the stability pact will consist of two regulations, which specify and expand on existing treaty provisions. The purpose of the resolution is to reflect the strong political commitment of the European Commission, the Council and the member states to a strict adherence of the pact and a timely application of the provisions which seek to ensure such adherence. Under the first regulation, member states of the euro area will be obliged to submit stability programmes. In these programmes medium-term, cyclically adjusted fiscal targets are set out. The cyclically adjusted target should be set at 'close to balance' or even at a small surplus, depending on the amplitude of the cyclical fluctuation of the country. This policy allows for the operation of automatic stabilizers, so that even in times of a cyclical downturn the upper limit will not be exceeded. The pact will provide for an important benchmark for the financial markets, which will certainly have a disciplinary effect on national budgetary policies. Non-euro member states will continue to submit similar plans, so-called convergence programmes, in which their policies are described, which should make participation in EMU possible.

The second regulation of the stability pact concerns the sanction mechanism of the excessive deficit procedure. The application of this mechanism, which only applies to the countries participating in the euro zone, will be clarified and expedited in such a way as to act as a real deterrent.

Of course, monetary stability in Europe and the working of the internal market may not be thwarted by exchange rate fluctuations between the euro zone and other EU currencies. For this reason, the European Council decided last year that the present ERM was to be replaced by a new exchange rate mechanism as from the start of EMU. The European Council in Amsterdam will adopt a resolution setting out the details of the new ERM. The new ERM will help those countries which will not join EMU right from the start to orient their policies towards convergence, in order to enable them to qualify for participation in the monetary union as soon as possible.

The changeover to the single currency has important legal aspects which have to be solved in advance for a smooth transition. Business and individuals must be sure that the introduction of the euro will not bring unexpected and unpleasant litigation. Based on interim consultations of the financial markets, substantial progress has been reached with regard to the legal framework for the euro. Certainty about the legal issues, such as the continuity of contracts, is one of the preconditions for a credible start of EMU.

On 1 January 1999, the exchange rates of the currencies of the participating countries will be irrevocably locked. From that same date, the European System of Central Banks (ESCB) will conduct its single monetary and exchange rate policy in euros. The use of the euro on the financial markets will be further stimulated by the governments of all participating member states, which will issue their new loans in euro. In 1995 sovereign issues accounted for roughly half of all the domestic bond issues. It may be assumed that governments are being followed by other major financial market players, banks and internationally operating companies in particular. Smaller enterprises and consumers will probably need some time before they are ready to undertake non-cash transactions in euro. It may be expected that such non-cash use of the euro in the retail sector will not really get off the ground before 2002, when euro banknotes and coins will be introduced. At most six months later, on 1 July 2002, the national currencies of all EMU countries will have been replaced in full by the euro.

A stable euro is likely to play a more dominant role in international trade. This will for instance hold for trade between the EU and the Central and Eastern European countries, which at this moment is usually settled in U.S. dollars. The more important the role of the euro in international trade, the more attractive it will also become as a reserve currency.

Let me finish my contribution to this book by expressing my confidence in the process towards European monetary integration. As far as the stability of EMU and of the euro is concerned, all necessary conditions will be met. An adequate application of the convergence criteria, together with the institutional safeguards embodied in the Maastricht Treaty, as well as the stability pact and the new exchange rate mechanism, will also guarantee sustained economic convergence after 1 January 1999.

December 1996

Acknowledgements

This book is the work of many Reuters correspondents, some bylined here, others not. Particular thanks are due to Sandy Critchley, now at Reuters Financial Television and former in-house EMU expert, for sharing her insights into the issues confronting financial markets. Henry Engler in Brussels provided valuable advice. We have also drawn on the expertise of Reuters Graphics Editor Corrie Parsonson and on that of Reuters Polling Unit. The London Treasury Desk, notably Rory Channing, Geoff Cornford, Mariam Isa and Adam Jasser, helped to commission and field the contributions. The chief correspondents of many Reuters bureaux made the time for their staff to write for the book. Above all, thanks are due to the central bankers, government ministers, officials, independent researchers and market professionals who have helped us to explain EMU through the series of interviews conducted in autumn 1996 on which this book is based.

Introduction: the economics and politics of EMU

Christopher Taylor, Visiting Fellow at the National Institute of Economic and Social Research, London

THE CONCEPTS, OBJECTIVES AND RISKS BEHIND EMU

The European Union is committed to forming an economic and monetary union (EMU) by around the end of the century. A monetary union is a group of countries or regions that use the same money, so the crucial step will be the permanent locking of exchange rates between EU currencies. But exchange rates will not remain fixed for long if there are persistent differences in the underlying monetary policies. Thus EMU will also require the merging of national monetary authorities. If this is done, and if the financial markets believe the arrangements to be permanent, the locked currencies will become perfectly interchangeable, and interest rates on similar financial assets will be uniform throughout the monetary union, even if separate national currency denominations continue to exist.

On some views, most of the benefits of monetary union could be achieved by the twin steps of locking exchange rates and merging monetary policies. But the European union intends to go further and replace national moneys by a single currency by the year 2002. This is partly in order to add credibility to the arrangements, by making them harder to reverse; partly to secure additional economic benefits; and partly because of its political significance.

It is less clear what economic union should entail. A loose economic union could be said to exist among a group of countries if there are no formal barriers to trade or payments between them, or to movements of labour and capital. But some views of economic union would go further, to include centralisation or harmonisation of all economic policies, especially fiscal policy and labour market regulation. These remain controversial issues in Europe. However, monetary union would not make much sense, and could hardly be sustained, without a single market in goods, services and capital, including especially financial capital. It was the agreement under the Single European Act of 1986 to complete the Community's internal market by removing the remaining barriers to trade in services and capital movements, and the subsequent legislative progress, that provided the opportunity for, and spur to, early monetary union.

Political motivations

There has never been any doubt that the main motivation behind EMU is political, and cannot be understood without some appreciation of European history and politics. The basic contention is that economic integration will promote political integration in Europe, so monetary union is seen as highly desirable by those who want Europe to become more closely integrated politically. Moreover monetary union has a special significance for them, in that money is widely acknowledged to be a powerful symbol of political unity. Hence their keen political interest in a single currency as a feature of EMU.

On a continent that has been ravaged by two major wars in this century, not to mention the recurrent conflicts of preceding ones, it is understandable that political integration has become, for many countries, a paramount objective. Among Germany's western neighbours, there is a powerful wish to integrate that country securely into the polity of western Europe by strengthening economic links in a way that would make hostilities difficult if not impossible. In France particularly, there is an additional ambition to raise Europe's political status to that of a global superpower by consolidating its economic strength, analogously with the U.S.; and other EU states probably share this vision, if to lesser degrees. The political logic of economic integration is also strong among most small EU states, many of which have collective security as a special goal. Germany's political interest in EMU is less easy to understand without reference to political morality. For many senior German politicians, the need for Germany to be securely anchored at the centre of a westward-oriented Europe into which it can contentedly settle, abandoning its historical eastward ambitions, has become a moral imperative since reunification.

But the drive to EMU is not simply a matter of power politics; it also reflects 'political economy' objectives. Thus, many of Germany's smaller neighbours dislike having their monetary policy effectively decided by the Bundesbank. Yet in the present situation they believe they have little alternative, because their economies are extensively integrated with Germany's through trade, and the trading advantages of the mark link are hard to resist. The penalty is that they have to follow movements in mark interest rates without question, which can be painful at times. So an arrangement offering a voice alongside the Bundesbank in monetary policy for the mark zone (as EMU would) has strong attractions for them. France shares a similar motivation, now that the 'franc fort' has become the accepted focus of monetary policy there.

For Germany, there can be no such motivation; indeed the prospect of losing control of the currency which is widely seen as Europe's most successful since the war is a worry to most Germans, and a considerable drawback to monetary union there. Nevertheless, increasing worries about the competitiveness of German industry have provided a new motivation for putting the mark into a fixed-rate regime, and some of Germany's economic misgivings about EMU have receded slightly.

There are of course a few EU states where notions of political union in Europe are unattractive, and for whom loss of monetary sovereignty would be highly unpopular. Britain is clearly one, together with one or two of the Nordic states. Denmark has decided on political grounds not to join EMU or certain other new areas of policy cooperation, although it might change its mind in due course.

Economic benefits from EMU

Although the EMU process is driven mainly by political motives, the economic pros and cons are potentially important in themselves, and continue to be closely debated. Least controversial among the expected benefits are the savings in transactions costs from removing the need to convert currencies in cross-border transactions within the Community. However, although useful and permanent, those gains will be fairly modest – probably less than 0.5 per cent of GDP on average, although larger for economies with relatively open economies (see Table 1) and for those with less efficient foreign exchange markets and payments systems. Foreign exchange costs are already quite minor for large transactions through the wholesale markets, and are therefore generally not a large burden for major companies. But even for individual travellers the increasing international use of electronically-based money transfer mechanisms is cutting the proportionately higher costs of converting small currency amounts.

Table 1:   **Basic Economic Indicators, EU States, 1995**

	Population million	GDP Ecu bn.	Exports* % of GDP	Exports** to EU-15, % of GDP
EU core-5:				
Germany	81.6	1846	23	12
France	58.2	1174	24	12
Netherlands	15.5	303	53	32
Austria	8.0	178	38	16
Luxembourg	0.4	13	91	44***
	163.7	3514		
Other EMU probables:				
Belgium	10.2	206	74	44***
Denmark	5.2	132	34	15
Finland	5.1	97	38	18
Ireland	3.6	47	76	45
	24.1	482		
EU 'periphery':				
Italy	57.3	831	28	12
UK	58.5	843	28	12
Spain	39.2	427	24	12
Sweden	8.9	175	41	21
Portugal	9.8	80	30	17
Greece	10.5	87	17	5
	184.2	2443		
EU-15	371.9	6440	29	15

*Exports of goods and services
**Exports of goods only
***Average for Belgium and Luxembourg

Source: European Commission

Possibly larger, but more debatable, are the potential savings in search costs costs of acquiring information about prices normally quoted only in foreign currencies. Some commentators believe that the benefits to consumers through greater price transparency could be substantial if everything traded on EU markets were priced in the same currency, but others are sceptical, since exchange rates are widely quoted in the press, and information on foreign prices can usually be obtained fairly readily. The significant international price differences known to exist among comparable consumer durables probably reflect factors like transport costs and administrative barriers whose elimination is more a matter for the single market than EMU.

One of the main benefits claimed for EMU would come from eliminating exchange rate uncertainty in cross-border trade and investment. Industrialists invariably point to exchange stability as a desirable but elusive feature of the European trading environment, without which the full advantages of the single market cannot be achieved. They have in mind not primarily the short-period, high-frequency, fluctuations that characterise many foreign exchange markets but rather the unpredictable longer-period swings observable in European exchange rates, which can destroy the profitability of investment in export facilities or foreign manufacturing operations. Unlike short-period volatility, these longer swings are hard to hedge against on conventional forward and futures markets. The benefits from eliminating them are also hard to estimate, but they are likely to be substantial.

Assessment of this benefit has focused on the differentials that exist between interest rates on strong and weak EU currencies which reflect, in part, exchange risk premia needed to persuade investors to hold currencies where there is some risk of depreciation. For Europe's weaker currencies, elimination of these differentials could be equivalent to reducing real (inflation-adjusted) long-term interest rates by perhaps two percentage points or more, and this would represent a substantial and permanent reduction in the cost of capital in those economies. The benefits would be lower on average for EMU as a whole, but even strong-currency economies like the Netherlands and Austria would probably gain usefully from their elimination. The result could be a significant boost to investment and GDP for EMU participants on average, implying on some estimates a (once-for-all) increase in GDP of the order of up to five per cent in the longer term. Such estimates may be conservative, in that they do not encompass all the possible sources of gain from exchange-rate stability.

A further, and for some countries potentially crucial, economic benefit sought from EMU is a lasting improvement in inflation performance. The

Table 2:   **Consumer Price Inflation, EU majors (% per annum)**

	1974–85	1986–90	1991–4	1995–7
Germany*	4.6	1.5	3.4	1.8
Netherlands	5.7	0.9	2.6	1.9
France	10.5	2.9	2.4	1.8
Italy	16.0	5.9	5.5	4.3
Spain	15.4	6.6	5.9	3.9
UK	12.0	5.0	4.5	2.7
EU-15	10.8	4.2	4.4	2.7

*Before 1991, West Germany

Source: European Commission, including forecasts for 1996 and 1997

argument is that countries with a history of domestic failure to control inflation should be able to improve their performance if they enter into a strong external commitment to price stability. Similar arguments for 'tying one's hands' were made in relation to the EMS, but they are believed more convincing in EMU because of the strength of the price stability mandate and guarantee of political independence to be conferred on the new central bank, and because a legally-binding treaty has more force than the more flexible intergovernmental approach of the EMS.

Unfortunately, EMU's potential benefits in curbing inflation cannot be quantified with any confidence. Although it is now widely accepted that price stability helps economic growth in the long run, at least in developed economies, the relationships are not well established, and it is admitted that the transitional costs of reducing inflation, once entrenched, can be severe. Secondly, although independent central banks have better inflation records than most governments, the causality is disputed. Where the domestic political atmosphere is conducive to price stability, it is unclear that treaty-based commitments are necessary to achieve it. The classic counter-example is Germany, where strong popular antipathy to inflation may be a more fundamental cause of price stability than the political independence of the Bundesbank, and where the worry is that membership of EMU may mean a deterioration in inflation performance.

For these reasons, the price stability payoff from forming EMU remains very uncertain, especially for countries which risk losing policy credibility in the move to EMU. In contrast, the balance of this argument for traditionally high-inflation economies must favour EMU, although the size of the eventual benefit is highly conjectural.

Other benefits could arise from EMU if the European single currency emerges as a global trading and investment currency on a par with the U.S. dollar and yen. Gains could arise from an international reserve currency which are akin to seignorage, the profits that accrue to authorities that issue money, such as the interest received on the securities held as backing for the note issue. To the extent that the new currency is held as money more widely abroad than the currencies it replaces, income will accrue to the governments that own the new central bank. Related benefits could accrue from savings by EMU authorities in their own holdings of foreign currency reserves as a result of locking exchange rates on a substantial part of EU trade. On some estimates, the surplus of foreign currency reserves held by central banks in the group likely to form EMU could be up to $100 billion, about one-half of their total reserves; but any long-run benefit from disposal would depend on the income that could be earned from alternative uses, including reduction of external liabilities.

Further benefits might arise from the expected greater attractiveness to international investors of European securities denominated in the new currency, as compared with those in existing currencies. It seems reasonable to expect that there would be some shift of international portfolio holdings in favour of single-currency assets, but its size and speed are hard to predict. The development of wider and deeper capital markets in the EU should be a strong positive factor for international investors, but it will be counteracted if EMU does not function well and if questions develop about the new currency's stability. Lastly, transactions benefits could arise if EMU enables a larger share of EU trade with third countries to be transacted in a domestic European currency, but such gains are likely to be modest.

Overall, therefore, the development of a new global currency for Europe should generate economic benefits, but their size, like that of the other potential benefits, cannot be quantified with any confidence. The same applies in the sphere of currency diplomacy. On the face of it, Europe should gain considerable influence in international forums like the G7 and the IMF if EU governments control a globally important currency, and this should assist global exchange stability. But this assumes that European ministers would speak with one voice on currency matters, which is by no means assured. The result paradoxically could even be a weakening, not strengthening, of global currency stability after EMU.

Economic costs and risks

The clearest cost from EMU will be the expense and dislocation involved in replacing national currencies by the new currency. Merely producing the new notes and coin and getting them into circulation will be a massive task. Apart from currency production and distribution, the main financial costs will be incurred by banks, all of whose information and accounting systems will need to be changed, and adapted to operate dual-currency systems during the three or so years in which national currencies will circulate alongside the new currency. The cost for major EU banks as a whole has been put at around Ecu10 billion for a 'big bang' conversion, the cheapest approach for banks, and perhaps double that if dual-currency systems have to be installed. Heavy direct costs would also be incurred by other financial institutions and by major cash handlers and inventory holders, such as retailers with extensive price lists, and businesses that rely on cash-handling machinery, all of which will have to be changed. Other businesses generally will encounter smaller but still significant accounting, IT and documentation costs.

Although substantial for the businesses involved, these costs would not be crippling. For example, British clearing banks have estimated that their operating expenses would be increased by some two to four per cent over a period of three years. These do not include the costs to individuals, which would be largely psychological. The mental effort and inconvenience of switching to a new money will no doubt make the conversion exercise highly unpopular both among households and small businesses. There must therefore be some risk, unless the exercise is carefully coordinated by national bodies, of confusion in the changeover phase which could create great difficulties for the banks and monetary authorities and, at worst, bring the financial system to a temporary halt. However, if this can be avoided, the overall costs and inconvenience of the conversion exercise, being once-for-all, should be comfortably outweighed for the economy as a whole by the permanent savings in transactions costs.

The same cannot be said of the potential costs that could arise from abandoning exchange rates and independent monetary policy as means of coping with major economic disturbances or deficiencies in national economic performance. Two types of concerns are relevant. Firstly, EU states may experience asymmetric economic shocks that call for different monetary policy responses, including possibly an exchange-rate change. Examples are the oil price shocks of the 1970s or German reunification in 1990. Secondly, there may be big differences between levels of production costs or productivity growth trends among EU states, for which exchange-rate movement may be a tolerable if imperfect response. Some observers fear that locking exchange rates and merging monetary policy in EMU could lead to heavy unemployment in countries hit by adverse shocks or experiencing productivity performance below the EMU average.

The answers must depend on a range of economic issues. EMU optimists hold, for example:

(a) that German reunification was a uniquely disruptive shock, unlikely to recur;

(b) that most EU states are sufficiently similar in terms of industrial structure, cost levels and adaptability to wage and price signals;

(c) that currency devaluation is not an effective mechanism because wage-bargainers are rational and far-sighted and because there is strong resistance to downward pressure on real wages;

(d) and because, partly through the competitive forces promoted by monetary union, labour market rigidities will be reduced through time.

Others take a more pessimistic view, pointing to:

(a) the large differentials in labour costs that exist within the EU on some measures at the moment;

(b) the high and rising rates of unemployment in some states; and

(c) the apparent success of recent currency depreciation in countries that left the ERM or devalued within it in 1992–3.

Although this debate leaves much uncertainty about the advisability of moving to EMU, the economic evidence suggests that Germany and its smaller neighbours could form a monetary union fairly safely. However, there is another group of mainly 'peripheral' countries which could not do so without considerable risk, owing to insufficient economic integration, structural dissimilarities, or deep-rooted inflationary tendencies. Some states are hard to categorise in this respect, but many experts would include Italy, and perhaps the UK, in the high-risk group. One of the hardest countries to place is France, whose participation in EMU would be essential, but whose credentials to do so in terms of labour market flexibility, integration with core group, etc., are mixed. Yet it is on the ability of the French and German economies to form a prosperous and stable monetary union that judgements of the project must essentially turn.

HISTORY: THE ROAD TO MAASTRICHT

Post-war beginnings

EMU is the latest stage in a process of economic integration in Europe which began with the Schuman Plan in 1950 to pool Europe's coal and steel resources, leading to the formation of the European Coal and Steel Community by treaty between France, Italy, Germany, Belgium, the Netherlands and Luxembourg in 1952, and the European Economic Community by the Rome Treaty between the same six nations in 1957. The EEC established a common market through the phasing out of internal trade barriers over a period of 15 years, a common external tariff on manufactured goods, and a common agricultural policy to stabilise and protect European agriculture. These objectives had been essentially achieved by the time the UK joined in 1972.

Although the primary motivation throughout has been political, with the vision and drive supplied mainly by French politicians and administrators, exchange rate stability has also been an important objective in postwar Europe, and has an earlier history. Both France and Germany had been interested in currency unions at various times in the preceding hundred years, but their efforts had proved rather unsuccessful, and had been subsumed by wider international arrangements. These took the form of the Gold Standard, which flourished from around 1880 until 1914, with an abortive revival after the first world war, and the Bretton Woods system, which was set up at the end of the second world war and functioned effectively as a mechanism for pegging exchange rates until the link between gold and the U.S. dollar was suspended in 1971.

Currency arrangements therefore did not feature prominently in Europe's early postwar steps towards economic integration, although they were in the background. Neither the ECSC Treaty nor the Rome Treaty mentioned the exchange-rate regime, and while the latter stated that EEC members should regard their exchange rate policies as 'a matter of common concern', it was not pursued. However, some ambitious thinking emerged in the 1960s. Jean Monnet's Action Committee for a United States of Europe in 1961 advocated a European Monetary Reserve System as a step towards a single currency, and the Commission's Action Programme of 1962 called for a 'second stage' of integration starting after 1970, which would include fixed exchange rates. But it was only when serious strains began to emerge in the Bretton Woods system in the late 1960s that European political ambitions turned seriously to monetary union.

The Werner Report

The true launching of the EMU process probably dates from the Hague European summit in December 1969, which discussed a timetable for EMU, based on a 'plan for action' devised by Pierre Werner, then Prime Minister and

Finance Minister of Luxembourg. The Werner Committee was set up in 1970 and produced its final report in February 1971. The Werner Report envisaged the creation of a fully-fledged economic and monetary union which would turn the common market into a single economy in three stages. The key requirements were the permanent fixing of exchange rates (but there was no mention of a single currency); a single monetary authority and monetary policy; unified capital markets; centralisation of fiscal policy at Community level, including methods of financing, taxation, etc.; strengthening and coordination of the Community's regional and structural policies; and closer cooperation between the social partners, industry, unions and government. The programme was endorsed by the Paris summit in October 1972, which called for completion of the transitional stages by the end of 1980.

The first major step to implement the Werner plan was the European currency 'snake' in 1972. This was an arrangement to limit fluctuations between participants' exchange rates to ±2.25 per cent, half the corresponding margin for non-U.S. dollar currencies in the Smithsonian Agreement of December 1971. It started with the EEC-6 currencies and was quickly joined by sterling, the Irish pound and the Danish and Norwegian kroner. However, it soon ran into difficulties: sterling was forced out after only a brief period, followed by the lira and French franc (twice, rejoining once). By 1978 only the mark and a few others survived in the grid.

The Werner plan never recovered from the snake's ill fortunes, and although the EC Council persisted with attempts to formalise policy cooperation, it was realised well before 1980 that the grand design for monetary union was not about to be achieved. Failure was blamed on the first oil price shock, which created big tensions between EC economies, but it was probably also due to the ambitious demands for centralisation of fiscal and structural polices, which few governments were ready to concede. Subsequent EMU planners were to take this lesson to heart.

The European Monetary System

By the late 1970s monetary integration appeared to be running into the sand, and with it all momentum for EC integration. Spurred on by a public appeal from Commission President Roy Jenkins in 1977, President Giscard d'Estaing in France and Chancellor Helmut Schmidt in Germany launched a joint initiative for exchange rate stabilisation which was to materialise as the European Monetary System. The declared objective was to create a 'zone of monetary stability in Europe'; there was no mention of monetary union, which was thought too remote to return to the agenda. But the goal of monetary union had not been abandoned, and there were several reports and draft action plans in the early 1980s, the outcome of which was the chapter on EMU in the Single European Act of 1986, which committed EC governments to early monetary union as a necessary step to complete the single market.

The EMS started in March 1979, and despite the 1992–3 crisis which nearly destroyed it, has proved more durable than its predecessors. The heart of the system, the Exchange Rate Mechanism, was an arrangement for currency stabilisation through a multilateral parity grid, with a fluctuation band of ± 2.25 per cent, later supplemented by a wider band of ± 6 per cent. When any two currencies reached the margins of their band, the respective monetary authorities were obliged to intervene to support the weak currency on an unlimited scale, although realignment was allowable as a last resort.

During the 1980s the ERM evolved from being an arrangement for exchange-rate stabilisation into a mechanism for inducing convergence on the monetary policy of the anchor country. This entailed the gradual abandonment of the original notion of policy symmetry between weak and strong currencies, and the progressive hardening of the mechanism towards a genuinely fixed-rate system – the 'hard' ERM. In the first few years of the EMS there were frequent realignments, which usually included some revaluation by the stronger currencies. There was then a phase in which realignments became less frequent as weaker-currency states made strong efforts to peg to the mark, which became increasingly accepted as the anchor currency by virtue of Germany's superior inflation record. This required willingness by those with higher inflation to emulate the thrust of German monetary policy, even if it meant high interest rates. The result was a large and sustained fall in inflation among ERM participants, and the perception gained ground that the system offered a powerful convergence mechanism. In this way, the ERM helped create the conditions for another attempt at monetary union by the end of the 1980s.

The Delors Report

The progress on inflation and the agreement in 1986 to complete the internal market generated a resurgence of Franco-German interest in monetary union, with the ERM as entry route. The outcome was a decision at the Hanover European summit in 1988 to appoint a Committee chaired by Jacques Delors, president of the Commission, and comprising EC central bank governors and a few independent experts, to produce a blueprint for EMU. The Committee reported in April 1989 and its proposals for a three-stage approach were endorsed by the Madrid summit in June, which decided to start Stage One in July 1990 and to convene an Intergovernmental Conference (IGC) on EMU as soon as possible afterwards. The impetus then and later depended heavily on support from German Chancellor Kohl and French President Mitterand.

Stage One of the Delors approach envisaged principally the completion of the internal market, including the creation of a single financial area, with free movement of capital and financial services across the Community; and consolidation of the ERM, with all EC states joining the narrow band. Stage Two would accomplish the transition to locked exchange rates, via a progressive hardening of the ERM, closer cooperation in economic policies, and the setting up of an embryo central bank, with the task of coordinating monetary policies and making the technical preparations for EMU. Stage Three would see the beginning of EMU proper, with permanent locking of exchange rates, a fully independent European System of Central Banks in charge of a single monetary policy, and in due course a single currency. There should also be binding rules to ensure that fiscal policy would be supportive of monetary policy. Unlike Werner, Delors avoided recommending a major centralisation of fiscal and other policies, and advised against setting rigid deadlines.

The Maastricht Treaty

After a year of intensive negotiation in the EMU IGC, the Treaty on European Union was agreed by the European Council at Maastricht in December 1991. Its ratification by national parliaments ran into unexpected difficulties and took nearly two years, suggesting that the political process had got ahead of public opinion, not least in Germany, which was last to ratify. These popular doubts partly reflected the esoteric nature of the subject, but also underlined that the process was principally driven by visionary politicians with little grass roots consultation.

The Maastricht Treaty is essentially a set of amendments and additions to the Rome Treaty. Although it also covers 'security and foreign affairs' and 'justice and home affairs', and foreshadows moves towards political integration, the EMU provisions are by far the most concrete. The treaty incorporates much of the Delors blueprint but there are important new features (see below).

Stage Two

- An elaborate selection process for EMU membership, guided by explicit convergence criteria aimed at measuring how far countries have converged.

The Council must use these criteria in assessing which countries are eligible for EMU.

- The European Monetary Institute, set up as forerunner of the central bank, but with only an advisory capacity in the policy field. This limitation was largely at German insistence and contrary to French instincts, and reflected German concerns to keep monetary policy in national hands right up to the moment of exchange-rate locking.

- A deadline (1 January 1999) for the start of Stage Three, in the event that an earlier start would not be possible. The EU fell back on this provision when it became plain in 1995 that an earlier start was not practicable. The 1999 deadline is supposed to apply regardless of how many countries qualify and of whether the general economic conditions are appropriate. It was inserted at the last minute under a special deal between President Mitterrand and Chancellor Kohl, and surprised other governments.

Stage Three

- An elaborate constitution for the new central banking system, giving pre-eminence to the European Central Bank within it. The strength of the ECB's mandate to maintain price stability, with only subsidiary regard for other economic objectives, its complete independence from outside interference, and its ability to direct national central banks on policy issues, mean that it is likely to be more single-minded in controlling inflation than any existing central bank – even the Bundesbank on which it is modelled. These features reflect German thinking, both in the central bank governors' committee, which devised the draft ECB statute, and in the IGC. That influence reflects in turn both the current ascendancy of the German approach to macroeconomic management, given Germany's acknowledged economic success in the past twenty years, and the need for EMU's leading protagonists to coax a largely hesitant Germany to take part.

- An 'excessive deficit procedure', which sets three per cent of GDP as a rigid limit on the size of national fiscal deficits, and outlines the way in which it will be monitored and enforced. This procedure already operates in Stage Two, but financial sanctions will be added in Stage Three, which means that EMU participants will incur fines if their deficits persistently exceed the three per cent limit. The scale of those penalties is to be determined in the course of negotiations for a Stability Pact, proposed in 1995 by the German government with the aim of bolstering fiscal discipline after EMU starts.

In setting limits on fiscal deficits the treaty followed the advice of the Delors Committee, but it totally avoided any strengthening of the machinery of fiscal policy cooperation in EMU, on which Delors had a number of modest proposals. Thus a feature of the Maastricht blueprint which is of some concern to the French authorities, among others, is the lack of a fiscal policy counterpart at EU level to the ECB, with its central control of monetary policy. Instead, fiscal policy is left in national hands, subject to observing the treaty limits, and this also reflects German thinking. This separation of powers could have important implications for policy in Stage Three.

In signing the treaty, all 15 EU states (including the three that acceded in 1995) have committed themselves to joining EMU, except the UK and Denmark, which obtained separate protocols enabling them to opt out when the time for decisions comes. Denmark has already done so. States that fail the convergence criteria will receive a 'derogation', which exempts them from the main rights and responsibilities of EMU membership but commits them to continuing their convergence efforts.

After Maastricht: ERM crisis

The Maastricht Treaty's emphasis on the ERM as the precursor of EMU induced a further hardening of the mechanism around 1990, at a time when acute stresses were developing in the economic fundamentals affecting currencies. Even though inflation rates were converging, the gaps in labour costs between strong and weak-currency states were still widening. As long as convergence commitments remained credible, the markets were prepared to overlook these problems, but where they came into question, confidence was apt to give way sharply. From early 1992, a series of events challenged the credibility of ERM commitments: a sharp tightening of monetary policy in Germany in response to overheating after reunification; a simultaneous weakening of the U.S. dollar reflecting policy relaxation there, which created tensions in the ERM; and referenda results and delays to ratification which cast doubt on the momentum towards EMU, even in France. The outcome was the currency turmoil of late 1992 and mid-1993, which drove a number of weaker currencies to devalue or leave the ERM, and ultimately a buildup of irresistible speculative pressure against the French franc and other stronger currencies. This precipitated a decision by finance ministers in August 1993 to widen the fluctuation bands to ±15 per cent, in a dramatic move to stave off collapse of the system.

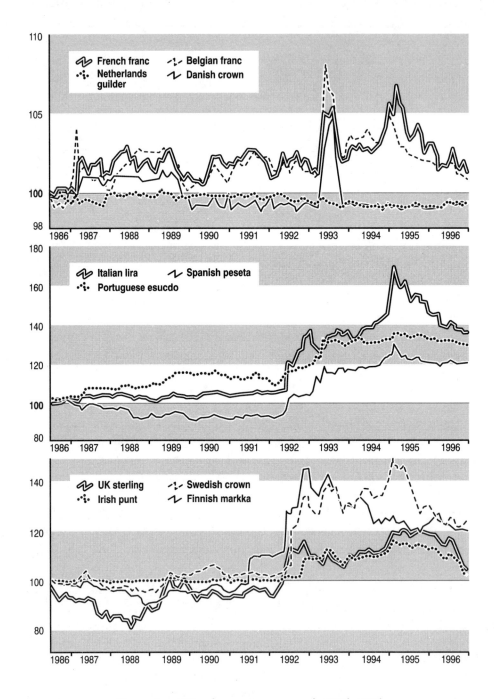

Figure 1: *EU exchange rates versus mark, 1986–1996*

EMU sceptics greeted the traumas in the ERM as evidence that the process was not viable. But such judgements turned out to be premature. The relaxation of the ERM bands was very effective in removing speculative pressure, and governments were quick to reaffirm their convergence commitments and back them up where necessary with policy action. The result was a fairly speedy restoration of stability among the stronger currencies around the mark, and a progressive stabilisation of the weaker currencies near their depreciated levels. A further period of severe turbulence in early 1995 was safely negotiated, and affirmatory statements from the Madrid European Council at end of that year appeared to convince the markets that an EMU on Maastricht lines would actually happen.

THE TRANSITION: FROM MAASTRICHT TO FRANKFURT

Even though the ERM had not been consolidated as the Delors Committee hoped, Stage Two went ahead in January 1994 with the establishment of the EMI in Frankfurt. The focus is now on progress towards meeting the convergence criteria and on resolving outstanding institutional and practical issues before Stage Three starts.

Meeting the criteria

The treaty's main economic criteria relate to inflation, fiscal positions, exchange-rate stability and long-term interest rates.

ECOFIN is to judge performance in 'early' 1998 on the basis of reports by the Commission and the EMI, as soon as complete data for 1997 are available. The decisions will be taken by qualified majority, excluding countries that have opted out, and will be subject to confirmation by the European Council. EMU is due to start on 1 January 1999 with as many states as are willing and eligible.

Most states will find the fiscal criterion hardest to meet. Assuming no major upset such as would cause another currency crisis, around 11 countries are likely to meet the inflation criterion by 1997, and ten will have been members of the ERM for the two years before the examination, plus Finland and Italy for a lesser period. The meaning of the exchange-rate criterion has been unclear since the ERM narrow band was abandoned, but Commission statements suggest that currencies which have been reasonably stable within the 15 per cent band for one to two years should meet the test. The posi-

The convergence criteria

1. Price stability: a rate of consumer price inflation over the previous year no more than 1½ percentage points above that of the three best-performing states.

2. Government financial position: a government deficit that is not judged by the Council to be excessive, according to two tests:

- a ratio of general government net borrowing to GDP no greater than three per cent, unless it has declined substantially and continually and comes close to three per cent, or the the excess is only exceptional and temporary, and the deficit remains close to three per cent; and

- a ratio of general government gross debt to GDP no greater than 60 per cent, unless it is sufficiently diminishing and approaching 60 per cent at a satisfactory pace.

3. Exchange-rate stability: participation of a state's currency in the exchange rate mechanism of the EMS while respecting the 'normal margins of fluctuation' for at least two years previously, without devaluing 'on its own initiative'.

4. Interest-rate convergence: an average nominal interest rate on long-term government bonds over the past year no more than two percentage points above that of, at most, the three best-performing states in terms of price stability.

tion is much less clear for currencies that remain outside the ERM, as may sterling.

Ordinarily interest rate differentials cannot be forecast with confidence, but bond yields on currencies which are expected to pass all the other criteria are likely to converge on those of the best inflation performers, as they have done in 1995–6 (see Figure 2); and this is also borne out by the implicit spreads in forward yields on long-term interest-rate swaps.

In contrast, prospects under the fiscal criterion remain highly uncertain. Most fiscal deficits have been on a declining trend since the low point of the European recession in 1993, but the slowdown in 1995 caused a setback and growing worries about meeting the criterion led to a sharp fiscal tightening in France and Germany, which may check the recovery. Aware of the risks, a number of governments have announced special expedients to cut deficits or debt which critics dismiss as 'creative accounting', and although some of these have been passed by the Commission, they may not survive scrutiny by fiscal hardliners on the Council.

Although the treaty gives pre-eminence to these criteria as tests of convergence, it does mention other factors to be taken into account, including 'the development of unit labour costs and other prices', the 'integration of markets', and balance of payments developments. On the face of it, none of those factors is liable to give major cause for concern: rates of increase in unit labour costs have tended to converge downwards, progress in creating the single market has been mostly satisfactory, and EU states' external current accounts have been near balance or in surplus. But the picture is less reassuring for real economy factors such as competitiveness and unemployment, which the treaty does not mention specifically but which are hard to ignore. Largely as a result of currency appreciation since 1989, unit labour cost levels in Germany and economies that have linked closely to the mark have moved appreciably above those of EU competitors, and also in relation to dollar costs (see Table 3). Moreover some of the core economies, including France and Germany, are experiencing historically high rates of unemployment (see Table 4), which show little sign of falling in the foreseeable future; if they were to come down, they could expose underlying balance of payments weaknesses and bring about a sharp market reassessment of the traditionally strong ERM currencies. Such considerations raise questionmarks about the advisability of starting EMU which may influence Council judgements, despite the treaty's silence on them.

Table 3: Movements in cost competitiveness, EU majors, USA & Japan

(Indices, 1991 = 100)	1986–90 (average)	1991	1994	1997
Germany*	100	100	114	116
Netherlands	105	100	103	103
France	104	100	100	103
Italy	93	100	76	74
Spain	86	100	82	86
UK	98	100	91	92
USA	113	100	92	91
Japan	115	100	138	123

*Before 1991, West Germany

Note: Indices are for relative unit labour costs in manufacturing, expressed in a common currency, in relation to all other main industrial countries' costs. An increase shows a deterioration in competitiveness.

Source: OECD, including forecasts for 1997

Monthly averages, in percentage points

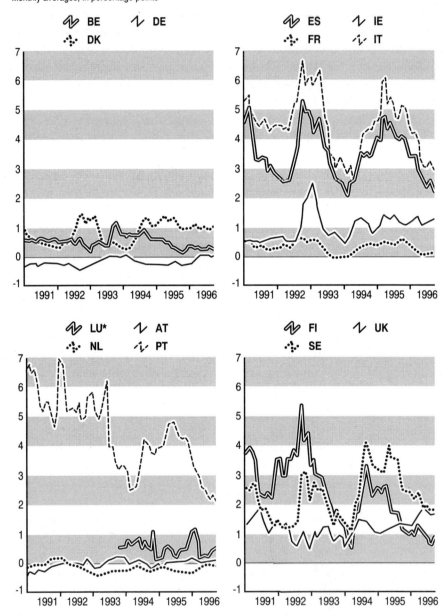

Weighted average of Belgium, Germany, France, the Netherlands and Austria. No Greek data shown.
*Comparable data are only available from 22 October 1993

Source: European Monetary Institute

Figure 2:   *EU interest rate differentials, 1991–1996*

Table 4: Unemployment in EU majors, USA & Japan

(per cent of civilian labour force, annual averages)	1974–85	1986–90	1991–93	1994–97
Germany*	4.2	5.9	6.7	8.9
Netherlands	7.1	7.4	6.0	7.2
France	6.4	9.8	10.5	11.8
Italy	7.0	9.6	9.4	11.7
Spain	11.5	18.9	19.2	22.9
UK	6.9	9.0	9.8	8.7
EU-15	6.4	9.0	9.5	11.0
USA	7.5	5.9	7.0	5.7
Japan	2.2	2.5	2.3	3.0

*Before 1991, West Germany

Source: European Commission, including forecasts for 1996 and 1997

Despite all these uncertainties, in late 1996 EMU looked set to commence on 1 January 1999 with around half the EU's membership. Assuming modest latitude in interpreting the fiscal criterion, some seven or eight countries seem likely to pass all the treaty tests, including the examination of central banking independence, on which most countries have either satisfied the EMI's requirements, or are prepared to do so soon. Crucially, Germany and France are likely to be judged eligible, together with their immediate neighbours, but probably not Italy, which despite recently announced fiscal measures seems likely to fail both the deficit and the debt tests. Denmark is assumed to maintain its opt-out, despite passing all the tests, although the pressure to relent would be strong if Finland and Sweden joined. At present, it seems likely that Britain will opt out of the first move to EMU, but in any case it might struggle to meet the test of central banking independence in time, since new legislation would have to be introduced from scratch. Britain might also fail the exchange-rate criterion if interpreted strictly (as may Sweden unless it joins the ERM soon).

It cannot be ruled out that up to 12 or so states will be admitted in the first group if the criteria are interpreted more flexibly, but it is more likely that three or four marginal candidates will be admitted in a second wave, perhaps in time to adopt the single currency, due in 2002. Nor can it be ruled out that the start will be held up for a year or so if France or Germany need more time to meet the fiscal criterion, or if there is a challenge in the German constitutional court. Finally, it cannot be entirely excluded that the process will be derailed.

Outstanding institutional issues

At the end of 1996, a number of important institutional and practical issues remained to be settled before the start of Stage Three:

Reform of the ERM

The realisation that perhaps a half of the EU might be left out of EMU initially, possibly for some years, has intensified concerns about policy links between the 'ins' and 'outs' after Stage Three starts. Attention has focused mainly on exchange-rate arrangements, although cooperation in other policy areas has also been raised. The Treaty said nothing explicitly about the future of the EMS, to which all EU currencies belong, even if they are not in the ERM. But it implied that some scheme would continue, if only to provide a later basis for the exchange-rate criterion.

Most potential 'outs' have an interest in reviving some form of ERM, in order to provide a focus for their convergence efforts, if possible with help from the EMU group. Potential 'ins' also have an interest in a reformed ERM, in order to avoid further depreciation of the peripheral currencies, which has become an acute concern to French and German industrialists. The only convinced sceptic has been the UK government, which is supportive of exchange-rate stability, anxious to preserve open access to the single market, but reluctant to be sucked back into formal exchange-rate schemes.

The upshot is that agreement has been reached on a reformed scheme known as ERM-II. 'Out' currencies will be pegged to the single currency on a 'hub and spoke' basis rather than through a multilateral grid. The normal fluctuation band will be relatively wide but other arrangements will be possible to suit individual circumstances. In principle, there will be a mutual obligation to support currencies at the bottom of their band, but the European Central Bank (ECB) will do so only if it sees no conflict with its price stability objective. The two key differences from the old scheme are therefore that all vestiges of policy symmetry will disappear: adherents will have to be prepared to follow the ECB's policy if they are to count on its agreement and support; secondly, in return for that, there will be greater scope for 'variable geometry' in the pegging arrangements. At UK insistence, membership of the new scheme will not be obligatory, but it is likely to be a requirement for countries seeking to join EMU. The scheme will come into operation when the decisions on Stage Three are made.

The stability and growth pact

The German government has been seeking a tougher commitment to fiscal discipline from potential EMU candidates. This has been a difficult issue because, although most countries support the principle that government finances should be put on a sound footing, there has been hesitation among Germany's partners. They opposed Germany's proposals for near automatic penalties, both as limiting national sovereignty and as limiting scope for legitimate fiscal manoeuvre in the face of an economic downturn. A stalemate on this issue was narrowly avoided at the EU's Dublin summit in December 1996. After much wrangling, agreement was reached on a compromise which, on paper, gives the Germans much of what they are seeking, but in practice may be difficult to implement. (See Chapter 1 for details.)

Introduction of the euro

The EU is also addressing the practical task of introducing the single currency, which is to be called the 'euro'. The Madrid Summit in December 1995 endorsed an EMI plan which envisages conversion to the new currency over a four-year timetable. This would start with an initial period of around eight months from the announcement of participating countries to the locking of exchange rates. There would then be a period of up to three years in which the euro would exist, as 'scriptural' (deposit) money only, mainly for wholesale transactions in the banking system and by the ECB, alongside national moneys at fixed conversion rates. Finally, in a concluding period of up to six months, euro notes and coins would be introduced in place of national currency, and the public sector and households would make their changeover.

This will clearly be a large and complex exercise for which countries should ideally start preparing now, but the uncertainties about membership and timing of Stage Three make this difficult even for those which have a high expectation of joining. Questions have been raised as to whether the changeover could be accomplished in an orderly way in the prescribed time. There is no real precedent. The closest recent example was the decimalisation of sterling, the British pound, in 1971. Detailed preparation for that took just over three years, even though the basic currency unit and all banknotes were unaffected and less than half the coinage was changed.

Questions have also arisen about what would happen if doubts emerge about national commitments to stay in EMU during the phase in which the euro circulates alongside national currencies. The EMI has asserted that 'there will no longer be foreign exchange markets between [national currencies] but purely arithmetical conversions' and that national currencies 'will cease to be foreign currencies in terms of each other'. At the Council's behest, the Commission has produced a draft regulation which provides for 'legally enforceable equivalence' between the euro and national currencies at the official conversion rate, without margins or fees. There are doubts whether legal devices like this will be sufficient to discourage markets from trying to drive a wedge between the conversion rates if confidence in some currency falters. If they are not, participating governments and the European System of Central Banks (ESCB) may be called on to back up their commitments by allowing unlimited conversion out of suspect currencies including the euro into, say, marks, should political tensions arise in EMU's early years.

Other questions arise about continuity of contract between the basket Ecu and the euro. Since the treaty was finalised, the understanding has been that the Ecu will cease to exist when Stage Three starts and Ecu contracts will then convert into euro equivalents at a rate of one to one, and the Commission has prepared a draft Council regulation to this effect. However, especially if the EMU group includes only countries with strong currencies, the euro will be, in economic terms, a stronger currency than the basket, and conversion of bonds on a one to one basis would imply a windfall gain for holders of Ecu assets at the expense of those with Ecu liabilities. This would raise troublesome questions of equity and could lead to challenges in the courts, at least on contracts written under non-EU law, as many Ecu bonds are.

The decision to adopt one-to-one convertibility between the euro and the Ecu raises other problems when considered in combination with a related treaty commitment – that the irrevocable locking will not affect the external value of the Ecu. These two provisions mean that it will not be possible to announce the euro's value in advance of the start of Stage Three, even though the conversion rates between national currencies will probably be pre-announced, as soon as possible after the EMU participants are named in early 1998. In the period from then to locking, the value of the basket Ecu in terms of the stronger EU currencies will almost certainly change, making it impossible to pinpoint euro conversion rates in advance. Accordingly, earlier hopes that it would be possible to select 'user friendly' conversion rates between the euro and national currencies, and that agents would know the euro's value before Stage Three starts, look like being disappointed.

Looking ahead to Stage Three

Stage Three will represent a major change of economic regime for countries that participate, and will have important effects on those that do not. It will be an enormous leap in the dark. Despite the institutional detail in the Maastricht Treaty and secondary legislation, it is still very unclear how Stage Three will work. It is yet to be decided how the ECB will conduct monetary policy, and the role of fiscal policy remains in some dispute.

FISCAL AND MONETARY POLICY

The formulation of monetary policy

The EMI has been studying how the ECB should set monetary policy. It produced its recommended framework in early 1997, although decisions must await the ECB's establishment on 1 July 1998. The treaty leaves no doubt that the maintaining price stability will be the ECB's 'primary objective', and its support for 'the general economic policies of the Community' must be 'without prejudice' to that objective. But it is not made clear what price stability means, or how it should be maintained.

In at least one important respect, the treaty added to the uncertainties by assigning reponsibility for exchange-rate policy to finance ministers, not to the ECB. In doing so, it bowed to governments' insistence on retaining their long-standing prerogative in this field, against the advice of economic purists. Thus ECOFIN would be responsible for any formal international agreements on an exchange-rate system involving the euro, and for any 'general orientations for exchange-rate policy'. In principle, this could lead to conflict, if EMU ministers choose an external exchange-rate strategy which is incompatible with internal price stability. In practice, the problems may be less serious than critics suggest, because the treaty provides that ministers may act only after a recommendation from the Commission and the ECB, and without prejudice to price stability; and because the ECB will be wholly independent in its use of monetary policy instruments, including foreign exchange market intervention and interest rates. Nevertheless, much will depend on whether governments in EMU can avoid confrontation with the ECB over the euro's exchange rate.

Although the ECB is unlikely to be indifferent to the euro exchange rate, it will strongly resist pegging to an external currency and almost certainly adopt an internal intermediate target for monetary policy. The choices then lie essentially between a monetary aggregate, such as the M3 money supply measure tracked for many years by the Bundesbank, and forward indicators of inflation, on the lines adopted by the British authorities after the pound left the ERM in autumn 1992, and subsequently taken up by several other EU states.

Given the German influence, the chances are that principal weight will be given to a broad money aggregate – probably M3. But past relationships between money and inflation, on which monetary targeting depends, seem likely to be undermined by the impact of EMU itself on how people and institutions in the region handle their finances. The result may be a compromise in which monetary targeting is supplemented by monitoring of leading inflation indicators, at least until the monetary relationships settle down. In that case, success will depend on the ECB being transparent in its policy actions, flexible in its choice and use of intermediate targets, but firm in pursuit of the underlying objective.

This may not be a straightforward task in a group of economies which still differ structurally in important respects. Government debt is still liable to be subject to differential credit risk in EMU, and the risk premia could be greater if some governments exploit the removal of traditional exchange risk to run persistent deficits, ignoring the mandatory limits. This might mean that the ECB's monetary policy would have an uneven impact across EMU states. Secondly, there are differences in the transmission mechanisms of monetary policy between countries, arising from differences in reliance on debt financing, particularly by households. Such differences are likely to be eroded in time, but they could complicate the conduct of monetary policy in the early years. While these problems would be most pronounced for Britain if it joins EMU, because of the prevalence of variable-rate mortgage and bank lending there, they could also be significant in countries like Italy where large volumes of short-term government debt are held domestically in private hands.

Thirdly, consumer price inflation is unlikely to be uniform across the EMU group. While competition and price transparency in Stage Three should lead to close inflation convergence in tradable goods and services, appreciable differences could remain among sheltered sectors, such as non-traded services and housing. In the past, persistent inflation gaps, of two per cent per annum or more, have been noted between tradable and non tradable sectors in some EU states; and there could be even larger gaps in wage inflation among sheltered sectors. If they continue, such gaps could pose dilemmas for the ECB, for it might have to choose between focusing on average inflation across the whole EMU group, or concentrating on areas where it is above average. Such problems are not unknown within national regimes, and they can lead to political tensions between regions.

The ESCB's monetary operations

The EMI has also been studying the operating instruments and procedures by which the ESCB will execute policy in Stage Three. There are issues here which will have far-reaching effects on Europe's financial markets, whether inside or outside EMU. Among the more contentious are the question of minimum reserve requirements (MRRs) for commercial banks within the ECB's regime; the degree of centralisation of market operations within the ESCB network; and access to the ESCB's central settlement system, known as TARGET. If adopted at a significant level and remunerated at below market rates, MRRs would impose a discriminatory tax on banks within the EMU area, which could lead to disintermediation and encourage offshore banking. The Bundesbank favours MRRs on the ground that they stabilise the banks' demand for central bank reserves and assist with monetary control. Yet the danger of making EMU uncompetitive with other financial centres is also recognised, and the outcome may be a compromise in which the EMI recommends comparatively low reserve ratios, remunerated at near-market rates.

The manner in which market operations are conducted by the ESCB will matter because it could affect the attractiveness of the EU's major major financial centres, including London. Important information can be obtained about prospects for interest and exchange rates through contact with active central banks. If the ECB is concerned about the cost and profitability of its operations, it will follow procedures which channel business to the most efficient centres, for example by distributing open market transactions on the basis of the most competitive tenders. Yet some central banks in the system may prefer business to be shared out more equally. It may therefore take time for ESCB operations to become genuinely market-led in Stage Three; but if and when that happens, the prospect is that Europe's money and foreign exchange markets will concentrate in even fewer, larger, financial centres than at present.

The central settlement system being developed for the ESCB by the EMI will link national settlement systems and is intended to provide cheap and reliable same-day clearing for wholesale payments in euros across national borders. Access to TARGET via their national systems would clearly be desirable for major banks seeking to conduct business in euros, whether or not they are located in the EMU area. However, the German authorities are resisting such access for banks outside EMU, on the ground that any provision of central bank credit to outsiders – even the intra-day credit needed to operate TARGET – would interfere with the ECB's ability to exercise monetary control. If this view prevails, non-EMU banks will be at a competitive disadvantage in the settlement of euro business, unless they establish subsidiaries in EMU centres, which would then be subject to ECB reserve requirements.

The Role of Fiscal Policy

Fiscal policy will be expected to support monetary policy in Stage Three, hence the treaty limits on deficits and debt, and the subsequent search for a stability pact. However, the loss of independent monetary policy and exchange-rate adjustment as methods for coping with asymmetric shocks at national level will put a greater onus on fiscal policy. Economic theory supports the view that fiscal policy will have more, rather than less, leverage over activity under fixed exchange rates, so there could be more incentive to use it for that purpose. The sharp division of policy responsibility in EMU, with control of inflation assigned to the ECB and responsibility for stabilising activity assigned to national governments, could exacerbate such tensions.

The German authorities have always feared that less-disciplined governments would use the freedom from traditional external restraints under EMU to pursue expansionary fiscal policies. If unchecked, this could negate one of the main benefits of EMU by pushing up real interest rates, penalising more scrupulous participants. However, if imposed too rigidly, fiscal limits might hamper legitimate freedom to use fiscal policy to counter shocks. On the face of it, a medium-term target of zero fiscal balance as proposed by the German government might seem reasonable, but for most economies, even Germany, it would represent considerable fiscal tightening compared with previous experience, as may be seen from Table 5. That should be manageable if there is a corresponding fall in private savings, preferably reflecting an increase in investment rather than consumption. Lowering of real interest rates might help generate that shift, but it cannot be relied on to do so; instead, incomes and activity might fall to bring about the necessary equilibrium in overall saving and investment plans.

Moreover, there is a risk that the deflationary forces in EMU could be even stronger if heavily-indebted governments take seriously the treaty injunction to reduce their debt stocks to 60 per cent of GDP. The arithmetic of debt reduction suggests that governments with debt stocks of more than 90 per cent of GDP will have to run substantial primary surpluses, excluding debt interest, if they are to get close to the required debt ratio in less than 20 years. Table 6 shows the constant primary fiscal surplus needed to reach the 60 per cent debt ratio under alternative assumptions about the initial debt ratio and how far the real interest rate exceeds the growth rate of real GDP. Failing a large private investment response, such policies would be very deflationary, and could drive unemployment to politically unsustainable rates in those states.

It should be possible to avoid these problems if the debt reduction and deficit limitation required in Stage Three are approached in a measured way, taking account of private sector responses. Unfortunately, there is little economic logic in the fiscal reference values written into the treaty, or in the numbers proposed for the stability pact. Yet some rules will be needed in EMU in order to give some reassurance against fiscal freeloading. The challenge is to devise the right rules, and it is not clear yet that this has been done.

Table 5: General Government primary and structural balances, 14 EU States, 1993–97

(Surplus (+) or deficit (-) as per cent of GDP, annual averages)

	Primary balance*	Structural balance**
Belgium	4.3	-3.0
Denmark	1.3	-1.1
Germany	0.6	-2.8
Greece	2.5	-9.2
Spain	-1.1	-4.8
France	-1.6	-3.6
Ireland	-1.1	-1.7
Italy	2.7	-7.0
Netherlands	1.6	-2.6
Austria	-0.9	-3.9
Portugal	0.4	-4.3
Finland	-3.8	-2.2
Sweden	-5.3	-5.9
UK	-2.9	-4.5
Total of above	-0.4	-4.3

* Financial balance of general government, excluding net interest payments.
** Structural component of general government overall financial balance (ie. after cyclical adjustment).

Source: OECD, including forecasts for 1996 and 1997

Even the best-devised rules on long-term fiscal performance would not ensure appropriate policy if national finance ministers' priorities clash with those of the ECB. Traditionally such matters would be resolved by close consultation between the monetary and fiscal authorities, but in the Maastricht model of EMU this is excluded by the insistence that the ECB will be immune from political interference. Understandable though this feature is in the light of postwar inflation experience, it leaves the EMU regime with a lacuna that could lead in time to policy errors. Assuming that French-inspired suggestions for an EMU fiscal council to act as a partner and counterweight to the ECB Council cannot be realised – although the proposed stability council could develop in that direction – it will take extraordinary skill and perspicacity on the part of EMU's finance ministers and central bankers to achieve an appropriate balance of fiscal and monetary policies.

Table 6: Arithmetic of debt reduction

Primary surplus/GDP ratio needed to achieve a debt/GDP ratio of 60 per cent:
Real interest rate gap* (percentage points)

a) after 10 years:				
Initial debt/GDP ratio (%)	1	2	3	4
135	8.5	9.5	10.5	11.5
120	6.9	7.8	8.7	9.7
100	4.8	5.6	6.4	7.3
90	3.7	4.5	5.2	6.0
80	2.7	3.4	4.1	4.8
(b) after 20 years: Initial debt/GDP ratio (%)				
135	4.7	5.7	6.7	7.8
120	3.9	4.8	5.7	6.7
100	2.8	3.6	4.4	5.3
90	2.2	3.0	3.7	4.5
80	1.7	2.4	3.1	3.8

*Excess of the real effective interest rate on government debt over the real growth rate of GDP

Source: Helmut Frisch, University of Technology, Vienna

WHAT IF STAGE THREE IS DERAILED?

The probability that the EMU process will break down before the critical moment of exchange-rate locking is small – possibly around 10 per cent – but it should not be ignored because the consequences for the Union could be very serious. Derailment would require more than just a temporary delay, such as might be caused by a challenge on some technicality in the German constitutional court: nothing short of a fundamental change of heart in Germany or France would suffice. Yet such a change is not inconceivable, especially in Germany, where popular opinion is heavily against the single currency, according to regular surveys done for the Commission. The same surveys have suggested, consistently since Maastricht, that French opinion favours the single currency – but that did not stop the 1992 referendum in France almost bringing EMU to a halt.

In either country, perceptions that the move to EMU is becoming too costly might quickly intensify, if economic growth fails to pick up as forecast, government deficits rise as a result, and further emergency fiscal cuts are imposed to meet the treaty criterion. Both governments have been obliged to announce sharp cuts in social security spending in the past year, and as their impact takes effect trade union resistance is hardening. France might attempt further window-dressing of the government accounts in order to finesse these difficulties, but it could be counterproductive if it led to similar stratagems elsewhere and a wave of heavily-indebted states threatened to qualify for Stage Three. That could cause a negative reaction among fiscal hardliners in the Bundesbank and the German parliament, and German political opinion might dig in its heels at the prospect of wide EMU membership. The approach of the German federal elections due in late 1998 could induce Chancellor Kohl's centre-right coalition into a last-minute rethink. The outcome could be that the EU would miss the 1999 deadline with no immediate prospect of retrieving EMU.

In that atmosphere, turmoil would almost certainly break out in the foreign exchange markets, with the weaker currencies becoming principal targets. A repeat of the 1992–93 crisis would be hard to avoid, with, on this occasion, the French franc, lira and peseta mainly in the firing line. Sharp interest rate hikes could be imposed in efforts to defend those currencies, making it more difficult for them to meet the convergence criteria. That could well lead to a political crisis in the EU, with bitter recriminations against Germany and threats to the continuation of the single market.

A crisis of this kind might be managed for a time if governments had to hand a package of measures to reassure the markets. These would need to include a modified ERM II anchored on the mark, a strengthening of economic policy cooperation at EU level, and strong government reaffirmation of commitments to continued convergence. But without a convincing plan for rescuing EMU it is questionable whether such a situation could be contained for long.

There might then be an inclination at the top of the French and German governments to go ahead immediately with a small monetary union of a few chosen countries, perhaps Germany, France and the Benelux states, via intergovernmental agreement, entirely short-circuiting the treaty. The institutional arrangements could be minimal – locked exchange rates supported by a common monetary policy run by a joint monetary council drawn from national central banks, and a mini-stability pact. However, it is questionable whether the German government would be willing to enter into such an exclusive arrangement, which would mean abandoning control over the mark with no achievement of wider German objectives in return. And unless the venture involved some prospect of extension to a wider membership fairly soon, it might antagonise the rest of the EU to the extent of threatening the union altogether.

Instead, German instincts might be to proceed more cautiously, perhaps aiming to enlarge the mark zone by offering to other small neighbours the kind of bilateral exchange rate arrangement agreed with the Netherlands when the ERM was relaxed in 1993. However, this would certainly antagonise France, whose ambitions for EMU would then be in danger of indefinite postponement. At this range, it is impossible to be sure how such a crisis would be resolved. What does seem clear is that if Maastricht-style EMU is derailed, it will not be possible to go back to 'business as usual' in Europe.

Bibliography

Arrowsmith J. and C. T. Taylor, *Unresolved Issues on the Way to a Single Currency*, National Institute of Economic and Social Research Occasional Paper 49, 1996.

Council of the European Communities/Commission of the European Communities, *Treaty on European Union* (Maastricht Treaty), 1992.

Commission of the European Communities, 'One Market, one money', *European Economy*, 44, October 1990.

Johnson, C. *In with the Euro, Out with the Pound*, Penguin, 1996.

Kenen, P. B., *Economic and Monetary Union in Europe: Moving Beyond Maastricht*, Cambridge University Press, 1995.

Taylor, C. T., *EMU 2000? Prospects for European Monetary Union*, The Royal Institute of International Affairs, 1995.

1

Calculating the odds on EMU

By Ruth Pitchford, Adam Cox, Mike Dolan and Phil Smith in London; Henry Engler in Brussels; Myra MacDonald in Paris; and Mark John in Frankfurt

Europe's quest for monetary union has driven the continent's financial markets, in pursuit of profit and in flight from loss, for nearly a decade. Funds have flowed into Europe's more debt-laden and inflation-prone economies in the faith that these countries can be transformed by sharing a currency with Germany, long viewed as a model of fiscal and monetary correctness. The money has fled to safe havens whenever political turbulence has stirred doubts about the EU's commitment to EMU. Yet the funds have flowed back into the region's riskier markets, renewing the cycle, whenever an EU summit meeting renewed the promise of an EMU reward.

Riding the tide of EMU sentiment has proved challenging for market strategists. Now calculating the odds on EMU has become a vital concern for those who plan business strategy and assess information technology needs within Europe's financial industry. It is here, in the wholesale markets where banks and securities houses trade foreign exchange and debt, that the new euro currency is due to make its debut on January 1, 1999. Their retail clients, whether major manufacturing corporations or family holiday-makers, are meant to carry on using the notes and coins of their national currencies, locked into irreversible exchange rates against the euro, until 2002. The practical demands of preparing to handle the new currency, with double book-keeping in euros and national currencies for the first three years, promise to spur a bull labour market for IT experts. For the planners who must commit their companies to major investment in preparing for EMU, the run-up to 1999 will be nerve-racking.

This book collates the efforts of Reuters correspondents in Europe, the U.S. and Asia to assess what EMU means for people working in the financial markets. We have asked central bankers, political leaders, Eurocrats and senior market professionals what impact they think the euro would have on monetary policy, political stability, drafting financial market contracts and writing computer software. We have inquired about the job prospects of the mark/lira trader and tried to sketch some post-EMU job descriptions for fund managers, bond strategists and equities analysts. We have examined what countries will have to do to become founder members of EMU, and which of them have the will to do it. We have checked out the euro's chances of maturing into a reserve currency. But first, we look at the currency's prospects of surviving its gestation period.

MARKET SWINGS, FISCAL AND SOCIAL TENSIONS

Political hurdles

When European Union leaders met in Madrid in December 1995, they generated a wave of confidence in EMU that was still rolling a year later. They set a launch date and a timetable for introducing the currency; they agreed that 1997 would be the crucial year for judging which economies were ready for EMU, and that early 1998 would be the judgement date; they pledged to issue new government debt in the single currency from the start; and they called the currency the euro.

The name was a compromise, inspiring criticism both on aesthetic grounds and because of its potential to create confusion in financial markets, where Euro- is the prefix for a currency held on deposit outside its country of origin. But the EU had to find a substitute for the single currency's previous name, the acronym of European Currency Unit. In 1992, the Ecu had fallen from grace along with the major bond market which it had spawned when voters in Denmark, viewed as a core EMU bloc country, rejected monetary union in a referendum. Ecu bonds became all but untradeable overnight: some liquidity gradually seeped back into the market, but by the time the EU had resumed its drive towards EMU, too many investors were cursing Ecu-denominated losses for the name to generate new confidence.

The euro proved a serviceable working title during 1996. In its name, EU finance ministers and central bankers leapt further hurdles in Verona in April, getting agreements in principle on a stability pact to maintain fiscal discipline within EMU and on a mechanism, dubbed ERM II, to link the euro with EU currencies which did not join in the first wave. At their Florence summit in June, EU leaders managed to sustain the markets' confidence merely by congratulating themselves on their progress towards EMU. When ECOFIN met again in Dublin in September, its members were able to hail the meeting as one of the most productive so far, elaborating plans for the stability pact and ERM II, and addressing anxieties about how financial market contracts could survive the transition to the euro. By the time Reuters polled analysts across Europe in mid-November, the averaged assessment was that EMU had an 82 per cent chance of starting on schedule.

The growing conviction that EMU was a done deal survived some remarkable developments. It became increasingly clear during 1996 that Germany, the architect of the stringent conditions for EMU entry laid down at the EU's Maastricht summit in December 1991, would have trouble meeting the criteria itself. Six years after German reunification, the bills for assimilating eastern Germany were still rolling in, threatening to push the government's budget deficit and its total debt burden in 1997 above the Maastricht target ceilings. France, EMU's other essential founder member, credited its 1997 budget plan with funds linked to privatisation, an accounting exercise which many analysts denounced as window-dressing. The markets decided that it was now safe to assume that qualifying for EMU had much more to do with politics than with a strict reading of the Maastricht Treaty. So did Italy.

Political tensions

At this point, tensions began to re-emerge. To the Bundesbank, Italy is the epitome of what the German central bank terms a 'less stability-oriented country', the sort of nation which should not expect to claim the mark's heritage as a founder member of EMU. Italy's conversion to the path of low inflation and debt reduction is too recent to win ready German approbation. Belgium has a greater debt burden than Italy, but is almost certain to qualify for EMU after years of success in shadowing the mark, squeezing spending and inflation, and, of course, hosting the European Commission in Brussels. In late 1996, Italy's leaders were making it plain that they intended to challenge all this received wisdom. Italian inflation had slowed dramatically, the lira had pegged itself to the mark again via the ERM, and the market was pushing Italian long-term interest rates down into the ranges demanded by Maastricht. All that remained was for Italy to claim the leeway that France had established on budgetary accounting and that Belgium was expected to win on total debt. Then, Rome argued, it would meet all the criteria for joining EMU in 1999.

The Italian claims helped to revive the Franco-German tensions which pose the main political threat to EMU. Germany raised objections to France's 1997 budget plan: the European Commission overruled the complaint. The Commission forecast that every EU member state except Eurosceptical Britain and outsider Greece had a chance of qualifying for EMU: simultaneously, the Frankfurt-based EMI offered a far more austere interpretation, saying that most EU countries did not make the grade as yet. Germany became more obstinate about the terms of the stability pact: senior French politicians began to voice new doubts about the benefits of a monetary union which left no fiscal scope for protecting and creating jobs.

There was a wider conflict, too, crucial to Europe's financial industry, over the design of TARGET, the future system for settling euro transactions. Countries due to remain outside EMU, especially Britain, were fighting for the access which their financial markets needed to compete for euro business. France and Germany found common cause in resisting the pressure. London-based analysts argued that they would have to give way because efficient euro settlement in Europe's dominant financial centre would be essential to smooth the new currency's launch. However, the TARGET dispute is peripheral to the question of whether EMU will happen.

Political resolve

Events were playing unexpected variations on the adage that monetary union will take place in Europe if France is able and Germany is willing. Suddenly there were doubts about whether Germany would be able to meet the strict terms of the Maastricht Treaty; and whether France would be willing to submit to a German-designed stability pact. Germany's dominant commercial bank, Deutsche Bank, raised its assessment of the risk that EMU would be delayed or cancelled to 45 per cent from 30 per cent.

But at the Dublin summit in December 1996, EU leaders once more rose to the occasion. Smaller EU countries, notably Luxembourg, Belgium and Ireland, played a crucial role in bridging Franco-German differences. The leaders wrestled to a compromise on the stability pact which freed them to endorse other essential details of how EMU would work. They finalised plans for ERM II; endorsed the urgent implementation of regulations to help financial markets plan for EMU; unveiled the prototype euro banknotes; and urged 'institutions, public authorities and economic agents to intensify their preparations for the starting date of 1 January 1999'.

Even so, there were signs at Dublin that the EU would have to clamber over a few more boulders on the path to EMU. The stability pact dispute had underlined the conflict between Germany's need to convince its citizens that the euro would be a worthy substitute for the mark, and the French conviction that political power must balance the ECB in steering the economic policies of the euro zone. Above all, the 1998 choice of who joins EMU will force into the open every national doubt and prejudice about the purpose and meaning of sharing a currency. 'I think we will see a few more crises ahead of us,' said Swedish Prime Minister Goran Persson.

Yet over the past decade, EU leaders have repeatedly surprised the markets with demonstrations of renewed determination to make monetary union a reality. Both France and Germany have invested a considerable degree of national prestige in EMU. Both fear that backing away from the project could wreak havoc with their painfully reconstructed post-war relationship. All told, progress towards monetary union has gathered powerful momentum.

What they say about EMU's chances

'To turn down the European currency would be to accept the domination of the dollar and the all-powerfulness of the financial markets.' French Prime Minister Alain Juppe, in his book *Entre Nous*, December 1996.

'Considering all the problems which still remain to be solved, there is a realistic chance of meeting the schedule (for EMU) ... . At the same time, one should guard against exaggerated optimism from markets which already stuck their necks out rather too far before the ... crisis in 1992.' EMI President Alexandre Lamfalussy, Handelsblatt, December 1996.

'I am sure the majority of the German population think they are paying a high price (for EMU). But they will be prepared to pay that price if they know that as a result Europe can live in peace.' German Chancellor Helmut Kohl, December 1996.

'I think the 1999 (start) date is inevitable. Failure to respect it would lead to such a crisis for our country (France) and our economy that I cannot imagine this catastrophic scenario.' European Commissioner Yves-Thibault de Silguy, November 1996.

'I get the feeling ever more clearly that it is going ahead.' British Chancellor of the Exchequer Kenneth Clarke, September 1996.

GAUGING EXPECTATIONS ON EMU

The path to monetary union hinges on convergence of long-term interest rates and the stability of currency exchange rates. The obstacles encountered, and advances made, are nowhere better seen than in the long-term charts of the French franc/German mark exchange rate and the spread between German and Italian 10-year bonds.

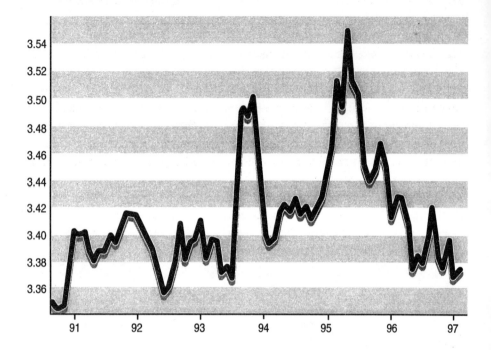

Figure 1.1: *Graph indicating mark/French franc rate*

Just as the Franco-German relationship represents the linchpin of monetary union, the franc/mark rate highlights the market's shifting views on the likelihood of EMU taking place. It has been a bumpy ride, although by late 1996 the cross rate was showing signs of stability. The current central parity rate around 3.3539 per mark was established in 1987 after a franc devaluation. From then until the early 1990s, the market did not stray too far from that level, although the franc was generally on the weaker side of the parity rate.

But as moves towards EMU gained momentum following the Maastricht summit, currency tension began to creep in. The first big blow was the Danish 'no' vote in a referendum on the treaty in June 1992. This coincided with a period of mark strength. German interest rates were high as the Bundesbank sought to quell inflation following reunification. By September the dollar had fallen to record lows against the mark and investors were flocking to the German currency as a bastion of stability. Anxieties about EMU ahead of a scheduled French referendum in September only added to the mark's appeal. The franc approached its 3.4305 per mark floor in its 2.25 per cent ERM band during this period but the resolve of the Bank of France and the Bundesbank held it. Sterling and the lira were not so fortunate. Both exited the ERM in September 1992.

The real pressure on the franc did not come until more than half a year later. Speculative investors, having profited so much on the sterling and lira devaluations, decided to have another attack on the ERM. The markets were out for blood and during July 1993, when the Bundesbank's support for the franc was perceived to be flagging, the pressures proved overwhelming. High-flying hedge fund managers sold the franc en masse. Billionaire George Soros, who had said before the crisis that he would not sell the franc, made a public statement that he no longer felt tied to his promise because the German central bank was not doing its bit.

By August 1993, European authorities were forced to revamp the ERM, widening the fluctuation bands to 15 per cent but keeping the central parity rates the same. The French franc weakened sharply but over time it regained its composure. After one last blowout, in late 1994, the franc has steadily improved and is now trading largely where it was before the European currency crises struck.

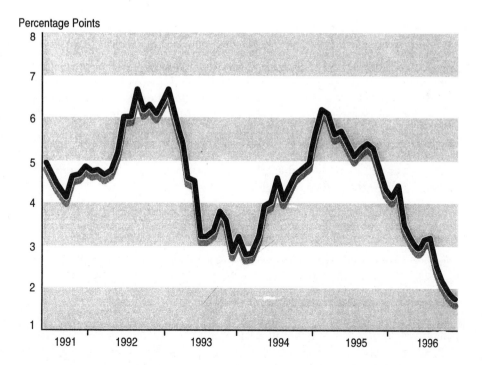

Figure 1.2: *Graph indicating interest rate differential between Italian and German 10-year bonds*

Italian government bonds have traditionally been dubbed 'high yielders' because investors have demanded a large interest rate premium to put their money into such a volatile market. During the currency crises of 1992 and 1993, the yield differential between the Italian BTP benchmark bonds and German Bunds widened out to 6.5 percentage points, bloated by Italy's plunging sovereign debt ratings.

After the ERM revamp, as market turmoil gradually died down, that spread narrowed dramatically before one last blowout in late 1994/early 1995. Since then, Italian fiscal reform and a falling inflation rate have raised its credit ratings and given the market confidence to chase after the large yield premiums on offer in the BTP market. As confidence in EMU grew throughout 1996, the spread rapidly dwindled to less than two points. At times it was smaller than the British Gilt/Bund yield gap, signalling that the market for the first time ever considered Italian government debt a better proposition than British bonds. Two points is the ceiling which the Maastricht Treaty sets on long-term interest rate differentials for EMU applicants.

How the markets rate EMU's chances

It is possible to get beyond the rhetoric and cynicism to find out how financial markets really rate the chances of EMU happening. There are at least five currency and interest rate instruments which market analysts scrutinise to assess whether investors believe the odds are on EMU. These indicators have to be used with some caution. To some extent they reflect how far and how fast EU economies are converging. Such convergence owes a lot to political competition to qualify for EMU, but it is also inspired by a global consensus that cutting state spending is good for countries in the long run. However, throughout 1996, these indicators showed a convincing bias towards at least a core group of countries launching EMU on January 1, 1999.

Implied interest rate spreads

National interest rate differentials are used in pricing foreign exchange and interest rate contracts like futures, forwards and swaps (see Glossary). By extracting this element of the price, analysts can work out how much of a risk premium the market is levying over German interest rates, the European benchmark, for products denominated in other EU currencies.

Some analysts are watching implied short-term rates to December 1998. One-week rates give a good indication of market confidence in EMU if they show French and German interest rates converging to the same level in December 1998.

More liquid implied five-year forward rates give a good indication of how the market ranks the chances of 'peripheral' countries joining EMU, maybe in a second wave, as well as measuring the overall degree of EMU optimism.

Five- and 10-year bond spreads

The difference between market yields on government bonds. They serve the same purpose as the implied interest rate spreads.

Mark/French franc exchange rate

One of the more obvious indicators of market confidence in EMU, given that most analysts see the Franco-German axis as a necessary, although not sufficient, ingredient for monetary union to go ahead. Confidence in at least the Franco-German commitment to monetary union can be gauged by the stability of this rate, although some argue that the level of mark/French franc may be a slightly flawed indicator because it's not certain yet at what rate the franc and mark would be irrevocably fixed. Despite the widening of the ERM's allowed fluctuation bands to 15 per cent, the rate returned to its old 2.25 per cent ERM bands during 1996, where it stuck through Franco-German and domestic tensions over cost-cutting and controversial accounting in drafting the 1997 French budget.

The mark/Swiss franc exchange rate rate

German investors concerned about the loss of the mark after EMU have been piling into Switzerland as the only alternative safe haven. The Swiss National Bank undertook major intervention in the money market during 1996 to counter such flows. This has muted the impact of German asset switches, but surges of EMU angst still affect the mark/Swiss rate.

The Ecu's actual/theoretical spread

This measures how far Ecu cash on the open market trades below its theoretical value, calculated from the values of the 12 currencies which make up the Ecu basket. Typically, the bigger the discount, the less confidence there has been in the Ecu becoming Europe's single currency. Liquidity drained from the

Ecu market after the 1992 crisis of confidence in EMU, and at times since then the discount has widened to more than three per cent. However, a European Commission proposal to make the Ecu convertible one-for-one with the euro helped to narrow the discount to 0.25 per cent in late 1996. If the market becomes confident that the euro will encompass only the stronger of the Ecu basket currencies, the discount should revert to the premium which the Ecu often commanded before the 1992 crisis. A continuing discount could reflect the belief that weaker currencies will be admitted to EMU, as well as more general uncertainty about the project.

German yield-curve kink

The yields on German bonds due to mature after the 1999 EMU start date sometimes ratchet sharply higher. London-based analysts say this often reflects concern about the stability of the single currency and the anti-inflation credentials of an ECB. They say the greater the size of that yield-curve kink, the more people think EMU will occur. Some Frankfurt-based analysts are sceptical, saying there are more mundane structural explanations for the phenomenon.

The JP Morgan calculator

US investment house JP Morgan has publicised its own method of calculating real-time market expectations of EMU, using bond yield spreads in the swaps market. It assesses what the spread would be if EMU takes place, what it is now and what the spread would be if EMU was not in the equation. It does not use nominal exchange rates or nominal bond yields because there is no certainty about what the fixed exchange rates will be or at what level bond yields will converge. JP Morgan says the one thing that is certain is that after EMU day, bond spreads in the swaps market between two member countries will be zero.

Finding the non-EMU level of swap spreads is more complicated. JP Morgan says it is not fair to simply strip out the EMU effect by looking solely at indicators such as inflation and budget deficits, because these have been heavily influenced by the policy push to meet EMU entry criteria. Comparing current spreads with an average historic spread is also vulnerable to misinterpretation because factors such as global deflation have helped to narrow spreads.

JP Morgan says a better way to estimate what European swap spreads would be without EMU, is to look at measures of risk such as volatility, inflation and default. Over the past 10 years, it says, around 80 per cent of the French-German 10-year spread can be explained by the behaviour of spreads outside Europe. The regression breaks down after 1994 when Europe treads a different path to the rest of the world – the EMU path.

So the calculator uses the zero spread assumed at EMU, the current spread and the estimated non-EMU spread, to assess the relative probabilities the market places in EMU happening in any one country and can look at their change over time.

In late 1996, the calculator classified European countries into three tiers:

● the core, such as Germany, France, the Netherlands and Belgium, where EMU is almost a complete certainty;

● a border group of Sweden and Denmark, where EMU probability was put at between 50 and 60 per cent, mainly due to public resistance to the project;

● 'peripheral' countries, such as Spain and Italy, where EMU probabilities were put at between 30 and 40 per cent because of doubts about fulfilling the entry criteria.

The stability pact

To give the euro maximum credibility, the EU has agreed on a mechanism to punish governments running high public deficits inside monetary union. Driven by Germany, whose obsession with monetary and fiscal rigour has become legendary, the 15-nation bloc has accepted the idea of a stability pact which would include fines on those unable to bring their deficits below three per cent of GDP. Only in the event of a severe economic downturn, inflicted by national disaster or an external shock, could a government plead exemption.

Franco-German tensions, the greatest risk to EMU, broke out in late 1996 over how to define the 'exceptional or temporary' circumstance that would let the offending country off the hook. Germany wanted a mechanism which would make the imposition of fines virtually automatic. France won the backing of most of its EU partners in arguing that the final say had to rest with elected governments. After hours of heavy-duty bargaining at the EU's December summit, a deal was done.

The result was a pact which will harden up an 'excessive deficit procedure' already annexed to the treaty (see Appendices), but still leave room for political manoeuvre. A government would be exempt from fines if its economy was in undisputed recession, shrinking by two per cent a year; or if it could convince other governments that it faced unusual economic difficulties which were not of its own making.

How the stability pact would work

These are the steps which the EU outlined in December 1996 for taking action against an EMU government whose budget deficit rose above three per cent of GDP.

- The European Commission would prepare an annual report on the offending country. 'As a rule', this would say the country should be exempt from sanctions only if its GDP had suffered an annual fall of at least two per cent.

- A new Economic and Financial Committee would give an opinion on the Commission's report within two weeks. This committee would replace the EU's monetary committee after EMU.

- EU ministers, the ultimate arbiters on sanctions, would also take into account any evidence that the offending government could provide 'showing that an annual fall of real GDP of less than two per cent is nevertheless exceptional in light of further supporting evidence'. A country could argue, for example, that the economic downturn was unusually abrupt or more severe than previous recessions.

- If the ministers were not convinced the government had a good excuse for heavy borrowing, they would make recommendations on how it should curb its deficit, with a clear deadline for taking action — four months.

- The deficit should be cut back to the three per cent limit by the following year 'unless special circumstances are given'.

- If a government failed to take the EU's advice, the EU would order it to hand over a non-interest bearing deposit. This would happen at most 10 months after the budget overshoot was first identified.

- The deposit would be converted into a fine after two years if the government's deficit was still considered excessive.

- The initial deposit or fine would be 0.2 per cent of GDP, with another 0.1 per cent for every percentage point that the deficit goes over the three per cent limit. The maximum fine would be 0.5 per cent of GDP.

EU leaders would back the pact with a resolution urging 'all parties to implement ... (the) regulations strictly'. If ministers did not act on a Commission recommendation to impose fines, they would be urged to 'state in writing the reasons which justify (their) decision not to act and to make public the votes cast by each member state'. Governments would pledge not to argue that their economic troubles were exceptional unless their economies were in 'severe recession'. In deciding how severe the downturn was, governments would 'as a rule' take a 0.75 per cent decline in GDP as a guideline.

EU diplomats said this last point was crucial in securing an agreement. The pact could not say anything which restricted the sovereignty of finance ministers' decisions unless the EU renegotiated the Maastricht Treaty, a step which no one wanted to take. This goes to the heart of the EU's decision-making process and France argued strongly against any erosion of ministers' sovereignty.

So the burden of proof falls on the offending government to show that its economy is suffering an exceptional downturn. The decisions reached at the Dublin summit were due to be formalised in a regulation expected to be ready in time for the next summit of EU leaders in Amsterdam in June 1997.

Germany said it was happy with the compromise. Juergen Stark, a senior finance ministry official, estimated that in the previous 35 years, only about 20 exemptions would have been granted to EU nations under the terms agreed at Dublin. A stricter pact, enforcing a two per cent fall in GDP as the only excuse for evading fines, would have produced 13 exemptions over that period, Stark said.

Does EMU need a stability pact?

The rationale for the stability pact is the risk that some EMU countries — or, at least, one of the larger states — could use their new-found freedom from exchange rate risk to borrow heavily. Sustained budget deficits in one or more countries could ultimately raise real interest rates throughout the EMU area and damage the credibility of the euro.

But the idea of imposing sanctions on governments which engage in expansionary fiscal policies has its critics. Among them is Willem Buiter, an economist at Britain's Cambridge University, who has argued that the link between currency and budget stability is tenuous at best. 'The idea that you need some sort of budget mechanism to ensure the success of EMU is absurd,' Buiter told Reuters.

To back their claims, he and other economists cite countries which run lofty deficits or have debt levels well above the norm and yet retain stable currencies. Belgium, a country whose total outstanding debt amounts to well over 100 per cent of GDP, is a case in point.

Besides, a set of rules which binds governments to tight budget policies might set in motion a deflationary spiral when combined with the future policies of a ECB wedded to price stability. The ECB's initial policy bias could be tilted towards monetary tightness in order to establish its inflation-fighting credentials. If it tries to keep real interest rates high against the backdrop of slow growth, high unemployment and budget policies aimed at achieving balance, economists in Europe and overseas worry that economic growth could suffer.

American officials, while publicly supportive of Europe's drive towards closer economic integration, have expressed concerns over the negative impact which tight budget policies would have on growth in the industrialised world. Their fears are heightened by Europe's lack of a fiscal transfer system on the U.S. model which could channel community funds to regions or countries hurt by a sharp economic shock.

Economists say if national governments inside EMU cannot demonstrate that such downturns are extraordinary, the fines could in fact deepen their budgetary troubles.

Some also question whether the temptation to borrow heavily will really be that great under EMU. They note that most big national debtors can benefit from inflation, by letting rising prices erode the repayment value of the funds which they borrow. If a Bundesbank-style ECB succeeds in stamping out inflation, then heavy borrowing will look less attractive to EMU governments.

Finally, even some EU monetary officials have doubts over how much allegiance politicians would have to the stability pact when faced with competing political objectives. 'I sincerely doubt whether a politician, facing re-election, would abide by Community legislation if it threatened his political life,' said one official.

A stability council?

The stability pact negotiations refocused attention on the idea of economic policy coordination within EMU, an issue not addressed by the Maastricht treaty but warmly embraced by countries like France. The French have insisted that elected governments should play a role in determining economic policy under a common currency. Fearful that the economic fate of those living under a monetary union will be dictated solely by the ECB, the French have proposed the idea of a 'stability council'.

The council would be a consultative body, with members able to make 'recommendations' on monetary policy. Germany is firmly against the idea of outside political interference in the ECB's decision-making, and its split with France over this has become increasingly evident in official talks between the two countries.

However, French President Jacques Chirac made it plain that he was not going to drop the idea. At the Dublin summit, he said there should be regular EMU summits to coordinate economic policy and act as a counterweight to the ECB. 'In a form which has yet to be determined, the council of ministers and the council of heads of state and government of the countries which are in the euro will constitute this power opposite the central bank,' he said.

G7 could be the model

One French delegation source said Chirac wanted to establish a body similar to the Group of Seven (G7) leading industrialised nations, which meets at the level either of finance ministers or heads of state and government. The G7, launched by France, has no formal secretariat, nor binding powers.

The question of how to step up coordination of economic policies within EMU looked set to become a major theme in the run-up to 1999. Officials also want to ensure that countries left behind in the first EMU wave are not left out of the decision making. 'We have to look and see how we can have intensified cooperation among the countries inside (the euro zone). But you cannot cut Europe in two,' said European Commissioner Yves-Thibault de Silguy.

Belgian Prime Minister Jean-Luc Dehaene has suggested the question of how to coordinate policies inside monetary union would depend on how many countries joined in 1999. But he added: 'there must be a political body opposite the institutional body which is the monetary authority'.

Any attempt to establish a political power to counterbalance the ECB will also have to balance France and Germany's different visions of exchange rate policies. While there is pressure in France to use the launch of the euro to push for a rise in the dollar to make European exports more competitive, in Germany there is resistance to using exchange rates as a trade tool. Chirac's aim of establishing a political grouping to coordinate policies inside EMU will therefore probably only be successful if it is clear that it is not going to do anything to jeopardise the independence of the central bank.

Social tensions

The stability pact is meant to underpin the post-EMU economy, but some analysts say the belt-tightening required may increase unemployment and generate serious social tensions.

Supporters of EMU say that in a world divided into large trading blocs, European firms must be allowed the benefits of trading in their own backyard without the burden of currency exchanges. Freer market access, lower transaction costs and easier travel between countries are all touted as compelling advantages of EMU that could actually boost employment across the continent long-term. Moreover, the reduction in Europe's national debt levels demanded for entry into EMU will free up funds currently absorbed by interest payments. In theory, this could be used to ease Europe's stubbornly high 11 per cent unemployment average.

But within EMU, countries will surrender the ability to devalue their national currencies to restore international competitiveness. This could have a drastic effect on employment. 'The main effect of EMU in the short-term is that it takes away a possible safety valve from the labour markets,' Steven Englander, international economist at investment bank Smith Barney in Paris said. He said that in the first two years or so after 1999, employment levels could rise because of the relatively healthy, low-inflation state of the economies of those countries that qualify for EMU. But after that, the collective wage bargaining systems still employed by a number of countries across Europe could prove too inflexible without the option of exchange rate adjustment.

'What then if a country makes a big mistake in its wage bargaining rounds?' Englander asked, noting that an excessively high round of wage settlements would make that country's products too expensive. That in turn could lead to serious job losses, unless the EU found other compensatory measures that could be 'very slow and very expensive,' he said.

All this would be less of a problem if EMU boosted cross-border labour flows which, nearly four years after the creation of the single European market, are still barely noticeable. But there is wide consensus that it will not. 'We do not expect to see vast amounts of cross-border movements just because of EMU,' said Norman Bowers, head of employment analysis for the Organisation for Economic Cooperation and Development (OECD). 'The portability of everything from qualifications to pensions will remain a problem, and then of course language is still an issue.'

In a July 1996 report, the OECD said western nations had to face up to a stark choice between persistently high jobless rates, or the freeing up of labour markets to create more jobs, while still condemning to poverty some of those in work. Employers generally regard the European labour market as less flexible than that of the United States, for example, largely because of the EU's high level of welfare provision but also due to less tangible cultural factors. That view, hotly disputed by Europe's trade unions and other worker groups, nonetheless appears to have found favour among Europe's governments, some of which are already putting through measures to free up their labour markets.

Cutting labour costs

Germany, which according to some estimates has labour costs up to double those in comparable U.S. industries, has launched an attack on the generous system of worker benefits once seen as underpinning the country's post-war economic miracle.

France, the other vital early entrant to EMU, has sought to cut its overall labour costs with moves to axe thousands of civil service and other public sector jobs. And Spain, which has the highest jobless rate in Europe, is now moving away from an old labour law under which companies were only justified in making redundancies if their survival was otherwise threatened.

But unions across Europe argue that higher productivity, not flexibility, is the long-term key to job creation and that governments should instead invest in measures to enhance Europe's output. 'Over the last decades it has been Germany and Japan that have invested the most in productivity, and that is why their currencies have over the long term been so strong,' said Hans-Georg Wehner, management board secretary of Germany's DGB trade union umbrella group. Wehner said that German labour costs looked high compared to those in the U.S. because of the huge appreciation of the German currency against the dollar since World War Two. Declared U.S. figures, which showed unemployment at around 5.5 per cent during 1996, excluded large numbers of jobless people who had not registered as such, he said.

German measures to slash 1997 public spending included: reforms to health and pension systems, cuts in sick pay entitlements and a relaxation of job protection law. The sick pay cuts in particular triggered protests by workers across German industry, led by hundreds of thousands of workers in the key metal and engineering sector. In late 1996, one of Germany's most powerful trade union officials warned that there would be more social strife to come across Europe over the austerity measures undertaken in the name of EMU. Ursula Engelen-Kefer, deputy head of the Confederation of German Trade Unions (DBG), said,'We need EMU. But it depends how it is shaped. If it is done the way (German finance minister Theo Waigel) Waigel wants it ... then there is the risk of huge strikes.'

Engelen-Kefer, whose organisation represents some nine million people across Germany, said the cuts in welfare systems meant that the poorest in society were suffering the most. 'The cost-cutting should not mean that you take money out of the pockets of the little man,' she said, calling for accompanying measures to stimulate the job market or protect existing posts. Instead of cutting social spending, she urged the German government to follow an Italian example — much frowned upon by the Bundesbank — and levy a one-off 'euro-tax' to cut the 1997 budget deficit. 'It would be much more intelligent to have a special tax for Maastricht,' she said.

Wehner said full employment targets and higher investment in the workforce were more appropriate long-term goals than creating a freer labour market. But such arguments have fallen on largely deaf ears. Unions and sympathetic political leaders in countries like Sweden have battled for the addition to the Maastricht Treaty of a specific commitment on employment. By late 1996, rising social tensions over unemployment were pushing more reluctant governments, notably those of France and Germany, towards making some sort of gesture towards recognising job creation as a priority under EMU. But few expected such a commitment to amount to much more than warm words.

If more left-leaning policies emerge in countries like Germany and Britain in the run-up to 1999, that might change. But whatever the shift in political balance in the run up to EMU, the fiscal tightness demanded by the Maastricht Treaty limits governments' scope for manoeuvre. That, some fear, may threaten the jobs of European workforces just as governments start to cut away the safety nets.

A CHRONOLOGY OF THE ERM AND STEPS TOWARDS MONETARY UNION

The exchange rate mechanism allows currencies to fluctuate within bands either side of their fixed central rates. After a crisis in 1993, the bands were widened to 15 per cent for all except the mark and guilder, which maintained 2.25 per cent bands.

1979

- March 13 – ERM formed. German mark, French and Belgian francs, Dutch guilder, Danish crown, Irish punt join with 2.25 per cent bands; Italian lira with six per cent bands.

- September 24 – First change to ERM parities: mark revalued, Danish crown devalued.

- December 3 – Danish crown devalued.

1981–3

- Five realignments produce: three French franc devaluations; four lira devaluations; three revaluations of the mark and guilder; a punt devaluation; and devaluation then revaluation of the Danish crown and Belgian franc.

1985

- July 22 – Mark, Danish crown, Belgian and French francs, punt and guilder revalued, lira devalued.

1986

- April 7 – Last independent French franc devaluation; mark, guilder, Danish crown, Belgian franc all revalued.
  Aug 4 – Punt devalued.

1987

- January 12 – Mark, guilder, Belgian franc revalued.

- September 12 – Basle-Nyborg accord grants central banks credit lines to finance intra-marginal intervention, to support their currencies within the ERM bands, but emphasises use of interest rate differentials as the best defence.

1989

- April 17 – Delors Report outlines three-stage plan for EMU.

- June 12 – Spanish peseta joins ERM with six per cent bands.

1990

- January 8 – Lira devalues and moves to 2.25 per cent bands from six per cent bands.

- April 23 – West Germany offers one-for-one conversion between West and East German marks, effective from July 1, prior to political reunification in October.

- October 8 – UK joins ERM with 2.95 mark central rate and six per cent bands.

1991

- December 10 – Heads of government agree the Treaty on European Union in Dutch town of Maastricht, paving the way for a single EU currency by 1999.

1992

- February 7 – Maastricht Treaty signed by EU finance and foreign ministers.

- April 6 – Portuguese escudo enters ERM with six per cent bands.

- June 2 – Danes vote no to the Maastricht treaty, with 50.7 per cent against, awakening market doubts about EMU and launching months of ERM turmoil.

- June 3 – France announces autumn referendum on Maastricht.

- July 16 – Bundesbank announces discount rate rise to record 8.75 per cent.

- June 19 – Ireland votes in favour of Maastricht, with 68.7 per cent in favour.

- September 3 – UK treasury borrows 16 billion Ecu to defend the pound within ERM.

- September 4 – Italy raises official rates by 1.75 points to defend lira.

- September 5 – EU finance ministers stress they have no plans for ERM realignment.

- September 8 – Finland severs markka's link to Ecu. Sweden raises interest rates.

- September 10 – British Prime Minister John Major rules out devaluation within ERM.

- September 13 – First major realignment of the ERM since January 1987: behind-the-scenes deal trades lira devaluation to 802.49 per mark for German interest rate cuts.

- September 14 – Bundesbank announces modest rate cuts: market sells pound and lira.

- September 16 – 'Black Wednesday.' Markets force pound, lira and peseta below ERM floors. Central banks intervene. Britain announces unprecedented two-stage rise in base rate from 10 to 15 per cent, then suspends pound from ERM and cuts base rate to 12 per cent. Sweden hikes overnight rate to 500 per cent.

- September 17 – After a six-hour meeting, EU's monetary committee suspends lira from ERM. Peseta devalued by five per cent. Britain cuts base rate to 10 per cent.

- September 20 – French voters approve Maastricht treaty, with 51.05 per cent in favour.

- September 23 – France and Germany launch counter-offensive against currency speculation. Exchange controls imposed temporarily in Ireland, Spain and Portugal.

- November 19 – Sweden abandons efforts to peg crown to the Ecu, renewing turmoil.

- November 22 – Peseta, escudo devalued. Markets attack punt, Danish crown, French franc.

- December 12 – EU summit in Edinburgh reaffirms commitment to Maastricht treaty.

1993

- January 1 – EU single market begins; Ireland, Spain, Portugal lift exchange controls.

- January 7 – Ireland raises overnight interest rates to 100 per cent.

- January 30 – Ireland devalues punt by 10 per cent, biggest single ERM devaluation.

- February 1 – Central bank intervention deflects market attention from Danish crown.

- April – Bank of France starts suggesting franc might share mark's anchor role in ERM.

- April 19 – EU finance ministers unveil 35 billion Ecu plan to create jobs.

- May 13 – Peseta and escudo devalued.

- May 18 – Danish vote in favour of Maastricht treaty at second referendum.

- June 21 – French intervention rate below German discount rate, first time in 23 years.

- June 21/22 – EU summit in Copenhagen calls for quick cuts in European interest rates.

- July 12 – Bundesbank intervenes to buy French francs.

- July 29 – Bundesbank ignores market speculation it will cut its discount rate to save the ERM, shaves half a point off less important Lombard rate instead.

- July 30 – Central banks fail to stop repeated French franc dips below ERM floor.

- August 1 – Emergency meeting of finance ministers and central bankers. After 12 hours of talks, early in the morning of August 2 they widen bands for all ERM currencies except the mark and guilder to 15 per cent. Mark and guilder maintain 2.25 per cent range.

- November 1 – German constitutional court rules in favour of Maastricht Treaty.

1994

- January 1 – Stage Two of EMU starts; European Monetary Institute founded in Frankfurt.

- September 6 – Germany's ruling CDU party suggests core countries launch EMU in 1999.

- October 17 – Germany's Chancellor Kohl wins fourth term.

1995

- January 8 – Austrian schilling joins the ERM with 15 per cent fluctuation bands.

- March 6 – Peseta, escudo devalued.

- May 8 – Jacques Chirac elected French president.

- December 15 – EU leaders confirm January 1, 1999, as start date for single currency.

1996

- October 14 – Finland joins the ERM with 15 per cent fluctuation bands.

- November 24 – European finance ministers and central bankers compromise on lira re-entry to ERM at 990 per mark after heated debate, with Germany pushing for stronger lira.

2

Which countries will qualify for EMU?

By Henry Engler in Brussels, Myra MacDonald in Paris, Richard Waddington in Lisbon and Ruth Pitchford and Astrid Zweynert in London

Reading the runes of the Maastricht Treaty is becoming a task of theological proportions for Europe's political leaders, central bankers and financial market analysts. The treaty sets out economic goals which countries must be seen to pursue if they are to be deemed fit for EMU on judgement day in early 1998. However, the treaty itself was the product of hard bargaining between Germany, anxious to reassure voters that it would be safe to surrender the mark, and its EU partners, who hope EMU will diffuse German influence over continental Europe's monetary policy.

The conflict shows. Protocols attached to the treaty do lay down some very specific goals on inflation, long-term interest rates, fiscal deficits and total state debt. But the treaty itself makes plain that the deficit and debt figures are target ceilings, cushioned by heavily qualified language to enable a political decision on admission to the EMU club.

The language of the treaty is meant to discourage politicians from interpreting the entrance criteria too liberally. The treaty emphasises that economies must have converged in a durable and sustainable way before they form a monetary union. Most economists would agree that such convergence is essential. EMU states will lose a favourite device for kickstarting an economy out of recession, the ability to devalue the national currency to spur export-led growth. Applicants need to be sure that they have enough control over their debt burdens to give up the safety valve of national currency devaluation.

However, the preoccupation with defining the words 'durable', 'sustainable' and 'convergence' looks set to rival the mediaeval European obsession with counting the number of angels that can dance on a pinhead. Hardliners tend to emphasise how long a country has spent converging. This lets in Belgium, the EU's biggest state debtor, on the grounds that it started running a primary budget surplus in 1985 in an economic reform drive which also helped to curb inflation and stabilise its currency. But it might exclude Italy, which adopted the EMU creed by slashing its budget into primary surplus only in 1992. Italy has since made bigger strides towards convergence than any EMU contender. But it started from the most precarious economic position and its conversion is too recent to convince EMU's hawks. As for the EU's lesser debtors, Ireland has set a precedent. The Commission said Ireland had met the

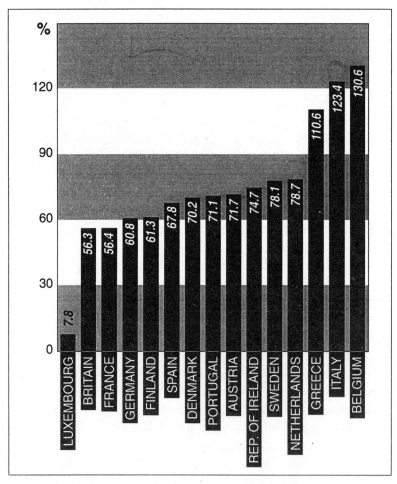

Figure 2.1:   *EU countries' debt (as a percentage of GDP, 1996)*

Source: European Commission Forecasts, Autumn 1996

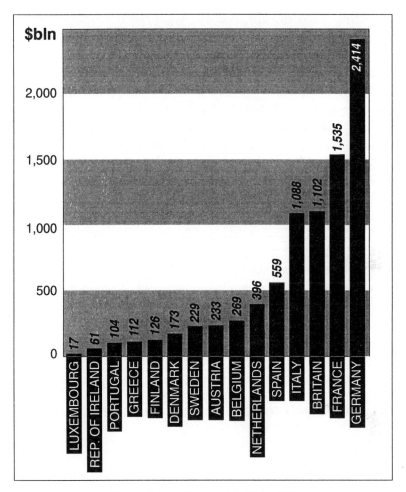

Figure 2.2: *EU countries' GDP, 1995*

Source: OECD, 1995

debt criteria when it cut its ratio from 117 per cent to just under 90 per cent of GDP in five years. By 1996, Ireland had whittled the ratio down an estimated 75 per cent and it was widely accepted that this performance would satisfy the 1998 auditors.

Another area rich in scope for interpretation is how budget deficits are calculated. The EU is due to make its 1998 assessment based largely on 1997 data. France ensured that fiscal number-crunching became an issue when it credited a transfer of funds worth 0.5 per cent of GDP from France Telecom to its 1997 budget, in return for assuming the state-owned company's pension liabilities.

Germany, Britain and the Netherlands complained that such one-off credits should not count in budget arithmetic. Eurostat authorised the plan, leaving some doubt as to how the EU could then disapprove of Italy's plan to use vaguely-defined 'treasury operations' and to levy a one-off 'Euro-tax' in 1997 in an heroic bid to bring its 1997 deficit within sight of the Maastricht target ceiling.

Spain and Portugal took pains to distance themselves from Italy, protesting at hardliners' collective term for the three economies, the 'Club Med'. They pointed out that just because all three countries entertained northern European holiday-makers at resorts of the Club Méditerranée tourism group, there was no need to stereotype their economies. The two Iberian countries have much smaller debt burdens than Italy, although they still suffer from greater inflationary pressures than the more mature economies of northern Europe. The EMI's 1996 report made some distinction between them, urging Spain and Portugal to pursue 'strong' measures towards convergence while exhorting Italy to 'very strong' action.

Decision-making will be complicated further if Germany itself misses the debt and deficit targets. It is highly unlikely to do more than creep above the ceilings, but that would put both the German ratios on a rising trend, a fact which states with bigger but declining debt burdens will be tempted to underline.

INTERPRETING THE MAASTRICHT TREATY

The EMU judgement

The 1998 judgement on who enters EMU will involve every major EU institution: the Commission, the EMI, ECOFIN and the European Council, with the European parliament entitled to an 'opinion'. The decision on who qualifies will probably be taken in April, when the EU hopes to have reliable economic data for 1997. Both the Commission and the EMI will offer their assessment of the 15 member countries. This will be weighed by EU finance ministers, then the heads of state and government will give the final verdict.

The EU's protocol on excessive deficits says the Commission should take into account 'all other relevant factors, including the medium term economic and budgetary position of the member state'. The decision-makers are certain to look beyond the decimal point in the three per cent target ceiling for 1997 budget deficits, towards the quality of economic convergence as well as towards political imperatives. As one German official put it: 'We have to get away from this bean-counter's mentality'.

There is a slightly clearer majority interpretation of the fifth convergence criterion, that countries should belong to the ERM in order to demonstrate exchange rate stability. At the time the treaty was signed, ERM membership limited currencies to fluctuation bands narrow enough to represent evident convergence. Britain and Sweden in particular argue that the 1992–93 crisis which eventually forced the EU to widen the ERM bands to 15 per cent changed all that, making ERM membership irrelevant in assessing currency stability. But the treaty specifies performance within the ERM as the litmus test on exchange rates. The EMI's 1996 report said there was a 'strong majority' in favour of applying the ERM membership clause.

However, an alternative has been mooted: using a mathematical formula involving a coefficient of variance to assess how much EU currencies have moved against each other. The Commission has tried out the technique and found that by this measure, ERM currencies varied less than those outside the ERM. At any rate, Finland's decision to join the ERM in October 1996 and Italy's re-entry the following month underline the expectation that the decision-makers will view ERM membership as an important token of political commitment to EMU.

What they call 'sustainable'

'It is important ... that the (EMU) member countries do not just reach the criteria through a breathless short-term effort.' Hans Tietmeyer, Bundesbank president, October 1996.

'I am not sure that the Germans are in a position to give us a lesson. They got into some dubious budget practices with the takeover of the Treuhand, the German agency for the privatisation of east German companies. And it is not certain either that they will fulfil the Maastricht criteria in 1997.' Jean-Pierre Gerard of the Bank of France's monetary policy council, *Le Monde*, November 1996.

'The decision (on who joins EMU) will be a political decision. It was never meant to be a technical decision.' Jean Claude Juncker, Luxembourg Prime Minister, October 1996.

'The Bundesbank assumes that we are dealing with a treaty that 15 states have approved ... and which one therefore cannot undermine on certain points which do not seem to fully suit at present.' Bundesbank vice-chairman Johann Wilhelm Gaddum, November 1996.

'The arguments of the fundamentalists will end up killing off the European currency with an overdose of criteria.' Former French President Valery Giscard d'Estaing, February 1996.

THE CONVERGENCE CRITERIA

- **Price stability.** An average rate of consumer price inflation during the year before the examination that does not exceed by more than 1.5 percentage points that of, at most, the three best performing member states.

- **Budget deficits.** Not to exceed three per cent of GDP, 'unless either the ratio has declined substantially and continuously and reached a level that comes close to the reference value; or, alternatively, the excess over the reference value is only exceptional and temporary and the ratio remains close to the reference value'.

- **Total government debt.** Not to exceed 60 per cent of GDP, 'unless the ratio is sufficiently diminishing and approaching the reference value at a satisfactory pace'.

- **Long-term interest rates.** Average nominal rates not to exceed by more than two percentage points that of, at most, the three best performing member states in terms of price stability.

- **Exchange rate stability** 'shall mean that a member state has respected the normal fluctuation margins provided for by the Exchange Rate Mechanism of the European Monetary System without severe tensions for at least the last two years before examination'.

Other considerations include

- **Central bank independence.** Every country wishing to join EMU has to make sure that a national government cannot influence its central bank's decision-making; and that the central bank's legal mandate gives it the primary duty of maintaining price stability. States really need to pass laws on this by mid-1998, when the ESCB and ECB are due to be set up. The EMI's 1996 report said that so far not even the Bundesbank met these criteria completely.

- **The real economy.** Decision-makers are also obliged to consider how far EU markets have integrated; countries' balance of payments on their current accounts; unit labour costs; and 'other price indices'.

- **The Ecu.** The treaty obliges the EU to consider 'the development of the Ecu', which may give some indication of the degree of market confidence in EMU.

The official view of convergence

Financial market analysts noted a sharp contrast in the two official views of convergence which emerged on November 6, 1996. The Frankfurt-based EMI concluded that 'at present a majority of member states do not fulfil the necessary conditions for the adoption of a single currency' and urged every EU country, except for economically unimpeachable Luxembourg, to try harder. The same economic developments confirmed the view of the Brussels-based European Commission that a 'significant, and probably increasing, number of member states' should prove capable of launching EMU in 1999. To a large extent, the two organisations were merely playing out their given roles as EMU's stick and carrot. But the contrasting tones of exhortation and encouragement also reflect a real conflict of emphasis in interpreting the Maastricht Treaty which EU leaders will have to resolve in 1998.

The Commission focused on economic growth, job creation and the extent to which member states were meeting the criteria. It said every EU state except Greece looked set to meet the inflation and long-term interest rate criteria, and all but Britain, Greece and Italy should meet the fiscal deficit target ceiling. Although most countries were unlikely to get total debt below the target ceiling in 1997, it believed most were likely to be able to demonstrate a declining trend. It took account of 1997 budget measures which had 'been presented in detail and backed with a sufficient degree of political commitment'. It said one-off budget measures 'should be complemented with other measures in order to achieve budgetary rigour thereafter' but found 'the scenario for 1998, indicating further improvements in member states' budgetary situations encouraging'.

The EMI adhered more strictly to the treaty's emphasis, focusing on the quantitative criteria. It did not assess 1997 forecasts or budget plans, but 'emphasised that the improvement of the deficit by measures with a one-off effect does not ensure sustainable consolidation and great attention will have to be paid to the substance and not only to the accounting methods used in measuring both deficits and debts'. It noted that EU states had to work harder on consolidating their finances in the face of persistent unemployment and an ageing population, putting upward pressure on welfare spending.

Focusing on 1996, it failed Greece, Spain, Italy, Portugal and Britain on the inflation criteria, and Spain, Italy, Portugal and Greece on interest rate convergence. It named only Denmark, Ireland, Luxembourg and the Netherlands as likely to squeeze below the deficit target ceiling in 1996. It allowed that other EU states projected deficit reductions, but noted that the German deficit ratio was under upward pressure. On total debt, it noted that only France,

Luxembourg and Britain were likely to keep their ratios below the target; Germany and Finland were likely to join the remaining 10 in breaching the ceiling; and of those 10, only Ireland and Denmark had so far achieved major debt reductions.

The Maastricht Treaty envisaged that EMU might be able to start in 1997 and specified that government leaders should make a formal assessment at the end of 1996 on which states met the criteria. However, when EU leaders decided to wait for January 1, 1999, the default date set in the treaty, they agreed to drop their 1996 assessment. Reimut Jochimsen, the Bundesbank's most outspoken hawk, criticised the omission, saying a trial run would have boosted market confidence in EMU and given companies a sounder basis for planning for monetary union.

Reuters poll on convergence

A few days after the EU's convergence reports were released, Reuters polled 41 analysts at banks, research houses, think-tanks and employers' bodies across the EU and in Switzerland to rate EMU's chances of starting on time. The averaged answers gave only an 18 per cent chance of a delay but predicted that only a core group would go ahead on January 1, 1999. The panellists were unanimous in expecting Austria, France, Germany, Luxembourg and the Netherlands to be founding members if EMU went ahead as planned, and more than 80 per cent thought Belgium, Ireland and Finland would also be part of the core. No one thought Greece would be ready and 20 per cent or less thought the other EU states would get in on time.

Reuters also asked 34 economists which countries would pass the Maastricht tests in 1997. Only Luxembourg got five out of five. For the others, most forecasters predicted the following:

- **Austria** would fail on a strict reading of the budget deficit and total debt targets. All the forecasters thought it would get close to the deficit target, predicting a deficit of 3.5 per cent of GDP or less, but most thought its debt ratio would be more than 70 per cent.

- **Belgium** was also likely to get within sight of the deficit target at 3.5 per cent or less, but its debt ratio was around 130 per cent in 1996.

- **Denmark** would fail only on a strict reading of the debt criterion. More than half of the respondents thought it could get the ratio down to between 60 and 70 per cent.

- **Finland** was thought likely to get its debt ratio below 70 per cent, with a third of respondents predicting it could slip within the 60 per cent target. It was expected to pass all the other tests.

- **France** achieved only minority backing for its claim to meet the budget criteria. Most forecasters thought the 1997 deficit would come in at between three and 3.5 per cent of GDP, but two thought it could be closer to 4.5 per cent. France was expected to meet the other criteria.

- **Germany** was forecast to have trouble with both the deficit and debt criteria. Most thought the 1997 budget deficit would be between three and 3.5 per cent of GDP and that the debt ratio would be between 60 and 65 per cent of GDP.

- **Greece** was forecast to fail on all the criteria. All the respondents saw a budget deficit of more than 4.5 per cent and a debt ratio above 70 per cent. Only one thought Greece would meet the inflation and interest rate criteria. Greece is not in the ERM.

- **Ireland** would pass on every test except the most purist reading of the debt criteria. Total debt is expected to remain above 65 per cent of GDP. However, this is a dramatic reduction from the late 1980s.

- **Italy** was not expected to meet the budget criteria. Most forecasters put Italy's 1997 deficit ratio at more than 3.5 per cent and some thought it would be 4.5 per cent or more. Italy's debt ratio was more than 120 per cent in 1996.

- **Luxembourg** got unanimous backing to meet all the criteria.

- **The Netherlands** is expected to have a debt ratio of more than 70 per cent.

- **Portugal** was widely forecast to run a 1997 fiscal deficit of between three and 4.5 per cent, although a few respondents thought it would hit the target. Forecasters put its 1997 debt ratio at 65 per cent or more.

- **Spain** was also forecast to miss the debt and deficit targets. However, some forecasters thought it could hit the deficit target and most thought it could get the debt ratio below 70 per cent.

- **Sweden** was forecast to have a debt ratio of more than 70 per cent. It could also be ruled out on the grounds it had not joined the ERM by the end of 1996.

● **Britain** was expected to run a 1997 budget deficit of between three and 4.5 per cent, although a few forecasters thought it could slip below three per cent. Its aversion to rejoining the ERM could rule it out of EMU.

What they say about government debt

'Deviation from the reference values should be granted sparingly by interpreting the words of the treaty in a carefully restrictive way.' EMI president Alexandre Lamfalussy, November 1996.

'Some of the countries which will surely be with the founding members will not have the 60 per cent of GDP to debt (ratio) ... . If you want to include Belgium, you have to look at debt as a tendency, not as a fixed level.' Portuguese Prime Minister Antonio Guterres, October 1996.

'In the case of the fiscal reference levels, the treaty does not require nations to hit the spot exactly ... . It would be desirable if the content of the treaty were acknowledged in Germany.' Bundesbank council member Hans-Juergen Krupp, November 1996.

'You can't pass judgement on the indebtedness of a country if you don't take into account the private savings rate. A country like Italy with a savings rate that makes it possible to cover all finanical requirements does not have an imbalance.' Italian treasury and budget minister Carlo Azeglio Ciampi, December 1996.

The politics of convergence

Since political leaders have the final say over who joins EMU, the EU's voters will inevitably help to sway the decision. For many EU politicians, that means a lot of hard work in the months remaining before April 1998. For many EU voters, the pain of austerity policies linked to EMU has dimmed any vision of European unity. 'The counter-attack (about the advantages of the EU) has been slow in coming,' said Peter Ludlow of the Brussels-based Centre for European Studies. 'Noble rhetoric is called for but there's nobody there to do it.' For another crucial group of voters, the dominant fear was that the euro might prove weaker than their national currency. But reassuring such voters that it will be safe to enter monetary union may mean keeping out some of the countries which are most anxious to join.

Reactions to the euro are mixed across Europe, ranging from enthusiasm in the Netherlands to the cold-shouldered aloofness of Denmark or the tortured indecision of Britain. In Austria and Finland, countries widely viewed as both able and willing to join EMU, European parliament elections in late 1996 revealed significant dissent: more than a quarter of Austrian voters chose the far right, anti-EU Freedom Party and Finns put some prominent Eurosceptics at the top of their voting preferences. Yet the acceptance gap between politicians and people is nowhere more pronounced than in Germany.

'The mark symbolises German identity and has filled the symbolic vacuum this country experienced after the (second world) war,' said Susanne Klunkert, a political scientist who specialises in European affairs at the University of Bonn. Analysts say the currency has come to embody both the successful rebuilding of Germany and its reintegration into the world economy and the community of nations. Now, the country's self-image is polarised between the satisfaction of having created Europe's most powerful economy and a nagging anxiety about how Germany is seen in the world.

'It's an added problem in accepting the euro that German politicians and the Bundesbank insist much more than anyone else in Europe on a tough interpretation of the Maastricht criteria,' said Hans Jaeckel, senior economist at DG Bank in Frankfurt. 'This has contributed to fears in the population the euro will not be as hard as the mark.' Many Germans are still haunted by painful memories of the 1948 currency reform, their second this century, when the Reichsmark was exchanged for new deutsche marks at a rate of 10 to one. 'For many Germans the euro smacks of another currency reform and a potential devaluation of their savings and pensions,' said Klunkert at Bonn University.

Italy, Spain and Portugal

Germany's next general election is due in late 1998, ensuring that the country's leaders think twice before admitting marginal candidates like Italy. But if Italy, Spain and Portugal end up as bridesmaids at the wedding of monetary union, it will not be due to lack of ardour for the single currency. Even a wave of opposition protests in Italy triggered by the centre-left government's 1997 budget plans focused on who should bear the brunt of tax increases rather than questioning the need to slash the state deficit for EMU. 'There is still a view that EMU is a crock of gold and all the suffering is worth it,' said one political analyst in Milan.

Until mid-1996, the odds on Europe's southern flank making the cut for monetary union were very long. But signs that there will be some flexibility in deciding who qualifies, together with genuine progress in putting economic houses in order, suddenly put them in with a chance. Even Italy — which faces the toughest task of the three — has seen a sharp narrowing in the interest rate premium that it must pay to borrow money, as investor confidence grows in Rome's financial discipline.

The economic reasons why southern flank countries are falling over themselves to join EMU can be summed up in two words: cheaper money. Italy stands to save huge sums as EMU drives it to sort out the chaotic state finances which have been a millstone around the neck of an otherwise dynamic economy. The markets rewarded Rome with a narrowing of Italy's interest rate differential to Germany which, economists estimate, cut the government's debt servicing bill by over $1 billion in 1996 alone. Each percentage point reduction in interest rates knocks the equivalent of 1.2 per cent of GDP off Rome's annual interest bill.

What they say about Italy

'The main European partners (have) suddenly speeded up their effort towards meeting the Maastricht criteria on convergence, linking this to the desire, wish and hope that Italy may be excluded.' Italian finance minister Vincenzo Visco, September 1996.

'No one wants Italy out of the euro.' Italian treasury and budget minister Carlo Azeglio Ciampi, September 1996.

'It would be extremely damaging to take such a crucial step in Europe without Italy, who has been with us since the Treaty of Rome ... . At the time of Italy's re-entry into the ERM, Germany gave too much the impression that it did not want Italy.' Jean-Pierre Gerard of the Bank of France's monetary policy council, Le Monde, November 1996.

'Italy will not face discrimination but it cannot expect privileges.' Hans Tietmeyer, Bundesbank president, November 1996.

'I have linked my fate to the euro.' Italian Prime Minister Romano Prodi, November 1996.

'It would be completely unacceptable if ... the decision (on EMU's founders) were taken ... based on the various resorts of the Club Mediterranee ... . What is being tested is the performance of each country and not that of its neighbours.' Portuguese Prime Minister Antonio Guterres, November 1996.

Political leaders may balk at admitting it, but many local economists also say that the three countries—comparatively recent converts to financial rectitude, need the discipline of the single currency to go on applying strict budgetary policies. 'I doubt that without this pressure from monetary union that we would have the progress on the public finances that we have had,' said former Portuguese finance minister and central bank governor Miguel Beleza.

Being outside the inner core of monetary union could also hurt big, export-orientated companies within the three states. But for southern Europe, EMU is far from being purely a question of economics. Portuguese Prime Minister Antonio Guterres says that Lisbon's main worry is that failure to qualify for monetary union would condemn the country to a European second division. With the European Union set to grow with the arrival of eastern European new members, countries such as Portugal, already geographically distant from the centre of European affairs, risked being left with no way to influence decisions. 'There will be a centre in the new Europe and that centre will be based on the countries that belong to monetary union ... we want to be part of that centre,' he told Reuters.

For Spain, the EU has been crucial to completing the country's evolution from an isolated, economic backwater under the dictatorship of Francisco Franco, who died in 1975, to a self-confident and thrusting democracy. For Italy, already one of the world's biggest economies, to be left out of EMU would be a blow to national self-esteem. But the near-unanimity amongst Spanish, Italian and Portuguese political leaders on the need to enter EMU has served to mask the fact that membership could have a significant economic cost, some economists argue. They say that Spain and Italy, in particular, suffer from severe rigidities in their labour markets as well as a burdensome bureaucracy that could condemn them to continuing high levels of unemployment within a system of fixed exchange rates.

France

Officially, in late 1996 France was united with Germany in emphasising that Italy still had work to do to prove itself fit for EMU. 'We have no doubts about Spain. Italy has expressed the same desire. We can only rejoice at that,' French President Jacques Chirac said. But if Italy is left out at the EMU launch, its determination to stabilise the lira might flag, leaving French industry vulnerable yet again to competively-priced Italian exports. Besides, hardline German demands on the stability pact were stimulating public dissent in unlikely quarters. Jean-Pierre Gerard, a member of the policy council of the Bank of France, accused Germany of snubbing Italy. 'There's a problem of loyalty to history,' Gerard told *Le Monde*. '(Italy) wanted the construction of Europe, with the Germans and the French. It would be a mistake to create the euro without them. At the time of Italy's re-entry into the ERM, Germany gave too much the impression that it did not want Italy.'

Gerard's comments reflected a surge of unease among the French political elite. From Paris, it looked as if EMU was being forced into a mould of increasingly austere German design. Austerity policies had already brought wave after wave of strikes in France and made Chirac's government deeply unpopular. Italy, a fellow G7 economy, could prove a valuable ally for France within EMU, helping to form a significant counterweight to Germany in asserting the importance of political and social pressures. The decision on whether to admit Italy to EMU as a founding partner with France and Germany is likely to have a significant impact in shaping the EU's future.

To its supporters, the euro is the key to making a federal Europe irrevocable. To its opponents, it signifies the loss of national sovereignty and amalgamation into a faceless entity. Psychological considerations work both ways – for and against the euro – as countries fear the loss of independence but don't want to be left out either. 'EMU is peddled as a political nostrum to cure all ailments,' Pedro Schwartz, chief economist at stockbroker Fincorp in Madrid, said in a 1996 lecture. 'The Germans want the union to stop them from falling into Nazi ways. The French want to be cured of an inferiority complex. The Italians want to become a nation. The Spaniards want to bury Franco. The Portuguese want to be French. The Greeks don't want to be Turks ... .'

3

Which countries want to join?

By Tom Heneghan in Bonn, John Giliardi in Frankfurt, Myra MacDonald in Paris, Paul Mylrea in London, Andrew Hurst in Milan, Sharman Esarey in Madrid, Garry West in Amsterdam, Nick Antonovics in Brussels, Steve Pagani in Vienna, Tony Austin in Stockholm, Steve Weizman in Copenhagen, Peter Starck in Helsinki, Dimitris Kontogiannis in Athens, David Brough in Lisbon, Carmel Linnane in Dublin and Michael Shields in Zurich.

GERMANY

It may be the euro's strongest backer but Germany has set such high hurdles along the path to EMU that outsiders sometimes think Bonn actually opposes the single currency. Within Germany, though, the political and business elites are all so pro-European that they ask not whether the euro will come but under which conditions it will arrive. The hurdles aim to ensure that Germans, who have a deep fear of inflation, will only exchange their marks for a currency with rock-bottom guarantees of long-term stability.

Veteran Chancellor Helmut Kohl firmly believes he can whip Germany and a few other states sufficiently into line to launch the single currency on time in 1999. But, in contrast to the East-West German monetary union Kohl rushed through before reuniting his nation in 1990, the EU plan depends as much on the economic nitty-gritty he disdains as the political manoeuvering he masters. 'This is not something Kohl can just push through in an act of political will. The numbers have to fit because the markets are out there waiting to pounce if they don't,' one Bonn-based European diplomat commented.

Germany's parliament, its 16 federal states, or its supreme court could all wield a veto in 1998 over the project that Kohl sees as the crowning of his long political career. Ironically, the one institution with the most influence over whether Bonn joins the single currency — the powerful Bundesbank central bank — has no formal power to block EMU.

Moreover, the EMU debate is being held on levels which sometimes complement, but sometimes contradict each other. First there is the popular level, where most Germans say they do not want to give up their mark. On the technical level, bankers and politicians debate how to interpret the Maastricht criteria and who will meet them. Above all this is a political level marked by broad support for further European integration and popular confidence that Kohl can best defend Germany's interests in Brussels.

To reach the single currency, Germany will have to clear five hurdles:

Public opinion

The best-known statistics in Germany's EMU debate are the opinion polls saying about three-quarters of the country's voters do not want to give up the mark. But pollsters contrast this with the broad support Germans show for European unity. Renate Koecher, co-director of the respected Allensbach polling institute, said about 40 per cent of the voters are against the euro, 20–25 per cent are for it and the rest are undecided. But she added: 'People are convinced the euro will come. They have accepted it, even if it is anything but a popular project. European integration as a goal is not questioned.' Kohl's Christian Democratic Union (CDU) party has launched a publicity drive to calm fears about EMU before it becomes a potential campaign issue in 1998. Efforts by Italy and Spain to join EMU at the start mean Kohl might have to take an even tougher line on the criteria for membership to avoid risking his re-election campaign. 'The German public will need to be reassured in an election year if the Club Med countries are taken in,' one Bonn-based European ambassador said. 'These are countries you take vacations in, not ones you let join in serious discussions.' Many analysts believe Germany is playing high-stakes poker with its strict line in preparations for EMU but could show some last-minute flexibility in the end to let it start.

The convergence criteria

If reports by leading economists in Germany are anything to go by, Bonn will fail to get its 1997 budget deficit below three per cent of GDP. Finance Minister Theo Waigel rejects the gloomy predictions and says cuts he made after those reports were drawn up mean the deficit will actually be only 2.5 per cent. But he has not let up the pressure on Germany and other potential EMU members to apply the Maastricht criteria strictly and avoid creative account-ing in the run-up to the euro. He added another hurdle in November 1995 when he launched his campaign for the stability pact, which the Bundesbank sees as crucial to EMU's success.

The political hurdle

The full German parliament, the Bundestag (lower house) and Bundesrat (upper house), must approve EMU membership before Bonn can join. They will vote shortly before the EU summit in June 1998, when the names of the founding members are known. Kohl, who has tied his political fate to the founding of the common currency, insists all members must follow long-term budget discipline. 'The Maastricht criteria must be met without ifs and buts, and that means in the long term,' he said in 1996. Except for a few Bavarian mavericks, Kohl's centre-right coalition is firmly behind his drive for the mon-etary union. The opposition Social Democrats (SPD) are pro-European with occasional populist leanings. But they seem to have backed off Euro-scepticism after the anti-EMU campaign in a March 1996 state election in Baden-Wuerttemberg backfired badly. The Bundestag ratified the Maastricht Treaty on December 2, 1992 by a majority of 543 to 17 after insisting it would have the final say over whether Germany joined EMU. In an accompanying resolu-tion seen as a guideline for its probable stand in 1998, the Bundestag stressed EMU was planned as a 'community of stability' and that currency stability 'must be guaranteed in all circumstances'.

The legal hurdle

Germany's supreme court could present another hurdle if it is asked to rule on the legality of any EMU deal in 1998. The Federal Constitutional Court plays such an important role in Germany that a rejection here would kill the project. The court ruled in 1993 that the Maastricht Treaty conformed to the German constitution but that parliament had to approve the move to a single currency. Would that approval remain valid if the monetary union agreed in 1998 did not create the 'community of stability' the Bundestag insisted on when it ratified the Maastricht Treaty? Judge Paul Kirchhof, the court's European affairs expert, recently worried some financial analysts by arguing the court would reject an EMU not based on the literal interpretation of the Maastricht Treaty's debt and deficit criteria. But analysts say Kirchhof takes a notably hard line on the Karlsruhe bench and few could imagine the court shooting down a monetary union that Bonn and Frankfurt supported. 'That would be a nightmare,' says

Norbert Wieczorek, the SPD head of parliament's European affairs committee. 'So we have to make the euro as stable as the mark.' Unhappy at Kirchhof's remarks, chief justice Jutta Limbach has refused to discuss the case in public, saying: 'I'm not going to say anything that will set markets in a spin.'

What they say in Germany

'A currency union without France is unthinkable.' German finance minister Theo Waigel, October 1995.

'If the German government fails to take a rigorous view of the criteria, those of us who oppose an overhasty union are certain to launch lawsuits ... . The sooner governments take a decision to delay EMU, perhaps for five to 10 years, the better.' Wilhelm Nolling, former Bundesbank council member, May 1996.

'We do not seek to exercise hegemonic influence, as some charge. We don't want to see a Europe where the big countries have the say and the smaller ones are appendages. That is not our idea of federalism in Germany and it is not our idea of federalism in Europe.' German Chancellor Helmut Kohl, December 1996.

'The insistent and overbearing nature of your speeches not only makes you unpopular — which you can certainly bear — but rather makes Germany as a whole unloved, something we have not deserved and cannot endure.' Former German Chancellor Helmut Schmidt, of Bundesbank president Hans Tietmeyer, *Die Zeit*, November 1996.

'I am an oak.' Tietmeyer's response.

'I continue to believe that the officials of the Bundesbank are campaigning against a single currency. Not all of them. But certainly (chief economist Otmar) Issing or Tietmeyer.' Schmidt, *Liberation*, December 1996.

The Bundesbank hurdle

With both parliament and the supreme court focusing on EMU's future stability, the advice the Bundesbank gives on the currency union could be crucial to its acceptance in Germany. Bundesbank President Hans Tietmeyer has indicated he saw some room for interpretation of the Maastricht criteria even though he wanted as strict an interpretation as possible. But the key to stability, as he and other Bundesbank council members stress in almost daily speeches, will be whether EMU members agree to sustain the budgetary discipline they showed when joining the club. 'We are convinced a stable European currency will be advantageous for all participants,' Tietmeyer said in November 1996. 'But it must have a stable basis, otherwise the danger that it could lead to economic and political conflicts is very great.' The main problem with EMU, Tietmeyer argues, is that member states will continue pursuing mostly national economic policies and have only their monetary policy in common. Only a solid stability pact could keep their economies in line. 'Centrifugal forces could quickly arise here if there is not at least a common measure of fiscal discipline, and it must be permanent fiscal discipline,' he says. 'We have to make sustainability the decisive criterion.'

Who's who in the Bundesbank

There are 16 members of the Bundesbank's decision-making Council, which is made up of two groups: permanent senior officials who make up the Frankfurt-based executive Directorate that conducts open market operations; and presidents of Germany's regional central banks. They are appointed for eight-year terms or until their 68th birthday.

The following were Council members in late 1996:

- **Hans Tietmeyer,** 65, president. Term expires in August 1999. Tietmeyer, a Christian Democrat (CDU), is an ally of Chancellor Helmut Kohl. Known as a monetary policy centrist, he joined the bank board in January 1990 after a career in Bonn ministries. Named president in October 1993, he wants a strict interpretation of the Maastricht Treaty and has pushed for a powerful stability pact. He believes ERM membership is needed to join EMU and has criticised 'window-dressing' measures to meet the convergence criteria.

- **Johann Wilhelm Gaddum,** 66, vice president. Term expires in June 1998. Gaddum, a CDU member and former president of the Rhineland-Palatinate bank, joined the Directorate in 1986 and was appointed to his current job in October 1993. A centrist, he is an expert on capital markets but has limited international exposure. Gaddum is sympathetic to public fears about the euro and favours strict treaty interpretation. He favoured a stability pact with automatic sanctions and converting existing German debt into euro debt as soon as possible.

- **Otmar Issing,** 60, chief economist. Issing, a professor who has no political affiliation, joined the council in October 1990 and is seen as a centrist on monetary issues. A proponent of the stability pact, he warns against softening EMU entry criteria. He is also critical of 'creative accounting' to fulfil fiscal criteria.

- **Wendelin Hartmann,** 59, Directorate member for payment systems and controlling. Hartmann, a technical banking expert with no political affiliation, joined in 1964 and was appointed to the Directorate in June 1992. He chairs a working group at the EMI on coordinating cashless payments under EMU. Hartmann is seen as a hawk on monetary policy. He believes the transition period between the euro's introduction and physical distribution should be shortened.

- **Helmut Schieber,** 58, directorate member for international relations who has no political affiliation. Joined in 1964 and the directorate in June 1992. A centrist on rate policy, he believes the EMU target start date of January 1999 will be hard to meet and entrance criteria should not be relaxed.

- **Peter Schmidhuber,** 65, Directorate member for legal and administrative issues. A Christian Social (CSU) member, he is an ally of Finance Minister Theo Waigel. Viewed as a monetarist hawk, he joined the Directorate in March 1995. He believes a timely start to EMU is possible if steps are taken to ensure stability and a delay could endanger the whole project.

- **Edgar Meister,** 56, Directorate member in charge of banking supervision. Meister, a Social Democrat (SPD), joined the Directorate in 1993 and is considered a favourite to replace Gaddum. A monetarist dove, he wants clear interpretation of EMU entry criteria. He notes public confusion on how the criteria will be interpreted and fears political pressure may push through the introduction of the new currency at any price.

- **Klaus-Dieter Kuehbacher,** 53, President of Berlin and Brandenburg state central bank. A former Bundestag member viewed as an outspoken SPD politician and expert on fiscal policy, he was appointed in September 1995. A monetarist dove, he wants EMU to start on time with a small group of nations rather than risk delay or softening the criteria.

- **Franz-Christoph Zeitler,** 48, President of Bavaria state central bank. A CSU member viewed as a monetary centrist, he was appointed in 1995. He oversaw the 1991 introduction of a 'solidarity surcharge' tax to pay for German unification. He is critical of nations using 'gimmicks' to meet entry criteria.

- **Reimut Jochimsen,** 63, President of North-Rhine Westphalia state central bank. An SPD member and former professor, he was economics minister of North-Rhine Westphalia before taking up his current position in August 1990. Centrist to dovish on monetary policy, he is a hawk on many EMU-related issues. He criticised France for its budget moves, saying Germany will not accept the euro if the criteria are eased, and believes five states seek to join EMU by fudging the criteria.

- **Hans-Juergen Koebnick**, President of Saarland and Rhineland-Palatinate state central bank. A former journalist and SPD mayor, he was named to his position in 1991 and as Rhineland-Palatinate bank president in 1993. A monetarist dove, he says forecasts that Germany may miss EMU criteria in 1997 are realistic and an EMU delay could be useful. He has said Italy, Spain and other 'Club Med' nations are unlikely to join the first wave.

- **Guntram Palm,** 65, President of Baden-Wuerttemberg state central bank. A CDU member, he was state minister before being being named to his current job in April 1992. Palm, a monetarist hawk, has warned other EU states against the use of 'tricks' to join EMU and backed a strict stability pact.

- **Ernst Welteke,** 54, President of Hesse state central bank. An SPD member and former state economics and finance minister, he was named to his job in 1995. A monetarist dove, he says an EMU delay to enlarge the group is unwise and could threaten the project. He sees some leeway in budget criteria but not laxity.

- **Olaf Sievert,** 63, President of Saxony and Thuringia state central bank. A non-party professor named to his job in January 1993. A monetarist dove, he says an EMU delay would be the beginning of the end and favours a small group. He sees the euro helping to solve unemployment problems in Europe.

- **Hans-Juergen Krupp,** 63, President of Schleswig-Holstein and Hamburg and Mecklenburg-Vorpommern state central bank. An SPD member and monetarist dove, he was president of DIW institute and named to his current post in December 1993. He says nations do not need to hit debt criteria exactly to qualify for EMU and sees room for manoeuvre, particularly on public debt.

- **Helmut Hesse,** 62, President of Lower Saxony and Bremen and Saxony Anhalt bank. He has no political affiliation and is a Club of Rome member. He was named bank president in December 1988 and given responsibility for more regional banks in November 1992. Hesse has made little public commentary on currency union but is considered a monetary centrist to hawkish.

FRANCE

France voted by a whisker in favour of EMU in 1992 and, if asked again, the result would probably not be much different. The country is still divided on the merits of a single currency, but polls show the balance still tips in favour. Officially, France is committed to launching the single currency on time in 1999, but there is a sizeable minority of doubters which goes across political party lines. The 1992 referendum, showing 51.05 per cent support for EMU, 'revealed a France with many faces, a France divided by multiple fault lines' as former European Commission President Jacques Delors put it at the time.

Those fault lines became glaringly obvious again in autumn 1996 in a renewed debate in France on the merits of monetary union. It took just a few comments by an ex-president with little residual political clout to highlight France's schizophrenic approach to its forthcoming monetary marriage with Germany. Ironically, they came from one of the founding fathers of the EMS, Valery Giscard d'Estaing.

His call for a fall in the franc to boost growth inspired a revolt against a decade-old link to the mark and was echoed even inside the Bank of France, bastion of monetary orthodoxy. Two members of the central bank's nine-member monetary policy council questioned the franc-mark link, long seen as the linchpin of the single currency project, prompting governor Jean-Claude Trichet to stress that he alone spoke for the bank.

Giscard d'Estaing spoke against the backdrop of a truckers' strike, partly caused by the effects of European competition, which was paralysing roads and choking the economy. That strike was ended by a government climbdown. A year earlier, the government had faced down public sector workers who took to the streets in protest against austerity policies meant to ensure France qualifies for EMU in 1999.

President Jacques Chirac, who in his 1995 election campaign flirted with the idea of a new referendum on Europe, was working hard to dispel doubts about the depth of his commitment to the euro. Few believed he would want to go down in history as the president who derailed EMU. But he had yet to gain the stature of former president Francois Mitterrand, whose close rapport with Kohl in the drive for monetary union had helped to ensure that it was based on a balanced Franco-German partnership.

That alliance was showing signs of strain in late 1996. Yet again, France and Germany succeeded in reconciling their ideological differences when they agreed a stability and growth pact, the word 'growth' was Chirac's addition, at the EU's Dublin summit. But the fundamental divide remained, between

French insistence on a political counterweight to the future ECB and German desire for watertight guarantees on the stability of the euro.

France's prime motive in pushing for the single currency was a determination to regain a share of monetary sovereignty. Without monetary union, it feared, Europe would be increasingly run by Germany with the Bundesbank setting Europe-wide monetary policy. So if it could not stand up to the Bundesbank, it could at least win a seat on the board by persuading Bonn and its other EU partners to set up an ECB.

The dispute over the stability pact was therefore central to the wider issue of selling EMU in France. When Chirac battled to defend the power of governments to define the limits of fiscal manoeuvre, he was also struggling to fend off his critics at home. But for Eurosceptics, any Franco-German tension makes it easy to exploit lingering suspicion and fear of Germany in some quarters after several bitter wars. During the stability pact negotiations, the Socialist opposition accused Chirac of capitulating to Kohl. Philippe Seguin, speaker of the national assembly in 1996 and an opponent of the Maastricht Treaty in 1992, struck the same chord in 1993 when he compared government austerity policies and neglect of unemployment to a 'social Munich', a reference to the pre-World War Two appeasement of Hitler.

More recently French officials have added a new concept to justify the single currency: 'globalisation', a fashionable buzzword used to sum up the idea that France can no longer compete alone in an increasingly interlinked world economy. Euro-enthusiasts believe the euro will usher in currency stability, lower interest rates and create a trading zone the size of the United States, boosting jobs and growth.

In fact, the 1996 debate on the merits of EMU erupted just as the pressure of financial market scepticism about France's chances of qualifying had lifted. France fulfils most of the Maastricht criteria, on debt, inflation, long-term interest rates and currency stability. The government made the Bank of France independent in January 1994, underpinning its commitment to a stable franc and stable prices and fulfilling a Maastricht requirement that central banks be independent by the launch of the euro. So for years, attention had focused on the difficulties of reducing the budget deficit to fit under the Maastricht target ceiling.

France dispelled most doubts about its ability to do that for 1997 by announcing it planned to use a 37.5 billion franc transfer of pension fund money from state-owned France Telecom to cut its deficit to three per cent of GDP. But while the scepticism was there, fuelling occasional speculative attacks on the franc, any real discussion of the franc-mark link, and the drive to monetary union which it symbolised, was taboo. If Giscard d'Estaing and others felt they could break that taboo, it was because there was no longer a threat from the currency speculators.

By the end of 1996, French doubts about monetary union appeared to have receded somewhat, at least temporarily. 'While in some people's eyes, the project (EMU) was uncertain, it is today on the right track,' said Finance Minister Jean Arthuis. 'The Dublin Summit has just dissipated any residual doubts.'

Officials said there could be no going back. 'Given where we are now, in December 1996, and given what has been said and done already, I don't believe the single currency will not be launched,' said French Treasury director Jean Lemierre. 'It seems unimaginable to me.'

But with unemployment at a record 12.6 per cent, and economic growth sluggish, there was plenty of room for controversy over EMU to burst to the surface again.

BRITAIN

Britain is a country of tradition and ritual: the changing of the guard at Buckingham Palace; annual bonfires to mark an attempt to blow up parliament four centuries ago; and always joining European institutions late. With the clock ticking away to the start of the European single currency, neither of the two main political parties shows any inclination to break the habit of two generations.

So, just as it did when the European Community began in the 1950s, Britain looks set to sit on the sidelines while Germany, France and other core countries forge ahead with a single currency. In late 1996, with less than six months before a general election which will end, or extend, an unprecedented 17 years of Conservative rule, neither of the main parties was prepared to commit itself to EMU. Prime Minister John Major had gone as far as he could to placate Conservative Eurosceptics opposed to European integration without actually ruling out entry, brandishing the opt-out negotiated at Maastricht and promising to decide later. Labour leader Tony Blair, employing his favourite tactic of occupying Conservative ground in a bid to nudge Major further to the right, has copied the government's wait-and-see line right down to the promise of a referendum if he decides to join later.

The result has been a frustrating lack of detailed discussion of what a single currency could mean for Britain and a growing fear that Britain may once again miss the boat. 'The "wait-and-see" option which dominates mainstream political thinking in the main parties will become increasingly untenable,' John Monks, the General Secretary of the Trades Union Congress (TUC) told a recent meeting on EMU. 'Greater clarity will become necessary or otherwise it is possible the UK will be excluded by a sort of default from the most important economic development in Europe since the war.'

With critics claiming the main effect of a single currency will be on jobs, Monks appears an unlikely champion of EMU. To see Britain's senior trade unionist arguing on the same side as business leaders and bankers makes it even more unusual. But it is a sign of the frustration of those in favour of the single currency that the country's political leaders were acting like rabbits frozen by the sight of car headlights as the election approached, leaving the field open to the Eurosceptics.

Senior figures from both Labour and the Conservatives say privately this game of political chicken over a single currency has been a mistake which will have long-term consequences. Leaving the floor to the strident Eurosceptics has charged the political atmosphere and encouraged anti-European sentiment. A recent British Social Attitudes poll showed the share of people wanting closer ties with the European Union had fallen to 29 per cent in 1995 from 37 per cent in 1994. Distrust of Europe has been heightened by the British tabloid newspapers' love of scare stories over Europe, like the spurious tales of EU regulations banning square strawberries, short bananas or curved cucumbers.

Eurosceptic Conservative MPs capitalise on this, warning of Britain being taken over by Brussels and of riots in the streets when austerity policies imposed by Europe begin to bite. But many leading politicians believe that polls showing a solid core of anti-foreign and anti-European sentiment give a misleading impression of Britain's complex relationship with its continental neighbours. Overlaid on the natural fears of an island race for what comes from beyond its shores is the clear belief that, in the modern world, Britain cannot afford to be isolated. Privately, they argue, a government committed to a single currency could win a referendum. In 1975, there was a two-to-one majority for continued membership of the European Community despite early polls forecasting a 'No' vote.

'The British people are indeed ambivalent about Europe,' Robin Cook, Labour foreign affairs spokesman and himself on his party's Eurosceptic wing, told parliamentary reporters recently. 'The British know that our place is in Europe, they have no serious intention of giving up that place, but they rarely manage to sound enthusiastic about it.'

Although it has not re-joined the ERM and could miss the three per cent of GDP deficit target in 1997, Britain is relatively well-placed to qualify for

EMU. Both Major and Blair see the Maastricht criteria as representing sound economic aims. Indeed, the fear among political and business leaders in London is more that the criteria for entry will be fudged rather than that Britain will be kept out by them. Privately senior Labour figures also believe Britain could get round the exchange rate clause — highly controversial in Britain after sterling's humiliating exit from the ERM in 1992 — by shadowing the euro without actually rejoining the mechanism.

But this still leaves any government which decides to take Britain into the single currency with a huge hill to climb, and little time to do it. It would have to rush a bill through parliament setting out the terms of Britain's entry and then call a referendum, all by the end of 1997. Parliament would also have to implement all the decisions of the EU Inter-Governmental Conference and grant independence to the Bank of England, which has been kept firmly under the government's thumb for decades. It would be sufficient for the government to show it could get the necessary legislation through before January 1, 1999. But even drawing up the legislation to hand control of monetary policy over to a central banker could split an already fractious Conservative party. As for Labour, it has already proposed giving the central bank more independence, but short of the level required under Maastricht. 'Gordon Brown (Labour economics spokesman) won't like the idea of taking over the Treasury and then handing power to (Bank of England governor) Eddie George,' said one Labour insider.

Labour's main fear, however, is that its first term — what Blair describes as his 100 days to prepare for the 1000 years of the new millenium — would be dominated by Europe, overshadowing key projects like plans for Welsh and Scottish assemblies. It is also nervous that a Labour government could find itself summoning voters to three referenda, one on a reform of the electoral system, one on regional assemblies and one on EMU.

One possible 1997 election outcome could hasten Britain's entry into EMU. Blair has signalled greater cooperation with the minority Liberal Democrats, the most openly pro-European of the parties. Some MPs believe Blair's vow to govern from the political centre could extend to a formal pact with the Liberal Democrats if he wins only a slim parliamentary majority, a tactical move which could tip the balance in favour of first wave entry into EMU.

Labour is in no doubt that, in the end, Britain is more likely to be in than to be out. 'If the single currency proceeds, I very much doubt in the medium term whether it's possible for Britain to stay out,' Cook told the Confederation of British Industry. It is a view that senior Conservative politicians believe Major shares but dare not utter for fear of inciting the Eurosceptics to new acts of defiance. The election is unlikely to bring Major any respite. Leading pro-Europeans, like former foreign secretary Douglas Hurd, are stepping down. Polls, as well as private soundings by at least one hopeful for the party leadership after Major, show most new Conservative candidates are heavily Eurosceptic.

For Labour, it is the opposite, with new candidates far more pro-European than the MPs they are likely to replace. Some Labour insiders have already suggested this could give Blair a weapon to help him to his avowed aim of governing not just for one term but for two — and beyond. If elected, they say, Blair could stay out of the single currency in the first wave, arguing that Conservative infighting had left too little time and poisoned public opinion. After a first term concentrating on domestic issues, Blair could then plant his flag firmly in the European camp for the next election in five years' time and ask for public backing to take Britain into a single currency. With Euro coins due to be introduced as legal tender in the single currency bloc in 2002, voters would have a concrete vision of what a single currency would mean, and Blair would be able once again to divide — and conquer — the Conservatives.

ITALY

Whether Italy succeeds or fails in a do-or-die effort to join a currency union by 1999, one thing is certain — for most Italians a lot more is at stake than bidding a long goodbye to their badly bruised lira. For many it is a stark choice between signing up to an elite club of prosperous nations or facing a bleak, lonely future on the fringes of Europe at a time when wrenching economic and social change is shaking the nation to its foundations.

Prime Minister Romano Prodi, sensing Italians are prepared to put up with a hefty dose of discomfort in the name of Europe, has staked his future on trying to ram Italy into EMU from the start. Opinion polls show a vast majority of Italians back him, even though many were wincing at the prospect of paying a 5.5 trillion lire ($3.6 billion) 'Euro tax' as the price of getting state finances into shape. 'We carried out a poll which showed that 80 per cent of respondents thought that staying out of monetary union would be a disaster,' said Paolo Natale, a polling expert at Milan market research house Abacus, in late 1996.

Critics of government policy, led by the chairman of car group Fiat, Cesare Romiti, believe Italy should take a little longer to ready itself for its European monetary adventure and be content with joining a year or two after the advance party. Prodi and his inner circle of advisers reject this, arguing that EMU membership at the outset offers a once-in-a-lifetime chance to engineer a sharp fall in interest rates and curb costs of servicing national debt.

Almost alone among major West European nations, Italy has no powerful lobby at home openly arguing a case for permanently staying outside a currency union. At the heart of the government's strategy is a belief that joining EMU offers Italy the best chance in a generation of putting its state finances back on an even keel and modernising the country root and branch. 'The aim is to use Europe to make reforms. People are willing to make sacrifices in the name of Europe that they would not make in the name of Italy,' said Patrick McCarthy, a political science professor at Johns Hopkins University in Bologna.

Also at issue is Italy's self-esteem, at a low ebb since the passing of a corrupt political order in the early 1990s whose collapse is still sending aftershocks through the body politic. Sluggish economic growth and high unemployment, particularly in the crisis-hit deep south of the country, have added to the sense of despondency at a time when an expensive but inefficient welfare state is widely seen to be under threat.

'Perhaps we do not fundamentally realise that a historical era is finished ... the period which saw the triumph of the welfare state is over,' said Vittorio Foa, one of the grand old men of Italy's left. 'Now everything has to be reinvented, thought out again, and it is not easy,' Foa told Rome daily *La Repubblica*. Faced with such awesome challenges ahead, many Italians feel instinctively that by binding themselves closer to countries with a stronger tradition of firm government, their chances of standing up to the chill winds of a global economy are greater. 'European unity is seen as offering the possibility of forging links with countries which are more solid,' said Natale.

History is also playing a part in Italy's campaign to stay with the front-runners in the race to form a currency union. Italy was a founding member of the original six-nation European common market in 1957 and the lira joined the EMS when it was launched in 1979. 'Italy has always played the part of a founding father in Europe since the 1950s. If they are late-comers to monetary union it would be seen as a backwards step,' said Lorenzo Stanca, chief economist at Credito Italiano in Milan.

To be sure of qualifying for EMU membership, Italy has to bring its public sector deficit down from a likely 1996 ratio of at least 6.5 per cent, a task which many economists liken to getting a camel through the eye of a needle. Prodi was aiming for 3.3 per cent in 1997. European Union Commissioner Mario Monti has said the government will have no choice but to pass an extra raft of fund-raising measures if there is any sign that it might miss its targets. Another fiscal squeeze could prove to be a tax too far even for Italy's prosperous middle class and some commentators now fear that the pro-EMU consensus would come under severe strain.

'If Prodi has to go to the country with an extra budget early next year I am not sure he will be able to get away with it,' said Sergio Romano, a former diplomat who is now a respected political commentator. Prodi, whose own future was clouded in late 1996 by a judicial investigation into his handling of a company privatisation while chairman of state holding company IRI in 1993, would probably have to resort to hiking taxes. The alternative is to cut spending, but Prodi has already promised not to lay a finger on a bloated pensions system — regarded as a prime candidate for heavy pruning — before 1998. 'If Italy looks as if it is going to have trouble making it (into EMU) it will be difficult to ask people to make more sacrifices,' said McCarthy at Johns Hopkins University.

Italian industrialists, who have profited from a weak lira, could clamour for a stay of execution on the grounds that Italy would not suffer from joining EMU a year or two later. But if the government balks it could be read by the financial markets, which have been betting on Italy joining a currency union, as a signal that pro-EMU resolve is weakening. 'If you want to dilute the government's policy of rigour you send a message to the markets. Staying out (of EMU) is a big risk,' said Romano.

SPAIN

It's a matter of honour, pride, and the sweet memories of past glory. For Spain, participation in Europe's single currency project fulfils its need to belong, to be accepted, to assume its rightful place at Europe's core after years at the edge under a fascist dictator and the fragile democracy that followed. Few Spaniards have grumbled at the austerity policies adopted to ensure Spain is fit for the launch, because the economic merits or drawbacks of the plan are of only secondary importance to them. They are inspired, instead, by a new international vision of Spain's role after decades focused on domestic politics. 'Spain wants to be taken seriously by its partners,' said a Western diplomat. 'Spain is one of the five largest EU countries and wants out of its fringe position. It can only claim this role if it is in European Monetary Union from the beginning.'

Despite high unemployment and government belt-tightening, public acceptance of the plan has been high. Future economic problems are unlikely to shake this commitment. 'There is no group that does not profess its European faith, that does not organise interminable congresses and forums about the European future and its effects,' wrote local financial daily *La Gaceta de los Negocios*. The conservative Popular Party government, which took over in May after 13 years of Socialist rule, adopted its predecessors' European economic policy with little fuss and set about revitalising the drive to whip finances into shape. King Juan Carlos, who rarely steps into national politics, told the country this year it was essential to be in the single currency, effectively clipping the wings of any political party which might have considered turning EMU into an issue.

Among Spain's major political parties only the communist-led United Left opposes the nation's European goal, considering that it is a plot by European elites solely for their own benefit. 'In Spain there is a broad consensus between the opposition and the government over the need for convergence, so (Prime Minister Jose Maria) Aznar made the (Socialists') 1994 ... declaration on convergence his own,' the diplomat said.

The government has put the public temper to the test, presenting a tough budget for 1997. It slashed the deficit to three per cent of gross domestic product, as required, from a huge 6.6 per cent in 1995, thanks to above-average revenue growth and severe cuts in spending growth. The government froze public sector pay to cut spending growth, causing some 200,000 people to rally in Madrid in late November in a protest demonstration. But there has been almost no resonance in society at large, where the plight of a salary freeze for public employees is unlikely to strike a chord when 20 per cent of the workforce has no job. Spain has the highest unemployment rate in Europe.

The government has launched an aggressive campaign to press unions and businesses toward a German-style consensus pact to crack open Spain's labour market and foster job creation. The country is within sight of meeting the economic criteria for joining EMU. Inflation has declined steadily. The peseta has stabilised and held firm after its most recent devaluation in spring 1995. Most dramatically, the difference in yield between Spanish bonds and their sturdier German counterparts has narrowed sharply, to around 1.3 points in late 1996 from 5.0 in mid-1995.

These economic benefits, combined with growth above the European average, may well have helped Spaniards come to terms with the budget cuts and other impending changes.

There is no sign of any fears in Spain like those that agitate Germans who worry about instability if they lose their hallowed mark. Nor would the peseta's demise signify the death of a major international currency, such as sterling.

For Spain, the bid to regain a bit of its past glory is well worth any temporary economic inconvenience. The fledgling government, backed by this strong national consensus, has already begun to flex its diplomatic muscle in the EU and beyond, seeking a higher international profile. 'Spain is right in thinking that the new integrative identity of the EU is not a fixed characteristic, but a dynamic process. Spain must be a part of this dynamic if it doesn't want to fall by the wayside,' the diplomat said.

THE NETHERLANDS

Other EU nations may be racked with division over EMU, but the Netherlands is racing wholeheartedly towards monetary union. Opinion polls show the Dutch are strongly in favour. Despite the prospect of losing the guilder, the Dutch currency for the last three centuries, Eurosceptics are hard to find in this tiny trading nation which has been a prime beneficiary of the the removal of trading barriers in Europe. The Netherlands serves as an economic model for neighbouring countries aspiring to qualify for EMU. Even the Bundesbank pays tribute to the Dutch, pointing out that the Netherlands has overtaken Germany in the past few years in the pursuit of a strong currency, low inflation and interest rates, steady economic growth and falling unemployment. These achievements are the result of 15 years work on making the country more competitive, helped by the close link between the guilder and the mark.

The Nederlandsche Bank is in practice one of the most independent in Europe but, to meet the Maastricht Treaty's criteria for central bank independence, parliament needs to abolish a 48-year-old law giving the government the right to intervene in the bank's operations. This is seen as a formality. Martin Brands, professor of modern history at the University of Amsterdam, said no Dutch government had made use of the law since it was enacted, underlining the country's long history of stability.

Opposition, where it does exist, comes from politicians who are concerned about the terms on which other weaker countries will join a single currency. Political analysts cite the Netherlands' long history of support for European integration in explaining the lack of opposition to EMU. 'Most Dutch would argue that European integration is in the Dutch interest,' said Dr Jan Rood, deputy director of studies at the Clingendael Institute for International Relations, an independent research and training foundation in The Hague. 'We have always profited from the (European) agricultural policies, which were favourable to the Dutch. The Netherlands is export-oriented. We're very interested in opening up European markets,' he added.

The Netherlands is home to some of the biggest companies in the world, including Philips Electronics and consumer products giant Unilever, export-oriented multinationals which were forced to expand long ago when they outgrew their domestic market. The Maastricht Treaty passed through the Dutch parliament in 1992 with little debate. 'In the view of the (political) elite, it's a logical follow-up of the market integration in the (European Union). It contributes to the stability of markets,' Rood said.

He said the Netherlands now had no influence over monetary policy and little influence over economic policy, independent of Germany, because of the close ties between the two countries. He argued that the Dutch would have a greater input into the operation of their economy under a single currency because they would have a seat on the board of the new ECB. Dutch central bank chief Wim Duisenberg will be the next president of the European Monetary Institute, the ECB's forerunner. 'The Dutch, in the end, have very little choice if the Germans and the French have EMU. We have only one option and that is to follow them. There's a feeling that the risks are worth taking,' Rood said.

The main political opposition to EMU has come from the conservative Liberals (VVD), a right-leaning partner in the Netherlands' three-party ruling coalition, which has threatened strong protests if EMU's convergence terms are relaxed. Dr Hans Hoogervorst, the VVD's finance spokesman, said his party saw benefits from a single currency but it also wanted to ensure the convergence criteria were met. 'We are more critical than other parties. That's because we have always seen this primarily and solely as an economic project. Many of the other parties are likely to close an eye if other countries do not meet the critera,' he said.

'(The Netherlands) is one of the countries that has the most to lose and the least to gain because we have such a strong currency with low interest rates and low inflation. We have to ensure that what we get into will be as strong. We have had that currency for three centuries and people are worried about sharing a currency with weaker countries. Now they can have (home) mortgages for 20 years fixed at seven percent (interest rate). Where else in Europe can you get that?'

Hoogervorst believes EMU cannot begin on schedule in 1999 if Germany and France do not meet the Maastricht Treaty's targets for reducing budget deficits and public sector debt. 'I think there should be a delay. There should be no question of it starting on time. What's really worrying is that nobody has really protested,' said Hoogervorst. The VVD voted in favour of EMU because it could see benefits in reduced currency speculation, lower transaction costs and competition for the dollar. 'There's very clear gains to be made. But unfortunately most politicians in this country are likely to agree with anything that the French and Germans decide. My party will create a big stink if the criteria are not met.'

But the VVD's concern is not widely shared. A survey by the Nederlandsche Bank in early 1996 found that 70 per cent of individuals and 80 per cent of companies considered the euro as acceptable as the guilder. The main complaint was a lack of familiarity with the euro.

Professor Andre Szasz, a former central bank board member, said the EMU debate was less controversial in the Netherlands because people had fewer illusions about their economic autonomy than some of their neighbours. 'We are a very open economy. There's no way we could pursue an independent monetary policy and accept whatever follows for the exchange rate,' he said. As for the austerity programmes which have been linked to EMU in other European nations, the Netherlands underwent the pain much earlier, during the 1980s. An explosion of public expenditure in the early 1970s led to a doubling of public sector debt to 80 per cent of GDP between 1970 and 1980. 'Then we started to gradually put our house in order. There was a lot of grumbling and a lot of worry that the welfare state would disappear, but this was to enable the welfare state to continue,' Szasz said. He said the Netherlands' own economic policies have led to its solid currency and low interest rates. 'I can only hope that EMU will be run in a way that doesn't change that, and that we don't exchange a solid currency for one that's less solid,' he said.

Professor Paul Verhaegen, director of economic affairs at the Confederation of Netherlands Industry, said the Dutch saw EMU as a natural progression from the creation of a single market in Europe. Like others, he believes that EMU is seen more in economic than political terms in the Netherlands. It will cost the country an estimated 7.5 billion guilders in total but will also cut transaction, administration and other costs by two billion guilders per year. 'In four years you get your money back,' said Verhaegen who, like many people in the Netherlands, believes that on this basis, it makes good sense.

BELGIUM AND LUXEMBOURG

Belgium and Luxembourg already have a monetary union and have warmly embraced the prospect of EMU. Opinion polls commissioned by the European Union indicate support for the project stands at more than 70 per cent of the populations. Both countries' economies are so tied to those of their large neighbours, France and Germany, that it is accepted staying outside a single currency area would be suicidal.

EMU has not been an issue in legislative elections and is unlikely to ever be so, unless the project is postponed or delayed. Both countries' next elections should normally take place in 1999, after the decision to lock exchange rates has taken place. As might be expected in two countries founded by the Great Powers in the 19th century, in neither has the project led to a debate about the surrender of sovereignty. EMU is described by policy makers as a logical step in the building of a more integrated Europe, a process Belgium and Luxembourg helped start in 1952 when they were among the six nations that founded the European Coal and Steel Community.

In Luxembourg, EMU is even seen as a way of winning back some autonomy: giving the country the opportunity to shape European monetary policy, and by association the external value of the Luxembourg franc, for the first time since it entered its currency union with Belgium on March 5, 1922. 'There is no debate. You have to consider that Luxembourg is the only country in Europe that does not have an independent currency ... we are the only ones who are really gaining something,' one government official said. The argument that EMU will give hard core countries more say in setting monetary policy also has weight in Belgium, where a six-year-old policy of shadowing the strong mark is periodically questioned by some exporting industries.

The broad level of support for EMU has given Belgium's coalition government of Christian Democrat and socialist parties the room to take tough and unpopular steps to clean up the country's notorious public finances. When Prime Minister Jean-Luc Dehaene first came to power in 1993, Belgium's secondary budget deficit still exceeded 5.5 per cent of GDP and debt was over 138 per cent of GDP. Under his latest budget, presented in October, they will be cut by end-1997 to under three per cent and 127 per cent.

Belgium argues its 10 trillion Belgian franc debt, while well above 60 per cent of GDP, is falling fast enough to meet the Maastrich criteria. Dehaene, now in his second term of office, went as far as saying in his budget speech that Belgium was already a 'de facto member of EMU'. The financial markets would appear to agree. In 1996 the yield premium of Belgian OLO bonds over Bunds collapsed from over 60 basis points to around 10.

Luxembourg's economic readiness for EMU has never been questioned. According to forecasts for 1997, its budget will show a small surplus and its debt, at around seven per cent of GDP, remains the lowest in the EU. Luxembourg has had to go out of its way to create public debt instruments in order to fulfill the Maastricht Treaty's long-term interest rate criterion. Its

OLUX state bonds, first issued in October 1993, now sell at a yield discount to Germany.

Both countries meet the Maastricht Treaty's other economic criteria on inflation and interest rates and on membership of Europe's exchange rate mechanism (ERM). Similarly they each run significant current account surpluses. The focus has turned instead to fulfilling lesser EMU criteria and preparing financial markets, companies and people for change. Both governments are preparing to switch over their consumer price indices (CPI), along with other EU nations, to a 1997 base year. Each has also brought forward legislation to bring its central bank statutes into line with the Maastricht Treaty rules on independence from political interference. Legislation to turn Luxembourg's Institut Monetaire Luxembourgeois (IML), founded in 1983, into a fully fledged central bank was in fact drafted as early as 1993. The government has waited however to present the draft law to parliament and IML officials expect that it will not be debated and voted on until early 1997.

Officials say some conflicts remain to be ironed out, such as what happens to the IML's present two-tier management structure. However, the government's power to dismiss the IML's board in cases of political disagreement will be removed. The IML is likely to celebrate its new status with a change in location: leaving its drab 1970s offices near Luxembourg's railway station for a period building elsewhere in the city. The search is already on for a suitable property, one official said.

Belgian legislation, presented in September 1996, modifying the structure of the 146-year-old Belgian National Bank (BNB) is also not expected to complete its parliamentary passage until 1997. The BNB has already, however, taken steps to meet another of the Maastricht Treaty requirements, setting up a real time gross settlement system (RTGSS) to link into TARGET. Belgium's Electronic Large Value Interbank Payments System, or ELLIPS, went live on September 24, 1996. Luxembourg's IML has begun work on building an RTGSS but is still a long way from implementation, officials said. The IML and 12 major banks are jointly studying the solutions being used elsewhere. 'We are not going to reinvent the wheel,' one official said.

Belgium and Luxembourg have also proposed converting their outstanding stock of debt to euros from January 1, 1999. The Luxembourg government has said it will also be the first EU nation to make such a promise law in a bill due to be passed at the beginning of 1997.

Belgium has gone further than most other EU nations in setting out when the euro can be used more widely in the economy, such as in company accounts and the public sector.

Luxembourg plans to publish a similar blueprint for the transition to the euro in the middle of 1997, after a series of brainstorming sessions between the government, industry and the IML.

Belgium plans to hold similar meetings in 1997, but the details remain sketchy. In November 1996 the government appointed a senior BNB official to the post of Commissioner General for the Euro to coordinate planning.

Each country intends to carry out wider information campaigns aimed at the general public in the course of 1997. Belgium's job is likely to be harder. In Luxembourg shops already accept several currencies and experimented with dual pricing in Ecus and Luxembourg francs as early as 1989, noted Luxembourg Banking Association (ABBL) Director Lucien Thiel.

Meanwhile, the cost of conversion is already being counted by the countries' financial institutions. Belgian banks estimate the arrival of the euro will bring a 35 billion Belgian franc bill for converting computer systems and training staff. They have asked for government help in meeting the cost, but that call in 1996 came against a backdrop of arguments about government restrictions on sacking staff and ever rising taxes. The ABBL estimates preparing for the euro will cost its members between eight to 10 billion Luxembourg francs. Luxembourg's stock exchange and investment fund industry are assessing the likely impact of the euro on their eurobond listings and multi-currency products.

Another symbolic loser will be one of Europe's few surviving private issuing banks. Banque Internationale à Luxembourg has issued legal-tender bank notes under agreement with the government more or less continuously since July 31, 1856. Issuance is now regulated to a maximum 50 million Luxembourg francs a year, a fraction of the country's total monetary needs. With EMU the BIL notes, the last series of which was printed in 1981, are destined to become collectors' items.

AUSTRIA

Austria's government and financial leaders are as confident of winning the race to join EMU by 1999 as they are of snow falling in the Alps in winter. 'I am convinced we can reach that goal,' central bank president Klaus Liebscher said, adding that any watering down of the strict criteria for entry or a postponement was out of the question. 'Not to take part in EMU would be a catastrophe for our economy,' Finance Minister Viktor Klima said. 'We cannot prevent EMU, we have to join it.'

But a large number of Austria's eight million citizens, who voted in droves to back EU membership in a referendum in 1994, have serious doubts, and the government has a hard sell ahead of it to persuade voters that their destiny, and their jobs, depend on closer economic integration within the EU. Waiting in the wings to reap the support of the disaffected is far-right leader Joerg Haider, champion of Austria's growing band of Euro-sceptics. He and his nationalist Freedom Party saw their vote soar in European Parliament elections in October 1996 to an all-time high of 28 per cent after a hard-hitting campaign against the Maastricht Treaty. Haider's score put his party almost level with the megaliths of Austrian post-World War Two politics, the Social Democrats and conservative People's Party, making his party the biggest far-right political group inside the EU and, he hopes, a beacon for anti-Maastricht voices in Europe.

The coalition government of Social Democrat Chancellor Franz Vranitzky has begun talking of meeting the EMU target date as if it were a badge of honour, a question of pride. Haider insists Austrian interests must come first. 'We want to reform Maastricht. We want a Europe of fatherlands, one that gives power to the people,' Haider said. The message was heard loud and clear: by farmers hit hard by the lower subsidies and tougher competition they have faced since Austria joined the EU on January 1, 1995; and by blue-collar workers who in the past two years have seen scores of factories close, or taken over by foreign firms bent on downsizing.

Unemployment is rising, insolvencies are running at record levels and exporters are struggling to make ends meet. But economists insist that Austria's economic woes cannot be blamed on the EU and say joining the Brussels club simply exposed deep-seated problems of poor competitiveness, a stifling bureaucracy and lavish government spending.

'These issues are all home grown. EU membership has just made it much more pressing to find solutions,' said Georg Busch, senior economist at research institute Wifo. Busch argued that the jobless rate would be higher if Austria were outside the EU and said net foreign investment worth $1.55 billion in the first half of 1996 was already triple the sum recorded for all of 1995.

Austria looks odds-on to meet most of the criteria for EMU with much progress made in achieving stability in exchange rates, inflation and interest rates. The Austrian National Bank already fulfils Maastricht Treaty rules governing the independence of central banks. Decisions over the preparation of the European System of Central Banks have been left in the hands of central bank president Liebscher and bank director Adolf Wala. They and Klima are all firm advocates of joining a single currency at its launch. Austria put the schilling into the EU's exchange rate mechanism (ERM) 10 days after joining the union.

'It is more important to have a core of stability at the start than to delay the introduction of EMU so that all European Union members can take part,' Wala said recently.

However, as in most EU states, ditching the national currency is a sensitive issue in Austria, regarded as little different from tearing up the red-white-red flag. With memories still alive of a weak currency and raging inflation in the 1930s, the schilling has become a symbol of stability. It has been pegged to the mark since 1979, forcing Austria's central bank to follow closely the monetary lead of the German Bundesbank. Austrians are big savers and murmurings of discontent can already be heard over a euro which many believe will be diluted by weaker currencies, reducing the value of their bank balances.

The European Commission forecast that Austria would meet the Maastricht budget deficit target in 1997, but this was not achieved without political pain. Tackling a ballooning deficit in 1995 forced a government collapse and a snap election. People's Party leader and Foreign Minister Wolfgang Schuessel said meeting the Maastricht criteria was central to his party's battle against Social Democrat intransigence over deep cuts in welfare payments, subsidies to state industry and a pensions system out of control. The two parties buried the hatchet and formed the next coalition, as they have for more or less the past 50 years, ditched finance minister Andreas Staribacher for Klima and agreed a two-year austerity budget to set them in line, at least on paper, for EMU.

Maastricht may be central to the EU's economic survival, but it does not look that way to the hundreds of men and women who are set to lose their jobs at the Semperit tyre factory in southern Austria because German parent company Continental is switching production to the Czech Republic where labour costs much less. Nor is it a popular message for the 90,000 construction workers out of a job as their industry slumps to its worst crisis in half a century, or those being made redundant by national grid Verbund or high-grade steel maker Boehler Uddeholm. It is a dilemma for Vranitzky's coalition government. Big economic and social change was clearly inevitable, but it has coincided with a period of turbulence within the EU as members struggle towards integration. For the Eurosceptics, the EU is the perfect scapegoat.

The next Austrian general election is due in 1999. Unless the government gets its message across by then, more disenchanted and unemployed voters may switch their allegiance to the anti-Maastricht party. Haider, who confidently predicts he will be chancellor in 1999, is waiting on the sidelines.

SWEDEN

Although a dramatic economic turnaround has put it on track to meet the entry conditions, Sweden is still months, if not years, away from deciding whether it wants to join EMU. With the ruling Social Democrats lacking direction and split on the issue, sentiment in a country which has a long tradition of independence and neutrality was evenly balanced for and against EMU in late 1996. 'We are a nation of free riders outside the walls, trading with both sides,' said Jan Herin, chief economist for the Swedish Employers' Confederation. 'Things are gradually changing and we are becoming more European, but the feeling of staying outside and seeing how we get on goes deep', he told Reuters.

Prime Minister Goran Persson and his Finance Minister Erik Asbrink have quietly tiptoed away from their once positive stance on EMU and are now uncommitted. 'If they are in favour, they should say so, if not, they should also say so. For many people, their final view will be dictated by the opinion of leading politicians,' said Kjell-Olof Feldt, a much-respected and pro-Europe former finance minister. Herin and Handelsbanken chief economist Carl Hamilton were agreed that the Social Democratic leadership would probably formulate its position in May/June 1997 ahead of a party congress in September. 'They have driven over the wishes of the party before and are scared to do so again,' said Herin.

If the country's largest party is fundamentally divided, other parties including the second-largest Conservatives are also split and unwilling to deepen the differences ahead of the next general election in 1998, Hamilton said. An opinion poll on November 27 showed 44 per cent of Swedes in favour of EMU and 40 per cent against – a volatile swing from only 21 per cent for and 54 per cent against on November 7. Between the two dates, the Italian lira had successfully re-entered the ERM without causing any political or financial market waves for Sweden, which now stood in a trio of European Union countries outside the ERM. These were 'Britain, which doesn't want to join, Greece, which can't, and Sweden which thinks it doesn't need to,' the tabloid *Expressen* commented.

In a country where the political debate consists largely of opinion polls, the latest surveys revealed deep uncertainty about the country's future identity. While the SDP remained uncommitted, the opposition Conservatives and Liberals were nominally in favour of EMU and the Greens, Centre, Christian Democrats and Leftists against. Even if the Social Democratic leaders finally decide to lead the party and country into EMU from the front, political commentators said they cannot count on a majority in the 349-seat Riksdag, the single-chamber Swedish parliament.

A government-appointed panel headed by university professor Lars Calmfors said in early November that the arguments against EMU entry in 1999 were stronger than those in favour. 'We felt it was a trade-off. The economic advantages of entering would be offset by some loss of political influence,' Professor Calmfors told Reuters. 'It would not take much to tip the balance,' he told a seminar in Stockholm on November 29. 'If it were only Sweden and Greece that did not join, it would be hard for Sweden to stay out in the long run.'

Neutral through two world wars and non-aligned in peacetime, a unique beneficiary of the terms of trade when Europe needed rebuilding, Sweden prospered on the northern fringe of the continent after 1945. Its labour market came to be known as the Swedish model and was the envy of the world. The twin towers of the LO trade union headquarters in Stockholm were a reassuring symbol of the harmony between organised labour and the ruling SDP. Sweden, it was whispered, had found the magic third way between capitalism and communism, in which workers assured of cradle-to-grave welfare would willingly switch from shipbuilding to carmaking if asked to do so.

By the late 1980s, however, Sweden's high wages and ever more generous benefits had begun to seriously undermine its competitiveness. Deregulation of capital markets led to a financial boom and bust, the collapse of communism redefined the need for neutrality, and suddenly Europe beckoned. Swedish voters may have taken their sceptical approach from the back-door way in which the government in 1990 announced it would seek membership of the European Economic Community (EEC). The momentous decision to abandon centuries of independence was buried halfway down a list of action points to tackle an economic crisis, what one newspaper called the 'most infamous footnote in Swedish history'.

But Swedish industry leaders from blue-chip companies like Ericsson, Volvo, Electrolux, MoDo and Astra and some trade unions recognised that although Sweden had joined the European Economic Area – grouping EU and some of the old European Free Trade Area (EFTA) – it needed to be on the inside if its voice was to be heard. Economists said Sweden had raised such a monster of state interference in the economy that it would need the external discipline of Brussels to bring its finances in order. In the debate about Europe, loss of neutrality, environmental concerns, fears about lower welfare benefits and the harmful effects of a more liberal policy on alcohol were set against the fears of losing access by Swedish export industries to European markets. The clincher may have been when EU negotiators allowed Sweden to keep 'snus', the wet snuff enjoyed by many Swedes but banned elsewhere on health grounds. In a referendum in 1994 Swedes voted narrowly in favour of joining the EU from January 1, 1995.

Sweden would have to amend its constitution to join EMU, to entrench the independence of its central bank. This would include changing the contract of the Riksbank governor, amending clauses on taking instructions from outside bodies, and removing its authority to issue banknotes. This would take time. 'To make constitutional changes requires two Acts of Parliament with an intervening election,' Robert Sparve from the Riksbank legal department said.

Sweden in late 1996 had the best inflation rate of any EU country — in fact, deflation of 0.1 per cent as charted by consumer prices over the 12 months to October. Handelsbanken predicted a budget deficit in 1997 of 1.6 per cent of GDP and state debt falling as a percentage of GDP to 74 per cent, a level which the EU might well interpret as acceptable. The markets were scaling down its long-term interest rates. But Sweden was resisting pressure to place its crown inside the ERM to comply formally with the fifth criterion, a stable two-year stint inside the currency grid. Politicians and Riksbank officials said in November that it was 'not an issue on the table at present'.

Unlike Britain and Denmark, Sweden has no opt-out clause on EMU and its position on currency stability has raised eyebrows among some European central bankers. Twice during October market sources said the Riksbank had intervened to keep the crown stable – but against what, and who was measuring? Belgian central bank chief Alfons Verplaetse told Reuters in Stockholm: 'This solution I personally can live with but only if the Riksbank declares a parity level for the crown.' Visiting Irish Prime Minister John Bruton said he could not see a problem of Sweden's qualifying for EMU if it had met the convergence criteria even if outside the ERM. Economics professor Johan Lybeck said the government was playing a difficult political game, but skilfully. He concluded, 'I'm certain Sweden will join by 2002 when it's time to pool currencies.'

DENMARK

With a strong currency, low inflation, falling debt and an independent central bank, Denmark has all the attributes of a founding member of Economic and Monetary Union but its citizens refuse to let it join. In a 1993 referendum voters endorsed the Maastricht Treaty, but only on condition that Denmark stay out of EMU. Entry would require a fresh plebiscite, an undertaking that polls indicate would risk another 'No' and one that Prime Minister Poul Nyrup Rasmussen is in no hurry to attempt.

'At the moment I see no reason to ask the Danish people to vote in a referendum,' he said during a November 1996 Vienna forum on the future of monetary union. 'We fulfil all five Maastricht criteria but we do not want to join. I say to the Danish people, I respect your decision and it will not be changed until the situation alters,' he added.

Analysts say that his position stems from the political imperative of not supporting a new poll until convinced that it is winnable, rather than from any basic opposition to the Euro project. Rasmussen, an economist by training, must also tread softly in order to minimise conflict within his own Social Democrat party, many of whose members oppose membership of the EU in general and EMU in particular. Economy Minister Marianne Jelved, a member of the centrist Radical Liberals in Rasmussen's coalition government, is openly committed to EMU but her political calculation is the same. 'I haven't changed (public) opinion yet. We shall have a new referendum when I think I can get a yes and not a moment before,' she said.

The Danish Confederation of Industry, the central bank and the main opposition Liberal Party all support early entry as essential given the country's close economic ties to the EU, particularly neighbouring Germany. More than half Denmark's industrial and agricultural production is exported and, of that, 60 per cent goes to the EU, with Germany buying the lion's share. Although Denmark has not had to submit to the painful austerity programmes that some other countries have had to endure in order to meet the EMU criteria, its business and political leaders have so far failed to shake their compatriots' gut aversion to the idea. A November 1996 survey by Danish polling institute Greens showed 53.4 per cent opposed to joining EMU with 30.4 in favour. The balance did not know or declined to answer.

Many citizens of this small, Lutheran country near the EU's geographical fringe see their language, culture and political independence threatened by deeper integration in a union which they view as dominated by French and German Catholics. A non-partisan group of 11 private citizens is challenging Denmark's existing EU membership in the courts, saying that in some cases the assignment of national authority to central EU institutions contravenes the Danish constitution. Should they win, legal experts say, the Danish government could be obliged to renegotiate its 1973 membership from scratch — and revise a mountain of EU-related domestic legislation enacted since.

Another option would be to amend the constitution, obliging Rasmussen's unpopular government to fight a general election which all recent polls indicate it would lose. Should it win, the law says that it must hold a referendum on the proposed change which has to be accepted by at least 50 per cent of the total electorate, not just those voting.

The government scored a point in preliminary hearings when the court refused the petitioners' request to have confidential government papers going back 20 years entered in evidence. But the outcome of the main hearing, expected to begin next year and continue well into 1998, remains uncertain. For the foreseeable future official policy is to maintain a kind of 'virtual membership'. 'Our policy will be that even while we are out we shall run our economy as if we had joined,' a senior central bank official said. There is agreement in principle with the EU's monetary committee that the crown will be confined within a tight band against the euro in a proposed exchange rate mechanism for non-member currencies.

Bankers are examining to what extent they will be able to participate in the new euro-banking system while remaining outside the currency union. Commercial banks are increasingly worried that they may have to set up satellite offices within the EMU zone in order to do business. Some local analysts, however, think Denmark is well out of the euro club, arguing that centralised direction robs member countries of a safety valve. 'The traditional stabilisers will be more or less put out of commission ... individual countries will be unable to stop a recession by lowering interest or adjusting exchange rates, only fiscal policy remains,' Lehman Brothers economist Keld Holm said recently. 'EMU is sold in many cases as an economic cure. It is not. It does, however, make economic and structural problems more visible, so that people ask themselves what they are really getting into,' he said.

Danes have long been asking themselves that question. The prospect of them finding a convincing answer before 1999 seems remote.

What they say about national sovereignty and monetary union

'A common monetary system welds member states into an indissoluble community. It will not leave untouched even those aspects of policy which have so far remained sovereign.' Former Bundesbank chairman Helmut Schlesinger, *The Economist*, September 1996.

'In a nation state, one has these common unifying forces like a common tax system, a common legal system, a central budget and a common social system ... . We do not have this form of solidarity on the European level. We won't have that in Europe for a long time.' Bundesbank President Hans Tietmeyer, November 1996.

'I am in favour of a pact for growth and solidarity ... . If someone is trying to impose on us an economic and monetary union in which the word "economic" is struck out and "monetary union" is reduced to a single currency and budget discipline, I say no. That is not what we agreed to in the Maastricht Treaty.' Jacques Delors, former European Commission president and mastermind of EMU, November 1996.

'The strong and independent central bank that will handle the common monetary policy on its own might lack a counterbalancing force in European fiscal policies ... (if this pushed the EU towards federation) the EU would be transformed into something completely different from the EU the Swedish people approved after some agony and a long and trying debate.' Swedish Prime Minister Goran Persson, *Svenska Dagbladet*, December 1996.

FINLAND

Finland is well placed to help found EMU, but political hurdles are scattered on an eager government's path to January 1, 1999 and beyond. Many Finns feel that by joining the European Union in 1995 they showed where they want their country to belong. Worried about their geographical location on the borders of a fast-changing Russia, they rushed to follow their western neighbour Sweden into the EU. Public debate about EMU has been more muted than in Sweden. However, opinion polls show less Finnish enthusiasm about EMU than about EU membership.

Finland leap-frogged Sweden to take the markka into the ERM in late 1996, with the Swedish crown still floating. But Sweden is Finland's dominant trading partner, and politicians of all parties paid attention to warnings from Stockholm that EMU was ill-suited to countries with high unemployment. Swedish unemployment is around 7.5 per cent, but the Finnish rate is twice as high. Studies show that Finns fear jobs will be lost, wages will come under pressure and their Nordic welfare state will come under fire within the monetary union. EMU opponents say that real economic convergence should be deeper than the Maastricht Treaty specifies for monetary union to work.

Finns, coping with longer distances and a harsher climate, live in a very different economic structure from that of continental Europe. Arctic villages like Utsjoki, about as far from Helsinki as is Paris from Rome, may see few benefits from the euro. '(German Chancellor Helmut) Kohl is not very interested in how people live in Utsjoki,' said Ulla Klotzer, leader of Finland's anti-EMU Alternative to EU movement.

But Utsjoki's problems do not trouble many Finns either, and the government has pushed on with a declared aim to secure a seat at Europe's top table. Prime Minister Paavo Lipponen argues that Finland cannot look after its own interests with just one foot in the EU. 'We must be part of the circle in the EU where decisions about the future of the union are made,' he said. Finance Minister Sauli Niinisto is selling the project under the slogan of eonomic security, appealing to numerous fears including the memory of a punishing recession after the Soviet Union collapsed.

However, the pro-EMU campaign has so far been hampered by the perception that the political elite is aloof and insensitive to ordinary people's concerns. Even within his own social democratic party, Lipponen is often accused of bullying. Niinisto, leader of the Conservative Party, is firmly committed to EMU and his party is backing him. Bank of Finland governor Sirkka Hamalainen is doggedly preaching the EMU gospel of low inflation bringing lower interest rates, sustained and stronger economic growth, and better jobs. But all three lack a populist touch. 'People have a very good instinctive feeling whether an argument rings true . . . if decision-makers sound credible people will support them,' said Esko Aho, who was prime minister when Finland joined the EU but is less enthusiastic about EMU. He now leads the opposition Centre Party.

In 1996, polls were putting public opposition to EMU at between 45 and 60 per cent. Opposition parties and one of the five parties in the coalition government have called for a referendum, but their leaders admit that a national vote is unlikely. Instead the decision is due to be made by parliament late in 1997, or more likely early in 1998. MPs will have at least half an eye on the debate in Sweden.

Some bickering has already started on a key issue which parliament's constitutional committee will decide, probably in spring 1997: the procedure for the EMU vote. The government line is that when parliament voted in 1994 in favour of EU membership, by a qualified two-thirds majority, it also approved the Maastricht Treaty, including EMU. The Aho government attached to the EU accession accord a unilateral statement that Finland will decide separately whether to participate in EMU, but nobody regards this as an opt-out clause similar to Denmark's or the United Kingdom's. Niinisto calls the statement an 'unofficial reservation'. If the constitutional committee follows the cabinet's cue, the legislature will vote on Finnish EMU entry by simple majority.

However, Aho says parliament could, by simple majority, give the government a political mandate to express Finland's wish to join EMU when EU leaders decide who qualifies. If the summit finds Finland eligible, Aho says the government should put before parliament the bills needed to adapt the constitution. Constitutional changes require a two-thirds majority, or a five-sixths majority to be declared urgent and take effect at once. With 45 MPs, Aho's Centre Party could block any 'urgent' constitutional change.

The 1.1-million member Central Organisation of Finnish Trade Unions (SAK) will decide its EMU stance in the autumn of 1997. Lipponen's Social Democrats will find it very hard to go against the union. Aware of this, SAK is demanding buffer funds to cushion potential EMU pains. Niinisto, the central bank and employers federations oppose the demand which — with other EMU-related labour market issues — was due to be settled in talks between government, union and employer leaders in spring 1997.

If the basic elements of a non-inflationary pay deal are in place in early autumn 1997, the government may include in its 1998 state budget proposal new income tax cuts to follow those laid out in the 1997 budget. By demonstrating that such cuts are possible for two consecutive years amid EMU-driven fiscal austerity, the government could hope to swing undecided voters — and through them, MPs.

But there are pressures within the coalition government, too. The Leftist Alliance, a junior government party, will poll its members on joining EMU in late 1997 and has pledged to respect the outcome. This has the potential to spark a government crisis, insiders say. By late 1996, government and opposition politicians alike were worried that the many issues would become dangerously interlocked with EMU, hampering decision-making on anything.

'The real problems may have to be faced by the next government,' says Carlo Erakallio, chief economist at Handelsbanken Markets. The plan is to defer until 1999 the constitutional amendments needed to enable the euro to replace the markka. If reluctant politicians feel forced by their leaders to take a divided nation into EMU, the next general election due in March 1999 could turn into an EMU referendum. The new parliament could be hostile and reject single currency-related legislation. 'This could become a big problem,' Erakallio said.

Central bank independence could yet prove another obstacle to early Finnish EMU membership. To meet the Maastricht Treaty requirements, Finland would have to abolish the board of parliamentarians which now serves as a political watchdog for the Bank of Finland. The risk of exclusion in 1999 is obvious if a central bank lacks independence, regardless of how well other criteria are met, finance ministry officials say.

But the parliamentary supervisors are unwilling to give up their role. 'We feel it could be dangerous to let go of all political control over our own currency,' one of them said. That view reflects a deep yearning to retain an economic weapon of last resort if Finland's vital forest industry suffers a cyclical downturn. Many think that weapon should be retained by avoiding EMU, especially if Sweden stays out.

GREECE

Greece is the only European Union state which has not met a single Maastricht criterion. But despite a background of public unrest, there is political consensus that joining EMU is crucial to the country's future. No one inside or outside Greece sees a chance of it participating in the first wave of single currency members but Greek leaders hold out hope for making it into the second round.

'We must succeed to be inside this nucleus if we want to play a role in matters that concern us. This is our future,' said Prime Minister Costas Simitis, not long after his socialist party won national elections in September 1996. The party campaigned on a platform of austerity that stressed the need for Greece to take part in EMU. 'Our economic policy aims to create the conditions so (that we can) participate in EMU with the second group of countries in 2000 or 2001.'

Simitis' austerity policies have generated a wave of dissent and have forced a public debate on EMU for the first time. The General Confederation of Greek Workers (GSEE), labour's biggest umbrella organisation, was joined by the civil servants union (ADEDY) in staging a one-day strike in November 1996 to protest against the 1997 budget and they have promised more protests to come.

To make up for years of lost time in moving towards EMU, the 1997 budget relies on elimination of a host of tax breaks and on a stream of revenues from new taxes such as a levy on government securities. The measures have angered many who face a drop in their real disposable income. The budget, as submitted to parliament late in 1996, aims to cut the general government budget deficit to 4.2 per cent of GDP in 1997 from an expected 7.6 per cent in 1996. Under Greece's official EU convergence plan for 1998, it has projected a fall in the deficit to GDP ratio to 2.4 per cent.

But is all this too optimistic? In 1995 Greece had a budget deficit representing 9.1 per cent of GDP. The country is making its projections on the assumption of a brisk rate of growth, forecasting a 3.3 per cent expansion in GDP in 1997 after a 2.7 per cent increase in 1996. At the same time the country plans a freeze on real spending and an overall 14.9 per cent rise in budget revenue.

Farmers, who benefited most from past EU policies and enjoy preferential tax status, have led the protests, which have included blockades of major roads and rail links. Like many in Greece, they are torn between a desire to hold onto the privileges they have enjoyed and a recognition that the country needs to be a part of EMU if its economy is to move forward. Ultimately the protesters say they want the Greek government to negotiate harder for their rights in Brussels.

For five years, the main political parties have staunchly backed joining EMU despite some differences over approach. Only the hard-line communist party and the splinter socialist DIKKI party reject EMU membership. The conservative New Democracy party suggests that Greece revise its 1994–98 EU convergence plan to spread the pain of adjustment over a longer period of time.

Financial markets and associations of employers have always been pro-EMU. Even labour unions have avoided criticising EMU directly. Yet despite the pervasive belief that EMU is essential, Greece had done little until the mid-1990s to meet even the technical goals required to get there. Aside from the economic criteria, one pressing need for Greece is to pass legislation to make the Bank of Greece independent.

The government is expected to grant independence to the Bank of Greece in 1997. Some officials attribute the delay to legal issues and the vague nature of the definition of independence in the Maastricht Treaty. Meanwhile the Bank of Greece ceased financing of the state's budget deficits from January 1, 1994 and the central bank is expected to lift remaining restrictions on capital flows. 'We have decided to do away with the very few remaining restrictions by the end of 1997,' a high-level central bank official told Reuters. Central bankers are also concentrating on the technical aspects involved with operations at the European Central Bank.

But to gain access to the single currency club, Greece will need to show markets and fellow EU authorities that the drachma is a stable and respectable currency. Greece has pursued a hard drachma policy which aims to combat inflation by letting the drachma slide less than would be justified by inflation differentials. The drachma depreciated by three per cent against the Ecu but Greek authorities are expecting their currency to be more stable than that.

'The drachma shadows the ERM and would have had no problem fluctuating within the broad 15 per cent band,' said one central bank official. 'We will address the issue of joining ERM at the proper time.'

Senior bankers, at least in Greece, are backing the official line. 'I have no doubt that Greece will make it to the EMU and sooner than many pundits think,' said Mike Paparis, treasurer at Midland Bank in Athens. George Georgiou, general manager at Bayerische Vereinsbank in Athens, said the drachma was already behaving as if it were part of the ERM and that it would face no difficulty within the ERM ranks.

PORTUGAL

Portugal's two main political parties are so enamoured of the euro that one opponent accused them of uniting to form 'The Party of the Single Currency'. The ruling Socialists and the opposition Social Democrats both believe the euro will take Portugal into the political hard core of Europe, fostering lower interest rates and faster long term economic growth. They say it will help bring billions of dollars of direct investment to Portugal as foreign companies take advantage of cheap labour and modern infrastructure financed by European Union (EU) cohesion funds over the past decade. Prime Minister Antonio Guterres says he wants Portugal to join the euro on January 1, 1999. He insists that Portugal must be considered for membership on its own merits, not lumped together with the other 'Club Med' countries, Spain and Italy. He says fiscal discipline and a privatisation programme that is bigger in relative terms that in most other European countries will enable Portugal to make the EMU grade.

'The Portuguese have been indoctrinated into the belief that the single currency is the only way forward for the country,' said Sally Wilkinson, economist with UBS. The main detractors are the Eurosceptical rightwing Popular Party (PP) and the Communists.

The PP, who have 15 seats in the 230-seat parliament, want a referendum on euro membership. But even opponents of the euro concede that the Portuguese would probably vote in favour of the European single currency. 'I think 80 or 90 per cent of the Portuguese would say yes to a single currency in a referendum,' said Vasco d'Orey, a university economist and card-carrying member of the PP.

Jorge Ferreira, head of the PP's parliamentary group, believes Portugal is not ready to join the euro and fears that the country would struggle to compete with its European partners within EMU. It was he who accused the government and opposition Social Democrats of effectively joining forces in blindly backing the euro. The Communists (PCP), who also have just 15 seats in parliament, say they oppose the euro because they do not want Portugal to lose control over its economic policy. 'The PCP oppose a dilution of the role of the state,' said Rui Martins dos Santos, politically independent chief economist of Banco Portugues de Investimento (BPI).

Economists saw little reason for any of Portugal's political parties to change their stance towards EMU over the next two years. They said Portugal would not have to adopt austerity policies as harsh as those confronting some other European countries, such as laying off civil servants or implementing a public pay freeze. It has a privatisation programme that was expected to garner at least 460 billion escudos in 1996, two to three per cent of GDP, and a similar sum in 1997. Economists said the state was unlikely to use its $5 billion in pure gold reserves as a cushion to meet EMU budget targets, but it could use gold to repay some state debt if it could do so without unnerving the gold market.

Portugal is not obliged to hold a parliamentary vote to accede to the euro, but analysts said a vote would almost certainly take place as it would undoubtedly pass with the support of both the government and the Social Democrats. The Bank of Portugal had already adopted nearly all the statutes required in order to meet the Maastricht rules on central bank independence, officials said. Bank of Portugal Governor Antonio de Sousa has said that the Bank would have no difficulty abolishing a statute that gives veto power to the governor, allowing him to suspend decisions of the board of directors.

Wilkinson at UBS said Portugal's biggest challenge was to meet a 1997 budget deficit forecast of 2.9 per cent of GDP, based on optimistic economic growth projections that depended on factors outside Portugal's control, notably growth in Germany. The government has already made progress on inflation and yield spreads over German Bunds had dropped to around 1.25 points in late 1996 from 5.2 in early 1995.

But analysts said a final EU decision on whether Portugal would join the euro from the start would be have to be qualitative rather than based purely on the 1997 outturn. 'The key issue is not that Portugal's deficit is three per cent of GDP, but Portugal's ability to show that keeping its deficit down is sustainable,' said BPI's Martins dos Santos. A Lisbon-based diplomat said, 'The EU member states will not bend over backwards to let Portugal in. But if it becomes necessary to bend the criteria to let a major country in, then Portugal could crawl in under its coat tails.'

D'Orey said a mood of Euroscepticism could surface if Portugal's application to join EMU were rebuffed. 'If the EU were not flexible, there could be a backlash in Portugal in terms of anti-European feeling,' he said. 'The Portuguese would feel that those guys (Eurocrats) are cheating us as we made all the effort required of us.'

IRELAND

Ireland is staunchly committed to EMU, but as the realisation of a single currency comes ever closer, fears are mounting of the potential repercussions for Irish business if Ireland enters EMU without its main trading partner, Britain.

The Irish government has remained unwavering in keeping the EMU entry criteria high on its fiscal agenda, with considerable success, and the Irish economy is booming. For the last four years Ireland has boasted the fastest growth rate in Europe. Its GDP growth rate hit double digits in 1995, running at 10.7 per cent year-on-year, against an EU average of roughly two per cent. Ireland also has the will of its people pushing it towards Europe. In 1972, 83 per cent of its people voted in favour of joining the then European Community.

Although concerns about joining Europe without Britain have become more vociferous of late, a 1996 survey of Irish business still showed a general acceptance that Ireland would be worse off staying out of EMU with Britain than entering EMU without its former colonial ruler. 'Staying out of EMU, as far as we are concerned, is more likely to give higher Irish interest rates and an unstable exchange rate,' a spokesman for Ireland's Central Bank told Reuters. 'We are working within a framework that we are going into EMU and the acceptance of Maastricht is not conditional on what Britain and sterling do,' the spokesman said. 'But that is not to say that we would not prefer to have sterling in.'

The risk for Ireland entering EMU without Britain is that it will be highly exposed to sterling volatility, trapped within the confines of a single currency without control over its exchange rate. Ireland's official trade statistics show a sharp reduction in dependence on Britain in the last 25 years but the statistics are not showing the whole story. In 1970, 66 per cent of Irish exports were exported to Britain with only 12 per cent going to the rest of Europe. In 1995, official trade data showed only 26 per cent of Irish exports destined for Britain and 47 per cent going to Europe.

The problem is the statistics are skewed by multinational transactions. Multi-national corporations currently account for half of all exports out of Ireland. These large transnational operations use Ireland as a backdoor to Europe and have little trade with Britain. This makes Ireland's dependence on Britain look artificially low. The bulk of indigenous Irish manufacturing exports are still going to Britain and their dependence on sterling is great.

So why doesn't Ireland take a risk averse view and follow Britain rather than Europe? Ireland has made many attempts to break its dependence on its former ruler. It decoupled from sterling, breaking its one-to-one link, in 1989. Since then Ireland has made great efforts to be a good European, struggling to keep the Irish currency at a credible level within the European Exchange Rate Mechanism (ERM). 'If Ireland was to stay outside EMU it is arguable that we could be in a vulnerable and isolated position,' Ireland's central bank governor Maurice O'Connell said. 'The markets would question our motives. The Irish pound might carry a significant interest rate premium,' he said. 'Staying out could also deter inward investment,' he added. 'One has to ask whether an Ireland semi-detached from the heart of Europe would remain such an attractive location for new overseas investment.' O'Connell also felt that Ireland may find it considerably more difficult down the road to satisfy EMU criteria. 'These are serious downsides that we should not underestimate.'

Finance minister Ruairi Quinn voiced similar sentiments. 'If we were to be outside the euro and declared to the rest of the world that we were qualifying to join a single currency but we were deciding for whatever reason not to join it, largely because of our dependence on sterling, I think we would compound our vulnerability,' Quinn told Reuters in late 1996.

Despite this relatively unanimous drive towards Europe, Ireland has changed little of a statutory nature or otherwise to underpin its commitment. A survey of Irish business showed that little or no effort was being made to accommodate the practical aspects of EMU.

Even Ireland's 1996 Central Bank Bill, which is currently going through parliament, makes no reference to EMU requirements that each prospective member should make statutory provisions to allow its central bank full independence. The Irish central bank spokesman said that while nothing had yet been changed, once the EMI produced a full menu of requirements the central bank would swiftly incorporate them. 'When this year's bill was being prepared there was talk about making some EMU-related changes that were reasonably obvious but ... it became clear that the EMI was still examining the issue and we did not yet know all the changes that would be needed. So it was decided that we would leave specifically EMU-related issues aside until the full menu was known.'

SWITZERLAND?

Swiss bankers and executives are whistling past the graveyard as they warily eye the approach of Europe's single currency, whose strength or weakness will help make or break Switzerland's stagnant economy. Business leaders fear that a weak euro, embracing the currencies of many EU countries, could spook investors and trigger massive flows of funds into the rock-solid Swiss franc, making exports even dearer and choking off economic growth. But the flagship banking sector and Swiss financial markets are putting the best face possible on their long-term prospects in the euro era.

For many bankers, the euro project is casting Switzerland in the light they find most flattering — the neutral, professional outsider whose discreet ways promise stability and prosperity. 'We are of the view that the function of Switzerland as a safe haven will remain, principally because in the longer term, banking secrecy will be called into question in many EU countries,' Bank Julius Baer analyst Hans Kaufmann said.

Some British politicians demand an end to banking secrecy in all offshore centres, and Luxembourg and Austria are already under attack for protecting confidentiality, he said in a study. But despite international pressure, the Swiss government has consistently spoken out in favour of retaining banking secrecy.

'In my view it is not at all visible that in terms of asset management there is a threat to Switzerland from monetary union,' said Christof Kutscher, head of investment consulting at Swiss Bank Corp in Basle. '(Clients) want to be offshore and Switzerland is still the premier choice of the offshore possibilities. It still has a better reputation than the Bahamas or the Cayman Islands or whatever else is available for offshore markets.'

Swiss banks do have some chinks in their armour, however. 'Swiss banks have an important position in foreign exchange trading, which is why they are bound to be hit by this,' Baer's Kaufmann said, doubting increased trading in other currencies would make up for lost cross-trading among European currencies. Banks could also suffer if Switzerland fails to join the TARGET cross-border settlement system, which powerful EU members like Germany and France want to limit to euro zone countries. A Swiss bid to join is on hold until Britain's status is resolved.

Some say Swiss banks will pay the price for having invested so heavily in their operations in London, which seems likely to remain outside the single currency area, at least at first. 'It is clear that Switzerland will be one the great losers of monetary union,' one senior Swiss banker said, forecasting Swiss banks would remain successful but only by moving more operations to financial centres within the euro zone. Kutscher disagreed. 'If you do currency trading you can do it from Timbuktu if you have the right computers and telephone links. I am not afraid Zurich will undergo a major shrinking process,' he said.

Swiss banks are likely to benefit from the alignment of interest margins to be expected after the euro arrives in 1999. Margins are now far higher abroad than in Switzerland, where interest income after deduction of reserves accounts for less than 21 per cent of banks' adjusted gross income, Kaufmann noted. 'It seems realistic to assume that at the point when European competitors are confronted with this problem, the process of structural reorganisation will already be over and done with at the Swiss banks,' he said.

The Swiss National Bank (SNB), which has been working hard to weaken the franc and boost the flagging economy, has made clear it will adjust its monetary policy if necessary to keep the currency from overinflating. It has even raised the prospect of tying the franc to the euro, but only as a last resort and only as a temporary measure.

Swiss voters in 1992 narrowly rejected joining the European Economic Area trade bloc, but some bankers think they could be persuaded to join the euro bloc in a few years if the currency is stable and the Swiss economy keeps shedding jobs. Meanwhile, Swiss markets are playing down the euro's impact. 'There is fear among my foreign colleagues that the smaller bourses will be made redundant with this decision (to start the euro). This doesn't have such a big influence here,' said Otto Naegeli, in charge of markets on the electronic Swiss Exchange.

Interest-rate contracts that face a big shakeout in Europe play a negligible role on the Soffex options and futures market, which remains driven by stocks and related equity instruments. 'All in all, it will be interesting for us what effect it has on markets, but I personally don't see any major impact. Nestle and Novartis and ABB and UBS will still be there. For shares this is not such a big problem,' Naegeli told Reuters.

Swiss industry, on the other hand, faces a major problem if the franc strengthens and the euro makes it simple for consumers to compare prices. This would test to the limit Swiss companies' insistence that their high-quality goods are worth the premium. Many banks and the Swiss Federation of Industry (SHIV) are advising companies to prepare to face the possibility that a strong franc makes exporting more difficult in the run-up to the euro.

'The pressure on margins will increase, and additional parts of the export industry threaten to be moved abroad,' Credit Suisse told clients in a recent mailing. 'On the other hand, rising demand for francs leads to lower interest rates, which promotes domestic investment,' it said. Nestle SA Chairman Helmut Maucher said the single currency would ultimately be advantageous by cutting transaction costs, but he added differing consumer preferences would limit savings. 'The differences between France, Germany, Britain, Spain and other places are not going to change because of a single currency,' he told reporters recently.

SHIV spokesman Rudolf Walser said it was hard to generalise on whether Swiss industry was ready for the day of reckoning, but he said he was not worried about the future because Swiss companies were used to dealing with a strong franc. 'I think about lots of things when I can't sleep at night, sometimes about economic subjects, but I have never thought about the euro,' he said.

4

Currencies: the 'ins' and 'outs' of EMU

By Myra MacDonald in Paris and Henry Engler in Brussels

FIXING EXCHANGE RATES FOR CURRENCIES WHICH ENTER EMU

Steeling themselves to abandon their national currencies, Europe's politicians want to be sure it is they and not financial markets who fix the exchange rates at which their countries will join a single currency. This is why central bankers and officials are considering announcing in advance how the rates will be fixed, rather than locking into monetary union on January 1, 1999 at whatever the currency rates happen to be on December 31, 1998.

'The guiding principle is that the sooner it is done, the better,' a Bundesbank spokesman said. Belgian Finance Minister Philippe Maystadt told Reuters it was important that European authorities made their decision well before the start of EMU. 'Everybody agrees you should have something which is not the rate of the day,' he said.

The theory is that whatever method Europe's leaders announce, markets will know where they expect rates to be at the start of monetary union and push the EMU 'in' currencies in that direction. Knowing that Europe's leaders have the power to fix the rates administratively, markets would be less likely than in past currency crises to call their bluff. 'This time the central banks have another weapon which is the legal stroke,' said Stefan Collignon, director of research at the Association for Monetary Union of Europe.

At issue are cross rates between national currencies. Europe's pledge to make the new euro exchangeable one-for-one for the Ecu means that the euro/dollar rate on the first day of monetary union will be the Ecu/dollar rate on the last day of 1998. The Ecu is a composite currency, based on a basket weighted according to each country's share in intra-EU trade. 'Fixing the euro rate against the dollar is not a monetary policy decision but the choice of a face value,' a working paper released in August 1996 by French banks and the Bank of France said.

The euro could then be left to find its own value, although there could be political tensions over quite how strong the new currency should be. (See Chapter 11.) Officials are looking at two main ways of fixing national currencies: using central rates in the existing ERM or using an average, an idea proposed by EMI head Alexandre Lamfalussy.

The central rates have the advantage of being agreed already as the correct reflection of economic fundamentals, but have the drawback of paying no attention at all to market rates. Using an average could address this drawback and the idea appears to be gaining prominence for the time being. 'We cannot take away market considerations,' European Commissioner for Economic and Monetary Affairs, Yves-Thibault de Silguy said in late 1996. He added, however, that it was premature to give an indication of how rates would be fixed.

Self-fulfilling prophecy

Collignon said it probably did not matter too much which method was used. More important would be the element of self-fulfilling prophecy through an early announcement. The idea would be to announce the method for fixing rates at the same time as the decision on which countries will join a single currency in 1999, a choice likely to come in April 1998. Since only those countries which have met Maastricht treaty criteria designed to bring economies into line will get in, there should be no fundamental reason for big currency swings.

Central banks, knowing they have the legal power to fix the rates, would be under no obligation to intervene in currency markets to prop up currencies. As a result the central bank buying that currency speculators required to mop up their heavy selling during the European currency crises of 1992 and 1993 would be absent. 'They don't need to intervene, and because they don't need to intervene the market can't test them out,' Collignon said.

And once EMU is launched, national currency banknotes will be nothing more than a numerical expression of the euro — so if, for example, you wanted to change all your francs into marks, you could do so. National banknotes will remain in circulation until 2002, but 'everyone will have euros, even if they are labelled francs or marks,' said Francois Chevallier, economist at Banque Francaise du Commerce Exterieur.

In the extreme case, marks, or euros, could be printed and other currencies burned, with the result that there would no difference in the net liquidity in the euro zone. That was not the case in the previous crises when the Bundesbank had to print marks to intervene on foreign exchange markets, posing a risk to the German money supply.

The overall aim of announcing the method for fixing rates early is to prevent speculators from ramping up currency rates in the run-up to EMU and taking the profits when these are then fixed at the higher level. Collignon said that this would also be a risk if rates in the months between April 1998 and December 1998 were taken into account in calculating the average. 'If you take the future into your average you have to have a hefty past,' he said.

Monetary officials say the EU is considering using the periods before and after April 1998 in any averaging method. But Europe's officials are likely to try keep everybody guessing until the last minute on how they plan to fix exchange rates. Otherwise, their early announcement would simply mean that speculation started earlier.

'They will be fixed and the world will discover the morning after they have been fixed,' Luxembourg Prime Minister Jean-Claude Juncker told Reuters. 'It would add to speculation if we organised a public debate on the question,' he added. 'The game is to run ahead of the markets before the markets start pushing the rates in a crazy direction,' ABN-Amro economist Philippe Brossard said.

Risk of competitive devaluation

Another motive for an early announcement is the desire to avoid a last-minute competitive devaluation by one of the chosen EMU countries. Economists argue the mere knowledge that such a move is possible could invite markets to put a higher risk premium on the debt of those with a strong motive to devalue. Belgium, for instance, with a debt burden well above the EU average, could save billions in interest costs through a last-minute devaluation.

There is a strong desire to settle the issue ahead of 1999, but there are also a few problems with the choices mooted so far. One concerns the influential role the Bundesbank would play if the central parity rates were chosen as the conversion rates in early 1998. For the next eight months, policy makers would have to guard against the risk that some external shock — an oil price rise or a US interest rate spike, for example — might disrupt Europe's currency and bond markets. Such a shock would put European monetary authorities under enormous pressure to defend the official rates against the ravages of the market. No central bank would feel the heat more than the Bundesbank. It is unclear at the moment how much appetite the Bundesbank has to assume such a risk.

Some analysts take the more sanguine view that heavy foreign exchange intervention by the Bundesbank and, say, the Bank of France would not have a great impact on inflation — the German central bank's primary concern — because within a few weeks or months any changes in domestic money supply would become meaningless. A potential shift from French franc to mark denominated assets during a crisis would leave the overall EMU zone money supply unchanged after the euro is launched.

A more vexing problem is how to reconcile an early announcement of the fixed rates with two existing EU commitments: to maintain the external value of the Ecu basket; and to ensure a one-for-one conversion between the euro and the Ecu. As a basket currency, the Ecu includes weightings for countries which are likely to opt out or be ruled out of EMU. How, then, can the authorities work out the cross rates for EMU entrants before they know the Ecu's value on the last trading day of 1998?

Many analysts say this problem will turn out to be hypothetical. They say the external value of the Ecu will probably converge with what market participants believe the value of the euro will be, which will in turn hinge on which countries are chosen and on the market's evaluation of the ECB's likely policy stance. If there is a good degree of economic convergence among the countries chosen, and if the ECB is seen as credible, the external value of the Ecu will probably approximate very closely to the future value of the euro. Some even argue that early announcement of the conversion rates would enhance the process and help to satisfy the Ecu/euro mandate.

LINKING THE EURO TO EU COUNTRIES OUTSIDE THE BLOC

The 'outs': ERM II

One of the most urgent tasks for EU policy makers in the run-up to 1999 is to create a mechanism to ensure stability between the euro and the currencies of the 'outs', the EU countries that do not qualify or choose not to join the first EMU wave.

The Dublin summit approved a new Exchange Rate Mechanism to bridge this gap. This ERM II 'would reflect lessons and experience gained with the present system and provide continuity,' the EU leaders said. The proposals

mark a sharp departure from the EU's current ERM,
the central role which it confers on the new European

The mark may be the informal anchor of the old E\
existing mechanism links currencies bilaterally through a c
tral parity rates. The euro would have unambiguous primac
II, a 'hub and spoke' system with the euro as the hub and th   ..rrencies
as the spokes.

The new system would be voluntary, with no country outside EMU forced
to join; and flexible, with each country's band narrowing as its economy converged on the EMU core. The standard fluctuation band would be 'relatively
wide, like the present one,' the EU communiques said, referring to the 15 per
cent bands agreed for the ERM after it was nearly destroyed by Europe's 1993
currency crisis.

How does the existing ERM work?

The European Union's Exchange Rate Mechanism (ERM), created in 1979,
is designed to keep currencies trading in a range around a central rate. At
end-1996, the grid included 12 EU currencies. Britain's pound, Sweden's
crown and Greece's drachma remained outside. All 15 currencies are part
of the European Monetary System (EMS).

Since August 1993, most currencies have been allowed to fluctuate by
up to 15 per cent above or below the fixed central cross rate against each
other. The German mark and the Dutch guilder trade informally within
2.25 per cent bands, the original range for all the ERM currencies until the
bands were burst open in a currency crisis in August 1993.

When a currency hits the permitted floor or ceiling value against another ERM unit, the two central banks concerned must intervene to hold it
within its band by buying or selling as required. This does not, of course,
apply to the three currencies outside the grid, although they are bound to
keep their currencies stable.

The ERM fluctuation limits are set as a percentage either side of the central rate. But when any two currencies move against each other, they will
not end up at the same percentage distance from the central rate. The
inverse of the upper limit of, say, mark/lira must equal the lower limit in
lira/mark. So a 10 per cent rise of the mark against the lira does not equal
a 10 per cent fall in the lira against the mark.

For example, if you take mark/lira at 1,000 per mark and there is a 10
per cent rally, you end up with 1,100. The mark is 100 lire higher. But if
you invert this in terms of the lira/mark rate, a 10 per cent move down

would equal a move to 0.0009 marks. Invert this and you get 1,111.11 lire per mark. This anomaly must be avoided when making sure the upper end of mark/lira equals its inverse in lira/mark.

For mathematicians, the EU Commission's guide follows:

Let x be the central ERM rate of, for example, mark per French franc. Then 1/x is the central rate of French franc per mark. The total band width is 30 per cent or 0.3.

The following conditions must be satisfied:
$[x(1+ru)]$ to the power of -1 = $(1/x)(1-rl)$
ie the inverse of the upper limit in mark per French franc must equal the lower limit in French franc per mark.
and ... ru + rl = 0.3, ie the total band-width equals 30 per cent
where ... ru is the upper range and rl is the lower range.

Putting the two conditions together yields the following quadratic equation:
ru squared + 1.7ru − 0.3 = 0

The solution to this is:
ru = 0.161187 (or +16.1187 per cent as the upper range)
rl = 0.138813 (or -13.8813 per cent as the lower range)

However, in ERM II, the trading ranges could vary, depending on how far each 'out' country's economy had converged with those of the 'ins'. An 'out' country that had met, say, all but one of the EMU entry criteria could opt for a narrower range against the euro. The communique was vague about the details, but it also allowed for bilateral agreements to narrow the target trading ranges for pairs of 'out' currencies.

Officials say the precise trading bands on offer are unlikely to be announced before the decision is made on who joins EMU. They are also hesitant to specify such bands for fear of pre-empting a formal interpretation in 1998 of what has become one of the more controversial EMU entry criteria, the measurement of exchange rate stability. The Maastricht Treaty sets two years of stable membership of the ERM as the test. However, when the treaty was agreed, most ERM currencies traded in 2.25 per cent bands. Britain and Sweden, whose currencies remained outside the ERM in late 1996, have both questioned whether the treaty wording retains any meaning since the ERM currencies were freed to fluctuate widely.

HOW A CURRENCY JOINS THE EXISTING ERM

- When the lira re-entered the Exchange Rate Mechanism (ERM) in November 1996, it brought the grid's membership to 12, leaving only Sweden, Britain and Greece outside.

- Any country joining or rejoining the ERM has to negotiate the rate at which its currency should join the system.

- Once a country has decided it wants to join, it asks for a meeting of the EU's Monetary Committee, a secretive grouping of finance ministry and central bank officials.

- The Committee, which normally meets in Brussels over the weekend to take such decisions, decides whether and at what central rate the currency should join.

- It is not unusual for a country wishing to join the ERM to contact EU monetary officials days before a meeting of the Committee to evaluate financial market conditions.

- Decisions can be taken very quickly, since the EU is routinely monitoring the economies of all its member states. A Monetary Committee meeting can be convened in a matter of hours, following informal telephone contacts between capitals.

- The Committee will grant the central rate which the applicant requested, unless the existing ERM member countries argue that rate is unsustainable and out of line with the country's economic fundamentals. Italy's application to re-enter in 1996 was approved at 990 lire per mark after hours of haggling. Sources said Italy had opened the bidding at 1,010 but other countries had sought a lira rate as strong as 950.

- If the Committee fails to reach an agreement, there may be a ministerial meeting the following day. This happened in the case of Italy's re-entry.

- There is no formal voting procedure for admitting new ERM members. Typically, a consensus among the members is found. The factors considered include how far the applicant country's economy has converged with those of the existing ERM members.

- Once inside, an ERM member must keep its currency within the agreed fluctuation bands and preferably as close as possible to its central rate.

- Currency turbulence in 1992 and early 1993 forced the EU to widen the ERM's fluctuation bands in August 1993 to 15 per cent either side of the central rates. Only Germany and the Netherlands still maintain the old narrow band of 2.25 per cent.

- An ERM member state must be prepared to take the lead in supporting its currency, through direct intervention or changed economic policies. It must accept a pre-emptive devaluation or revaluation if the central rate becomes untenable.

- The markets drove the pound out of the ERM along with the lira in September 1992. Britain has not rejoined the currency grid. Greece has never been a member. Sweden is contemplating membership.

- Countries including France and Germany insist that ERM participation is a precondition for joining EMU. Sweden and Britain have argued that currency stability, not formal ERM membership, is the key. This debate is set to rage until EU leaders meet in early 1998 to decide which countries qualify.

The ECB's central role

The bands and central rates would have to be agreed by EMU finance ministers, the ECB and the 'out' central bank governors and finance ministers. The European Commission and the new Economic and Financial Committee would have a say too. But countries which opted out of both EMU and ERM II would be excluded from the decision making.

The new mechanism would give the ECB undisputed dominance in deciding whether to support 'out' currencies which run into market turbulence. The ECB's ultra-independent mandate would rid ERM II of the ambiguities which shroud the original exchange rate mechanism. In the 1992 and 1993 ERM crises, markets never knew quite how far the Bundesbank, formally obliged to defer to the German government on exchange rate policy, would be prepared to go in selling marks to defend other currencies. The Dublin agreement makes plain that the ECB would not have to go very far at all.

The communique says ERM II currencies should get unlimited and automatic central bank intervention to keep them within their trading bands — but only 'in principle'. The ECB and the 'out' central banks would have the right to suspend intervention unilaterally. Under monetary union, central banks' sole priority would be to keep prices stable by limiting the supply of euros. No 'out' country could expect the ECB to bloat the euro money supply to defend a threatenened currency. Nor is there any suggestion in the Dublin accord that the ECB should be obliged to prove that intervention was becoming potentially inflationary before it pulled out of the foreign exchange market. In practice, ECB intervention could well prove very limited and far from automatic.

The Dublin accord seeks to address what many regard as a major, related weakness in the original ERM, a tendency for countries to cling to unsustainable central rates for far longer than could be justified on economic grounds. Under ERM II, the ECB would have the right — along with any other party involved — to initiate a confidential realignment procedure. Monetary officials say that in practice, the suspension of ECB intervention in defence of an 'out' currency would act as a trigger for a realignment.

Ministers would have a role in monitoring the operation of the mechanism. But 'the division of responsibilites will need to respect the independence of the ECB and the non-euro area national central banks', the Dublin communique said.

5

Profits, pensions and equities trading

By Dale Faulken, David Holmes, Caroline Allen and Kate Kelland in London, Pierre Tran in Paris and Clifford Coonan in Frankfurt

AN INVESTMENT REVOLUTION

Tens of millions of Europeans are about to be swept up in an investment revolution. Momentum is already building for a transformation of the European savings industry and monetary union could give the process a final, decisive push.

The EU's efforts to create a single European market in goods and services is exporting Anglo-Saxon practices to continental Europe, changing corporate culture. An ageing population is forcing governments to question their ability to maintain state-run pension funds into the 21st century. EMU is set to accelerate the pace of change, forcing the private pension providers that cater for small investors to look beyond government bonds and national markets.

The outlook for equities trading is unambiguously bullish compared with the mixed picture for the government bond and foreign exchange markets. Job cuts are inevitable in the forex market, especially in smaller European centres; and there are sharp differences of opinion on whether EMU will give birth to a euro bond market to rival U.S. Treasuries, or just kill the volatility that now enlivens European government bond trading. Equities trading has a much better chance of retaining its volatility after EMU and may well attract investors away from bonds, because companies will retain their inherent diversity and economic growth data will still move share prices.

PROSPECTS FOR CROSS-BORDER EQUITY TRADE

For investors, the single currency would encourage cross-border equities trading by removing currency risk. Major banks and securities houses are already restructuring their equities departments to take a sectoral rather than national approach to European shares, comparing Volkswagen with Renault rather than with Allianz. For companies, EMU will remove currency hedging costs and conversion fees, help them to plan with greater certainty and possibly boost investment by reducing interest rates.

Pension fund deregulation in particular should be spurred by the knowledge that the ageing of Europe's population will put unbearable pressure on government finances in coming decades unless there is a mass move now into privately funded pension schemes. Pensions will also have to become portable across EU national borders if labour mobility is to compensate for the loss of national flexibility under EMU in combating recessions.

These factors should combine into two major forces pushing pension funds to increase their European equities holdings. First, freed within the euro bloc from the need to match national currency assets and liabilities, they could add substantial liquidity to new pan-European trading systems. Second, if deregulation threatens to cost them their protected domestic markets, continental European funds will come under pressure to increase their overall equities allocation to improve performance. As for national stock exchanges, analysts say they have little option but to combine or compete with exchanges offering remote, screen-based, pan-European equities trading.

Scope for protectionism

EMU's impact on the equities market still depends heavily on how far monetary union encourages the EU's cautious moves to deregulate the investment services industry. The Investment Services Directive, the EU's blueprint for a single market in fund management, has many critics who say that some of its provisions in fact strengthen government powers to keep foreigners off their territory.

A protectionist interpretation of the directive could slow the pace of change in Europe's equities markets, but not halt it. Just as London's 'Big Bang' revolutionised trading practices, curtailed long lunch hours and submerged hallowed British financial houses beneath global investment banks in the 1980s, so the forces of European integration could transform the continent's investment culture in the early 21st century. 'Big Bang' may seem with the perspective of history as an early tremor rather than the earthquake itself,' said Bank of England director Pen Kent.

A liberalising force

In Britain, academics, bourse officials and fund managers agree that EMU would herald a dramatic rise in the volume and value of share dealings throughout Europe. The euro should prove a driving force behind the harmonisation and enhancement of cross-border EU share trading. 'Monetary union will act as a far more powerful force for liberalising European market structure than any directive or piece of legislation ever could,' said Dr. Benn Steil, chief economist at the Royal Institute of International Affairs.

Steil believes that institutional investors, afraid of seeing the value of their shares fall due to an unattractive exchange rate, tend to stick to their own domestic listed shares. A single currency would not only increase cross-border turnover but would fundamentally change the structure of equities dealings in Europe. 'After the currency risk is removed, domestic exchanges and electronic dealing systems throughout Europe will have to compete against each other head-on with virtually nothing to distinguish them,' he said.

Steil's view, based on a 12-month study of the structure of European bourses, is shared by the chairman of the Amsterdam Stock Exchange, Boudewijn Van Ittersun. 'It will increase cross-border investment and there is no doubt about it,' Van Ittersun said. Dutch shares are popular among international investors but currency risk is still a major deterrent for many foreign institutions. 'We have the disadvantage today in Holland where we have a strong economy but a small-based currency, which limits the potential for investors,' Van Ittersun said.

Many fund managers, too, see benefits in the single currency. Kees van Rees, managing director of Shell Pension Fund Management in Amsterdam, said the fund had lost heavily due to currency exposure over the last few years. 'Last year alone we lost well over 2.5 per cent on currencies ... The currency is the important factor.'

But the euro would not necessarily in itself guarantee any immediate jump in European share trading, strategists said. Market professionals believe that existing structural barriers across Europe will continue to inhibit institutional investors from any dramatic move towards cross-border asset allocations.

'The single currency will not solve some of the underlying problems, such as accounting differences and the different valuation parameters that are used throughout Europe,' said Andy Hartwill, equities strategist at Société Générale

Strauss Turnbull. He said stockbrokers throughout the EU had for many years been offering advice to institutions looking to invest in a wide variety of shares throughout Europe — but with only limited success. 'This pan-European sector approach has been going on long before there was talk of a single currency,' Hartwill said. 'We have been confronted daily by complicated calculations on valuations.'

OPINION Juergen Schrempp, from Stuttgart, Chairman of Daimler-Benz AG.

Some believe they could debate long and hard as to whether the advantages of European currency union are really that large. But sticking to plans laid down by the Maastricht Treaty regarding stability has now become a question of European credibility. The loss of public confidence if the project collapses would be dramatic and hardly repairable in regions that are now taking unpopular steps to fulfill the Maastricht criteria. And the hard currencies from countries like Germany and France would experience a massive upward revaluation if a 'no-euro' scenario were to unfold. In the wake of such a decision, the existing disadvantages of Germany as a production site would become even worse.

For Daimler-Benz, Europe is simultaneously a central production and employment centre. For us, there is no alternative but to continue European integration and for currency union to take place. It is not just about the possible advantages of currency union. Rather, it is also about the costs of a 'no-euro' scenario. The controversial discussion about the January 1, 1999 start of currency union, the possibility of delay, the number of participants and the interpretation of stability miss the heart of the matter.

We cannot go into the next century debating if country 'X' at a particular time 'Y' will land exactly on the public budget deficit target of three per cent of, or the new debt target of 60 per cent of, Gross Domestic Product. I am not talking about easing the stability criteria. But the Maastricht Treaty has provided room for manoeuvre. The contract intentionally provides for flexibility — flexibility that should be used in a way that will keep stability in mind. This should take into account efforts made so far and the political will for a lasting policy directed at securing monetary stability.

Stability criteria, or the orientation toward them, will be regarded internationally as supporting economic policy. Economic policy will be quantifiable and therefore comprehensible and their effects will be controllable.

The EU's Investment Services Directive (ISD), which took effect in 1996, is supposed to be the pass key that will allow brokers and bourses in the EU to unlock investor capital. Although the ISD does allow banks and brokers to operate throughout the EU with virtually the same freedom as they enjoy in their home markets, it has not yet addressed such problems as diverse accounting practices or taxation differences.

In addition, equity holdings of EU pension funds, both domestic and cross-border, are strongly influenced by regulations on minimum funding and portfolio composition. French institutional investors, for example, have to invest heavily in domestic government bonds. 'We are funding the budget deficit,' said Denis Kessler, President of the Fédération Francaise des Sociétés d'Assurances (FSSA).

In 1996 France was considering lifting a ban on private pension funds. Such funds would have a 65 per cent ceiling on their bond holdings, leaving the way open for hefty investment in equities. France's stock market association (SBF) believes the introduction of private pensions would generate a natural flow of investment into shares because they offer higher long-term returns.

Some dispute whether the pensions burden will automatically push funds into equities, which are generally perceived as riskier than fixed income products. They say there is a counter-argument that such huge liabilities inspire caution, and therefore bond investment. Hartwill at SocGen said the pecking order for asset allocation in Europe was still biased towards domestic bonds first, followed by domestic equities and then foreign bonds. 'Foreign equities come in a distant fourth. Over time that will change as monetary union encourages cross-border flows. But it won't happen overnight. It will take place over a very long period of time,' Hartwill said.

Young Germans seek more risk

However, in Germany there is already a new generation of younger investors which is prepared to try to balance risk and reward. They are shifting into equities, urged on by a growing consensus that share-owning will help to generate the higher returns needed to fend off a 21st century pensions funding crisis.

The 1996 flotation of Deutsche Telekom was central to Germany's efforts to develop a share-owning culture. Before the flotation, only 5.5 per cent of privately-held financial assets in Germany were invested in shares, compared with 21 per cent in the U.S. 'It could make the breakthrough we all want and install an equity culture in Germany,' said one Frankfurt options trader. Rolf Passow, the head of Germany's fund managers' association, agreed. 'The Telekom float ... has done a whole lot to get this word "share" onto people's lips.'

Joerg Franke, a senior management board member of Deutsche Boerse, expects the euro to give the German stock market a boost. He said the exchange would offer equities products based on sector indices, anticipating a move towards sectoral rather than national trading. The Boerse sees its future in its range of electronic trading possibilities. It has opted for a market model-based trading system designed to concentrate liquidity in an order book, increase transparency and stimulate liquidity. Initially the bourse planned to get rid of floor trade altogether, but the Finance Ministry indicated it would like to have more trading options available.

Creating value in France

The euro would force French firms to focus on creating value if they wanted to attract international investors, Paris-based analysts say. Once currency risk disappeared, sector analyses, radical changes in asset allocation rules and a tougher approach among fund managers would put the spotlight on management objectives. Individual offerings would be scrutinised without the traditional country and currency risks. 'The universe for allocation for investors, particularly international ones, after 1999 will no longer ... be geographical but will become a universe of issuers,' said Monique Bourven, chairwoman of State Street Bank said.

She said the euro zone would represent 25 per cent of world market capitalisation, against 40 per cent in North America, 20 per cent in Japan and 15 per cent for the emerging markets of Asia, South America and the rest of Europe. A major question would be whether Europe could succeed in attracting more capital than other regions. French investors were already making a tentative choice, with figures showing net growth in SICAV mutual funds focusing on European stocks, against a net outflow from French equity funds.

Colette Neuville, head of the ADAM small shareholders' group, said French companies' profits had fallen 36 per cent in the last five years while those of British and U.S. firms had risen respectively by 52 and 75. The scope for improvement was attracting international investors, but French companies would have to show 'they can create value and create more value than their foreign competitors' if they wanted to retain foreign investor interest.

Neuville described the French economy as changing to liberal capitalism from 'administered capitalism,' which had sought to satisfy the demands of management and employees. But fund managers, themselves facing greater competition for savings, would put companies under greater pressure to show profitability and explain strategy and objectives. Corporate managers would have to demonstrate each unit's profitability, show that one part of the group was not subsidising another, and justify acquisitions — which could be destroyers as much as creators of value.

Private pension funds should help to address a severe lack of French equity capital, said Jean Gandois, chairman of the CNPF French employers' federation. Shares accounted for only 22 per cent of total institutional flows in France in the first half of 1996, against almost half in the U.S.. French market capitalisation amounted to just 33 per cent of GDP, half that in the U.S. and a third of the British ratio. Gandois urged the French authorities to make flotation procedures easier and told companies they must provide more information and make greater efforts to improve corporate governance. 'It's an essential point,' he said.

IMPLICATIONS FOR FUND MANAGEMENT

EMU would sort fund managers into global players or niche operators. The implications for London's fund management industry, controlling huge investments in Europe, are radical. But in late 1996, plans for change were still in their infancy. Some said that many fund managers at the heart of the global industry were betting, wrongly, that monetary union will not have an immediate impact on their investments. 'They hope they will be able to convert slowly, to think about all the ramifications,' Nigel Morgan, economic strategist at Old Mutual International Asset Managers said. 'But it will be like reunification of East and West Germany — people found there was no interim. They had to make the leap and clear up the mess afterwards.'

Monetary union would pose three major challenges for funds, forcing them to reassess their corporate strategy, investment methods and IT needs. Strategically, EMU would force fund managers either to build a pan-European presence or to specialise and serve niche markets. 'From 2000 there will be room only for the very big managers and the specialists, no middle ground,' said one U.S. fund manager. 'You need big muscle and deep pockets to get into Europe — which is what U.S. groups have in abundance.'

But would investors prefer a local firm over a global name? Fund groups who have already made their first forays into Europe testify to the need for a strong local partner, often necessitating a joint venture or a branding arrangement. 'This is essentially the same debate as whether money is better managed locally or from a global centre,' said Peter Ludvig at actuaries Wyatt Watson. 'The jury is still out on that one. If you're a huge fund and you want to access a niche market like U.S. small tech stocks, you might do better to find a local manager, but most big houses have global analysts.'

Although doubts about the political will to see EMU through were dissipating, few in 1996 saw Britain in the first round. This worried many London-based investment houses, because they know that if EMU went ahead without Britain, their influence on a growing and potentially lucrative European investment market might dry up. But views differ widely. 'I don't think there will be much impact to start with. In 30 years time it will all be pan-European, sure, but things move very slowly,' said one European fund manager. 'Besides, London differs from European markets in everything from accounting standards to management styles.'

More mergers

Morgan at Old Mutual said the transition may not be as smooth and manageable as that. He believes EMU would affect both the investment and the corporate strategies of investment houses and banks. 'Those who can't either grow or specialise will wither or get caught in between, so we expect more international mergers building on the national activity recently.'

Stephen Cohen, director at Mercury Asset Management (MAM), sees EMU accelerating the trend for institutional investors to take an increasingly pan-European view. 'It's sometimes difficult to distinguish between a French or German company and a European one,' he said. 'Soon there will be euro-denominated shares and a centralised European stock exchange, perhaps cross listing on several exchanges. Pricing anomalies will disappear. If you want to buy a chemical company you'll look for the cheapest in Europe, never mind where it is based.'

Richard Davidson, European strategist at Morgan Stanley International, sees increased pressure for restructuring. 'Cross-border holdings are going to be a lot more important in company shareholder structures,' he said. 'And the pressure to restructure will grow because in the past, entrenched domestic holdings have not demanded the same longer term returns.' Cohen says EMU would certainly promote cross-border flows, 'which conventional economics tells us is a good thing. If distinctions among currencies go, then accounting and corporate governance differences will also reduce,' he added.

But previous attempts to free up cross-border capital flows in Europe have met with limited success. In 1996, many countries still imposed curbs on how much may be invested internationally and demand a minimum holding in domestic bonds or equities. Investment managers wanting to do business in Europe were only just coming to grips with the demands of the EU's Investment Services Directive and Capital Adequacy Directive. None doubted that the market was waiting to be opened up but most knew they would meet fierce local competition and make an expensive outlay before any benefits appeared on the bottom line.

IT implications

Some British funds see little immediate impact on their portfolio operations if EMU goes ahead without Britain in 1999. Portfolios would remain sterling-based and London-listed stocks would still be quoted in sterling. But fund groups doing business inside the euro bloc would have to overhaul information systems. For up to three years after 1999, they would have to run euro portfolios alongside home currency portfolios, taking account of the base currency of their investor and measuring it against newly produced euro-denominated indices. As EMU developed, currency-specific portfolios would be abolished for the euro zone. 'It is going to be systems-intensive,' noted one fund manager. But he admitted his company had 'not scrutinised the operational side ... We are frankly more concerned about what the year 2000 will do to our computer systems.'

Cohen said that theoretically there should be no problem adding a new currency to any adequate system. 'But you'd have to evaluate how to convert, say, a mark portfolio into euros and how to recalculate all the book costs. Everyone is going to have to do some work. The better existing systems will need less.'

Even while planning went ahead for EMU, there was still widespread scepticism in London about the benefits. Many fund managers believed monetary union was being forced ahead before economies had converged properly. Wyatt Watson's Ludvig said it was almost impossible to predict in detail the fallout from such a fundamental change to the European markets. 'It's like a global merger — BT and MCI — there are sure to be benefits of scale but you won't really know how successful it has been until it has been running a while. EMU is a merger of countries ... there will be an overall benefit, but also some rationalisation along the way.'

EUROPE'S PENSIONS CRISIS

European pension funds will have to overhaul their structure and strategy with or without EMU, fund managers say. A 1996 World Bank report called pensions funding in mature economies 'the biggest crisis of our time,' but many European governments have been loath to risk the voter backlash which could be whipped up by wholesale reform. The sheer size of the industry, estimated at end-1994 to hold assets of some $1.45 trillion in 12 EU states, precludes any rapid action. But a clutch of studies show present funding plans may not meet projected liabilities and ageing populations are likely to place an ever greater strain on government schemes.

'The extent of unfunded pension liabilities in certain of our European partner countries casts serious doubt upon the long term sustainability of their finances,' said a report from Britain's parliamentary social security committee in 1996. It put the net present value of public pension schemes in the UK at 19 per cent of GDP, France at 98 per cent, Italy 113 per cent and 139 per cent for Germany.

Conventional wisdom has been that the funding squeeze will usher in a golden age for private pension providers in Europe. Politicians are already urging them to grab a share, but fund managers who have tried say it is not easy. 'There is this rosy vision of private providers cleaning up but actually it's a cut throat business,' said one U.S. fund manager. 'Protectionism is rife and a local presence and credibility is essential. It is also very expensive.'

European pensions consultant and author Debbie Harrison agreed. 'Very few have actually won mandates in this tough, fragmented market ... only in Belgium, Denmark, the Netherlands and Switzerland have local managers lost significant market share to foreign institutions.'

Most fund managers expect European pension funds to remain overweight in their home market where their liabilities are. 'Local equities are correlated with local salary and inflation conditions,' said one. 'You can remove the currency effect with EMU but there is still the influence of the local economy.'

However, funds would watch EMU for opportunities for improved cross-border access, both as pension fund providers and as investors. The European Commission tried to set up a Pension Fund Directive aimed at harmonising the industry continent-wide, but tax practices and fund structures proved too diverse. In 1994, after four years of wrangling, the initiative was shelved. 'Europe is a real mixed bag on tax. It is the main obstacle to harmonisation and cross border investment,' said Peter Ludvik at actuaries Wyatt Watson.

OPINION Giovanni Agnelli from Turin, Honorary Chairman of the Board of Directors of Fiat Spa.

EMU is an important means of reinvigorating the political pact that binds western Europe ... Italy's failure to join the EMU would weaken not just our own growth prospects, but also the very survival of the European political design. Without Italy, Europe would lack a major player, not just in terms of size, but above all in ability to strike a balance between the various partners.

Hence participation in EMU is something we owe not just to ourselves but to Europe as well ... Decisive economic factors are also at stake ... .

By contrast, non-participation would open a period of uncertainty and reduced competitiveness for those left out of the inner circle. Let us not forget that business needs a frame of reference that is as stable as possible in order to operate efficiently. Productive investments demand at least medium-term planning, which risks being overwhelmed by the instability of exchange and interest rates ... .

The European manufacturing system will do everything in its power to ensure that as many countries as possible meet the Maastricht parameters in time ... . It is clear that Italy, together with Greece, has the farthest to go. In particular, Italy is burdened by a public debt that is twice the size recommended by Maastricht. The servicing of that debt restricts government investment in infrastructure, research and training to an extent that is extremely worrying: in the medium term it could have dangerous repercussions on our ability to remain competitive.

However, if we examine trends rather than the numbers alone, Italy looks better placed than some of her partners. Since 1992 and despite suffering the worst recession since World War Two, the country has in fact made significant progress ... . Nevertheless, if it is to have a fighting chance of receiving a positive review in 1998 of its convergence performance, it cannot afford to relax its efforts in the public finance sector ... .

Since there is so little room for manoeuvre on either the taxation front or the battle against waste ... it is critical that the social partners commit themselves to a 'stability pact' that will last the life of the present legislature. One essential feature of that pact must be to give new momentum to the income policy as the only way to achieve a drastic cut in inflation and hence a further reduction in interest rates. This could be decisive in lightening the burden of public debt and stimulating manufacturing investment.

All the measures needed to make our economic system more efficient and competitive must be implemented. This means drastically reducing the role of the state in the economy, expanding the market and strengthening competition by privatising the financial system and the public utilities. It will also be necessary to reform the tax system ... (and) upgrade public spending in the strategic areas of infrastructure, training, and research ... .

The Italian government has shown its intention of speeding up the economic reform process with a view to joining the EMU in 1999 ... . If the Italian government can give further credible, consistent, and coherent signs that it is moving in this direction, it will certainly be able to count on support of the nation's manufacturing system, workers, and public opinion at large. In this way we can consolidate what we have already achieved in terms of economic integration, as well as build a stronger Union stable enough to handle both the imminent challenges of enlargement and the growing European involvement in a wider world context of sweeping change.

Pension funds would feel the impact of EMU whether their home states participated or not. Monetary union would focus attention on widely differing national preferences in asset allocation. British pension funds generally hold a high proportion, up to 80 per cent, in equities and foreign assets. European funds are traditionally heavily weighted in domestic bonds with at most 40 per cent of their portfolios in equities. Germany, the Netherlands and Switzerland hold more real estate than other funds, while Portuguese schemes favour cash.

'With most European funds there are many restrictions on asset allocation, limits on what you may invest in equities and bonds, at home and abroad,' Ludvik noted. Fund managers say some restrictions are bound to remain, if only because in some centres the capitalisation of the pension funds is larger than the local equity market. Tony Dolphin at AMP Asset Management sees a rapid move to a single euro debt market after EMU gets started, with 'a much slower move over maybe 20 years to a pan-European equity market with firms quoted on what will be "regional" exchanges — London, Frankfurt or Paris.'

That would radically change the asset allocation of pension funds, stunting the geographical diversification which is a major factor in controlling risk. Among global funds, the weightings 'UK' and 'Europe-ex UK' are widely used, but after EMU funds might have to increase holdings in the Far East, North America or high-risk emerging markets to diversify. 'It will depend if Europe is viewed as a truly single market and whether investors start looking at sectors rather than countries,' said Ludvik.

EMU might prompt some convergence of investment styles. 'There is a move in Germany, where pension funds are currently very much invested in bonds, to take on more equity investment because they have to, and perhaps UK schemes, as they get more mature, will take on more bonds,' said AMP's Dolphin. Pensions consultant Harrison said France may yet follow Germany, where corporate schemes are funded by the book reserves in the company balance sheet. This allows the company to use the capital and provide an employee benefit. There has been a limited shift to external funding in recent years but 54 per cent of total pension payouts are still on the book system, down from 62 per cent in 1985.

There were signs in 1996 that European governments were waking up to the looming pensions funding crisis, often pushed into action by employers' organisations feeling the strain of contributions. Germany faced pension charge rises in 1997. Italy was pushing through legislation on private pensions, and some trade unions were interested in setting up their own schemes. A French poll in December 1996 showed the public backed the move to establish private funds in 1997 but the Spanish state still offered generous provisions.

The sooner the problem is addressed, the better, industry experts say. The crisis may not be apparent yet, but if governments do not act soon, Europe will be in deep trouble when the baby-boom generation starts retiring around 2010.

CORPORATE DESIRES AND ANXIETIES

In December 1996, British management consultant firm KPMG released a survey showing most top European companies had made no attempt to estimate the cost of EMU to their business. Of 301 major European firms questioned for the poll, carried out in July and August, only eight per cent quoted a figure for the cost of the changeover. Yet 93 per cent of those surveyed said they expected the country in which they were based to join EMU at some stage.

'Many companies are seriously unprepared for the big changes EMU will bring,' said Alan Reid, European head of KPMG Management Consulting. 'Given that over half of all respondents believed their country will enter EMU at the earliest possible date, the 80 per cent of companies that have failed to undertake such a fundamental estimate have very little time in which to prepare.'

The telephone poll surveyed finance directors of firms across all sectors employing at least 5,000 people and with a European headquarters in one of the member states of the European Union. Britain, Ireland, France, Germany, Italy, Austria, Greece, Spain, Portugal, the Benelux countries and Scandinavia were included. Not one firm, asked to state the key issues it faced in the area of international business on trade, mentioned the euro. But prompted into addressing EMU, nearly half said they would put it towards the top of a list of important issues.

While almost three-quarters of top European companies said they expected to benefit from EMU, two-thirds of them said they had no strategy for coping with it, although half of those said they were in the process of developing one. German-based firms were best prepared, with 52 per cent saying they had a strategy already in place. Only 19 per cent of British-based companies and 25 per cent of Italian-based organisations had a working plan. However, 69 per cent of firms based in Italy said they were developing plans for EMU.

Very few companies were prepared to estimate the extent to which the changeover would tip their balance sheets. Of those that did, the projections ranged from one to 65 million sterling ($1.6 to $106 million). Information technology (IT) was picked out as the area expected to need most spending, but only four per cent of the 301 firms said they had completed a pre-EMU review of IT systems. In the whole of Britain, Spain, Portugal, Greece and Austria, not one firm had completed a review, although two-thirds said they were undertaking one. More than a third of companies surveyed across Europe had not yet started looking at IT preparations.

British reserve

It is not that companies are actively antagonistic to EMU — a revolution in Europe's finances that could open up markets for their products and make their borrowing cheaper. The 15 EU member states make up a trading bloc of 356 million people with GDP totalling $8.4 trillion in 1995.

At the most basic level, companies would gain from EMU by avoiding the cost of exchanging currencies when moving goods within the euro zone. Deutsche Bank economist Josef Auer has estimated that German firms alone would save some 40 billion marks annually in such transaction costs.

Yet there are risks, too, that exporting the monetary discipline of Germany would impose an uncomfortable straitjacket for other economies.

It is in Britain that such concerns are most public. Polled in 1995 on their views towards EMU, some 30 per cent of members of the Confederation of British Industry said EMU would not be beneficial and could even be harmful to their interests, against 49 per cent who would welcome a single currency. Memories of Britain's 23-month struggle with recession while sterling was in Europe's Exchange Rate Mechanism (ERM) may be one reason why some firms were still queasy at the thought of an outside body exercising financial authority.

OPINION Michael Smurfit, from Dublin, chairman and chief executive of Jefferson Smurfit Group Plc, an international paper and packaging manufacturer with operations in Europe, the U.S. and Latin America

European monetary union is not only good for the countries of Europe, it is essential. It is not sustainable that a single market can operate to its optimum efficiency without the existence of a single currency. Those countries that can meet the necessary economic criteria will find monetary union good for business, good for internal trade and good for financial discipline.

However, I would like to caution that in trying to rigidly create the Europe of the future we are in danger of destroying the good things about the Europe of the past. I understand that the Irish government needs to control public expenditure to stay on track for EMU but I am concerned about the impact this will have on economic growth rates — industry's lifeblood.

Indeed toward the same goal, throughout Europe, government leaders are preparing to administer massive doses of fiscal frugality which is aggravating vested interests and making investors nervous. This has produced a manifest dilemma.

If the various governments succeed in pushing through their austerity programmes, then the drop in government spending that follows could endanger economic recovery. But if social unrest and parliamentary opponents succeed in blocking the cuts, then most countries can forget about meeting the requirements for monetary union. Such a failure would lead to a damaging loss of confidence in European stock and bond markets. I believe the main governments will do what they must to achieve EMU — it is a political priority. And while there will be some convenient moving of goals and targets, the outcome will see a reduction in EU budgets of very significant proportions.

Therefore, Europe's only hope for economic growth lies firstly with Bundesbank rate cuts — not something you can depend upon — and secondly on the arrival of the much-vaunted economic recovery. I regret that it is my prognosis that Europe will not be a good environment in which to do business for the next year or so.

This may also be true for Ireland. Our excellent growth rates have to a significant extent been dependent on Europe and on the special funding we have received. While this funding has been justified, to allow us to upgrade our infrastructure given our peripheral European location, it will not last forever.

EMU or not, there is a problem of high social costs Europe-wide. Such costs have always compared unfavourably with the U.S. and this has become even more the case since President Clinton's recent welfare reforms. European governments have always been of the view that they have a responsibility to correct the social inequalities created by a market economy. Whether right or wrong, such a philosophy has delivered expensive social support systems that give young people no incentive to accept lower paid, low-skilled jobs. These systems contribute to the problem of long-term unemployment as welfare recipients are not inclined to seek jobs. Europe's unemployed in excess of one year is five times the U.S. average.

Clearly Europe is operating at a structural disadvantage and this must be a concern as we face up to globalisation and the threat posed by fast-growing Asian economies.

Continental conviction

Companies in Germany and France are more enthusiastic, perhaps reflecting that they would have more to gain, at least initially. For major German and French corporations, EMU offers an end to the devaluation of weaker currencies that has made imports from other EU states more competitive than their offerings. In contrast, many in Britain credit sterling's ejection from the ERM in 1992 with kickstarting an economic recovery.

Mercedes, the luxury carmaker unit of Daimler-Benz, exemplifies the outlook of many of the country's major industrial groups. 'German business finds it unacceptable that hard-won productivity gains simply disappear abroad due to currency fluctuations,' said Mercedes chief executive Helmut Werner. He said there was no doubt the euro would come and urged European industry to get ready.

Stephan Schuster, head of Deutsche Bank's fundamental issues group, told a 1996 London conference that companies should hasten preparations in areas including treasury management, banking and IT systems, all of which were likely to become more centralised under EMU. Deutsche's chief economist Stephen Bell told that conference that time was running out fast for companies which had not yet begun their EMU planning. 'If we have scared the living daylights out of you,' Bell said, 'then maybe that will help.'

6

Jobs at risk: the exotic alternatives

By Kate Kelland, Abigail Levene, Andrew Reierson and Adam Jasser in London,
Christopher Pizzey in Singapore and Danielle Bochove in Chicago

From Scandinavia to the Mediterranean, scores of dealers, analysts and even central bankers are wondering if they will still have jobs after 1999. The euro has the potential to wipe out large turnover for trading financial instruments in as many as 15 currencies, which would drive securities and banking houses into sharp cost cutting to make up for that loss. Some experts say as many 50,000 jobs may be cut across Europe's financial sector, but others say the impact on employment would be a barely noticeable net negative. Foreign exchange traders would be in the firing line as the European cross rates that have held their attention and paid their salaries for years dissolve into one currency. 'Assuming we get five or six major currencies in — marks, guilders, French francs, Belgian francs, Luxembourg francs and Austrian schilling — then a lot of those traders will be out of work,' said John Langton, the Zurich-based chief executive of the International Securities Market Association (ISMA).

CONSOLIDATION IN THE FINANCIAL INDUSTRY

Smaller financial centres should watch out, since their currency business is generally focused less in international trades such as the yen and the dollar, and more on European cross rates, analysts say. 'The big players in small markets are going to be thrown into a much bigger pot of stew,' said John Leonard, a European banking analyst at Salomon Brothers in London. 'In banks in places like Belgium, the Netherlands, Germany and France, maybe 15 to 20 per cent of the foreign exchange revenue is sensitive to EMU. I'd expect them to try and get at least half of that back on the cost side,' Leonard said.

Others envisaged a similar imbalance in the effect on foreign exchange-related jobs in different centres, but said other avenues may begin to open up. One London-based analyst said many banks were saying that traders could be redeployed into exotic markets or into the currencies within Europe, particularly those in the east, still jostling for places in political or monetary union. Matthew Elderfield, director at the London Investment Bankers Association and soon to be ISDA's director of European policy, saw a similar scenario. 'The percentage volume of EMU-area cross currency trades is actually quite small in London,' he said. 'In other financial centres, the proportion of EMU-area trade tends to be much bigger — and although that will disappear and some people will lose their jobs, it may be that some traders will move into dollar/euro or dollar/yen trading.'

In bond markets, the euro's impact is less definable. While some analysts say inevitable shrinking in the volume of debt available for trading would mean personnel levels will also have to fall, others argue a single European debt market would rival the U.S. Treasury market in depth and liquidity, allowing bond traders to stay put. And despite the strict criteria for EMU entry, perceived credit risk discrepancies between participating nations would still create spread trading opportunities. 'You're still going to have national bond markets and there will still be credit differences between them,' said Elderfield.

A bigger and more tangible threat confronts the estimated 160,000 central bank staff in the 15 potential EMU countries which may eventually melt into a single European body, one banker said. The creation of the European System of Central Banks will mirror the U.S. Federal Reserve System, which employs just 25,000 people, and highlight thousands of duplicated jobs, analysts said. Analysts pointed to small pockets of Europe's financial industry, such as fund management and corporate finance, which could benefit from the euro's birth. But overall they said the outlook was likely to be negative, and certainly unclear. 'You have to be careful of how many jobs would have gone anyway as a result of technology rather than purely because of EMU: the two are linked together,' said ISMA's Langton.

Others said a definitive assessment of the euro's threat to jobs in the financial sector will be difficult until the identity of the 'ins' and 'outs' is revealed. 'The likelihood is that up until the irrevocable fix (of national currencies against the euro) there will be an awful lot of jockeying for position and oppor-

Table 6.1:   Mark trade against other EMS currencies, as a percentage of total foreign exchange trade in each EU country

Country	% foreign exchange trade in mark/other EMS
Britain	9.5
Germany	15.4
France	27.1
Denmark	13.5
Belgium	13.5
Netherlands	21.4
Italy	17.1
Sweden	24.4
Luxembourg	13.0
Spain	20.4
Austria	11.3
Finland	33.5
Ireland	37.7
Greece	13.1
Portugal	26.8

These percentages were calculated by Reuters from data given in the Bank for International Settlements April 1995 survey of foreign exchange and derivatives activity. The BIS data used, which include mark/Ecu trade, show daily average turnover in spot, outright forward and swap trade. These BIS data were adjusted for local but not cross-border double-counting and were not adjusted for estimated reporting gaps. On the same basis, the BIS calculated that global foreign exchange trade totalled an average $1.57 trillion daily. Adjusted for cross-border double counting and reporting gaps, the global BIS figure is $1.19 trillion.

Reuters calculations show that mark/sterling trade accounts for 1.8 per cent of global foreign exchange trade and 3.2 per cent of London's foreign exchange trade. Total global trade in the mark against all other EMS currencies, including sterling and Ecu, is 8.9 per cent of all global foreign exchange trade.

tunity to make money,' said David Clark, honorary president of the Association Cambiste International (ACI), an umbrella organisation for forex groups around the world. 'You wouldn't close the lira/mark desk, for example, because lira/euro trading may still be there afterwards. And even if Italy were in the first round, there would be so much jiggery pokery as it goes in that you're going to need your traders.'

A euro trading mentality

If EMU succeeded, market mindsets would have to alter. Some believe dealers will begin to consider countries in terms of trading blocs rather than as national entities, so that a dollar/euro trade would reflect the sale or purchase of the EU trading bloc against the U.S.. That would suggest an enhanced role for euro/yen, mark/yen's replacement, as it was used to play Europe off against Asia. 'Whereas before you could diversify and buy a little bit of marks and a little bit of francs, you're going to have these massive shifts into one bloc,' said one London-based merchant bank trader. 'It could cause more volatility in the long run.'

David Deakin, treasurer at Bank of Bermuda in Guernsey, believes the euro will be a true force to be reckoned with. 'I question whether people will think of the dollar as the be-all and end-all unit of account,' he said. 'They might, but there's no reason why they should when you've got something that has the clout of the European Union behind it.'

While the amount of speculative trading would depend on the euro's stability against external currencies, trade flows should continue unabated, experienced market operators said. 'In terms of the trade part, there's no reason why the amount of euros needed to be bought and sold against the dollar should be any less than the sum of the (EMU) currencies now bought and sold against the dollar,' said Graham Cocks, vice-president, treasury, at Bank of Boston in London. Investment flows are tougher to predict. 'That depends on the euro region's need for inward capital and its ability to export capital,' said Cocks. The European drive to cut government debt should mean less bond issuance and that threatens to reduce investment streams, he added.

But as sovereign European currencies gave way to the euro, just which economic data would operators use to make their trading decisions? That question prompts many different answers. Some believe data from individual EU states would remain crucial as investors choose assets. The euro's arrival should minimise currency risk, leaving players to make decisions by weighing yield differential versus credit risk and assessing their ability to sell a bond on to someone else, they say. Others believe national statistics, especially those of Germany and France, would be important in the early stages of monetary union but only until more countries joined and pan-European data gathering really took off. Bank of Bermuda's Deakin said pan-European figures would be key. National data would be watched only 'to the extent that people look at the Detroit purchasing managers' index or retail sales in the German states,' he said. 'U.S. trade figures are more interesting than Hawaii or Texas trade figures.'

With confidence so high in the euro's credibility, the role of the Swiss franc might appear in jeopardy. But most are convinced it will always have a place in investors' hearts. The franc should remain a safe haven from jitters over monetary union, and benefit as a potential EMU member if all goes well, market watchers said. It is also seen continuing to profit from faith in the Swiss economic and political system.

'The Swiss franc has the ability to win significantly if the whole thing (EMU) is messed up, yet even if it runs smoothly I don't see bundles of money coming screaming out of Switzerland into the euro,' said Cocks at Bank of Boston.

One thing is sure. If European currencies are subsumed into the catch-all euro, forex traders will have to adapt to survive in an unpredictable environment. For the inflexible mark cross trader the alternative is clear, said one treasury manager: retirement. 'It's a question people joining the market or young people in the market will have,' he said. 'What will they be doing in three or five years' time?'

PROSPECTS FOR MATURE CURRENCIES

Chicago worries, too

The angst is not confined to European traders. In Chicago, derivatives experts say EMU would bring sweeping changes to the U.S. foreign exchange options market. Despite doubts about whether monetary union will succeed, the EU's plans were already sending tremors through the industry in 1996. U.S. exchanges and over-the-counter (OTC) dealers were beginning to discuss the impact of the euro on a market that trades well over $20 billion worth of contracts a day. Brokers expected a substantial drop in trade of options on European currencies, and a reallocation of some of that business to the emerging markets and to European interest-rate options.

The Chicago Mercantile Exchange (CME), which trades options on currency futures, has appointed a committee to study the 'major opportunities and significant challenges' posed by EMU. The Philadelphia Stock Exchange, which trades options on currencies, was seeking regulatory approval to list customised and standardised options on the euro.

However, the OTC markets will feel the impact most. OTC trading accounted for 87 per cent of foreign exchange options traded in the U.S in the first quarter of 1996, according to the Comptroller of the Currency Administrator of National Banks in Washington, D.C. According to the Federal Reserve Bank of New York, that accounts for $19.9 billion of trade a day. Of that, roughly half is done in contracts which include European currencies.

'Certainly there's going to be an impact on everybody's business,' said one OTC dealer with a major investment house. 'Putting those all into one currency has got to decrease business by, I think, 30 per cent or 40 per cent.'

Dealers said they expect to see such losses mitigated by several factors, the most obvious being gains in currency options activity in Latin America, Asia, and Eastern Europe. Options trade in emerging markets is already growing and should get an extra boost as some of the options business lost through monetary union shifts to other markets, they said. 'A trend, obviously, is that you'll see a growing amount of business from the non-first tier currencies,' said Oliver Jefferson, vice president at Société Générale. 'But that won't replace the reduction in business for those currencies that disappear.'

The lifeblood of the options industry is volatility and Jefferson cited the Dutch guilder as an example of what may happen to other options in potential EMU currencies as 1999 approaches. The guilder tracks the mark so closely that there is virtually no need to use options to hedge against sudden swings in the cross rate. 'What happens to an options market, if there's no volatility, is it disappears because there's no purpose in having options,' he said.

However, Jefferson believes the euro itself could offer new options trading potential, because an amalgamation of European currencies is likely to be more volatile than the mark. For that reason, euro options could be more liquid than mark options — which are already very liquid — a fact which could help mitigate some of the loss of business, he said.

Greg Kaldor, vice president of currency option sales at Bank of America, said there could be a spike in options business in the run-up to EMU as speculation intensifies about which currencies will make the grade. This effect would be particularly dramatic if there were repeated delays in launching the euro. And while the need to hedge currency risk may disappear, EMU could produce greater volatility in European bond markets, increasing demand for interest rate derivatives. 'We expect to see more interest in options on bond spreads between the euro countries,' Kaldor said.

Another dealer was looking for an increase in some exotic currency options to fill the void. He cited one complicated range binary option, which dealers sardonically refer to as a SCUD (secondary currency unhedgeable derivative). The option is based on one currency but becomes valuable or worthless depending on the movement of a second. Such instruments are currently very illiquid but could become more common when some European 'plain vanilla' options are phased out, he said.

But Jefferson disagreed, maintaining that highly speculative options are unlikely to ever become widely used. 'I don't think the development of the products has anything to do with the introduction of a currency union,' he said. 'There's always new products ... . The question is how many of these ideas are really practical or how many are just bets that you could make by going to a casino.'

Hunt for new forex trades

Traders and investors would have to be flexible and innovative in their hunt for income sources to replace the mark crosses. The Australian and New Zealand dollars, the currencies of Eastern Europe and of Asia's 'tiger' economies, and Latin American currencies such as Mexico's peso, are all cited as potential plays for the mark-deprived investor. 'There are a lot more currencies to deal in than just the odd European one and I think people will concentrate on that,' said a London-based treasury manager. A veteran trader at a British merchant bank said, 'The banks are diversifying even more and looking at some of the exotics to replace some of the ones coming out.'

Investor demand for these markets is growing, with foreign investors and commercial lenders set to put a record of around $225 billion into emerging market economies in 1996, according to the Institute of International Finance in Washington. By late 1996, banks in Asia were already looking at implications for their own business in anticipation that the euro would boost exotic currency trade. Some banks were expanding their forex trading teams, while brokers were eyeing the region with hopes for salvation if business dies away in other zones.

'With mark/French franc disappearing, there's going to be (forex) traders looking for something, anything, to trade. Exotic currency volume is bound to benefit from this,' said one trader at a U.S. firm in Singapore. A proprietary dealer at a U.S. bank in Singapore said his firm was looking into expanding its exotic currency trading desk. 'I'm not saying it's all to do with the euro, but the bosses say it's definitely a factor in their thinking,' he said.

The head of treasury at a European bank in Singapore agreed. 'Banks are already beefing up their (exotic currency) desks here. They've brought in some fairly senior people to do this and the euro has to be one of the factors.' He noted that the euro would take away several potential areas of profit for proprietary foreign exchange trading and it was natural for firms involved in that business to look elsewhere. 'Look for an increase in (Malaysian) ringgit, (Indonesian) rupiah and, to a lesser degree, (Thai) baht trade,' he said.

Desmond Supple, senior emerging markets economist at IDEA in Singapore, agreed that exotic currency trading, especially against the yen, would get a fillip from the creation of the euro. At present virtually all exotic currency trading is conducted through the dollar. 'When it comes to trade and debt flows, the yen is far more important to this region than the dollar,' he said.

Asian currencies

Southeast Asian currencies are typically linked to a basket of currencies. The exact arrangements differ. The first factor is the extent to which regional currencies are allowed to fluctuate around the central rate determined by the basket. In Thailand, there is almost no flexibility. The spot rate can only differ by 0.2 per cent from the basket rate. But in Indonesia, that figure is eight per cent.

In a 1996 report, Deutsche Morgan Grenfell said the term 'basket' was a little misleading. 'Pegging a currency to a basket implies that the currency tracks the value implied by the basket relatively closely. That is only the case for the Thai baht,' the report said. Elsewhere currency management is usually more flexible, with a less clearly defined target rate. However, the baskets have something in common in that they are all heavily weighted towards the U.S. dollar and, to a lesser extent, the yen.

The exact weights and the extent of correlation are not normally disclosed. For example, the Monetary Authority of Singapore says it 'monitors the external value of the Singapore dollar against a trade-weighted basket of currencies, with the objective of promoting non-inflationary sustainable economic growth.'

Using regression analysis, Deutsche Morgan Grenfell came up with the following U.S. dollar and yen weightings in the baskets. It did not estimate what other currencies might be in the baskets.

	U.S.$ weight	Yen weight
Thai baht	82.39	10.37
Malaysian ringgit	71	22
Singapore $	82	8
Philippines peso	71	1
Indonesian rupiah	99	0

Deutsche said there is probably only one true currency basket in the region, Thailand's. Indonesia has embarked on a crawling devaluation against the U.S. dollar. 'In the case of Singapore and Malaysia central banks take the value of the dollar and the yen into account ... but the extent to which this basket is tracked and the composition of this basket tends to vary significantly over time.'

Of the other currencies, the Hong Kong dollar has enjoyed a highly successful peg to the U.S. dollar at a central rate of HK$7.80. The Chinese renminbi became fully convertible under the current account in late 1996. Current account convertibility covers payments for trade in merchandise and services such as shipping, banking and tourism, as well as private transfers. Full convertibility is not expected for some time, probably years.

Gap before exotics open up

However, the Asian 'tiger' countries are unlikely to free their currencies fast enough to enable them to fill the trading gap left by the euro straight away. 'Basically, all the currencies in this region will ultimately become fully convertible and that's when things could really take off,' said the head of treasury at a European bank in Singapore. Like IDEA's Supple, he saw the yen as a focus for increased Asian exotics trading. 'For example, over 60 per cent of Indonesia's debt is denominated in yen. Indonesia does huge trade with Japan. At present we see some commercial flows in yen/rupiah, but very little in the way of what I call real trading. Real trading, where proprietary traders move in and start having some fun, will come. I guess it'll happen within three to five years and the euro should hasten the process.'

The proprietary dealer at the U.S. bank in Singapore said that until volatility picked up in exotics — possibly when the euro was established – profits would not be as great as those offered by trading the mark. 'The central banks try to keep a lid on volatility out here. They're establishing repo pacts between each other to help fend off the speculators. Remember that volatility is what makes traders (like me) money and at the moment we haven't got too much volatility,' he said.

Many London-based analysts agree that the disappearance of major European forex trades would not ensure a shift to emerging markets. Any EMU-led boost to exotic currency volumes is likely to be a relatively small factor in the growing trend to trade markets like the Czech koruna or the Thai baht, they say. 'There will be a shift of resources of traders, salespeople and banking infrastructure to trade these currencies but obviously that cannot run ahead of end-user demand for foreign exchange products,' said Peter von Maydell, senior currency economist at UBS in London.

Liquidity is a major problem. Few of the exotic forex markets approach the depth of the major cross currencies, the U.S. dollar, the German mark, and Japanese yen. While traders are focusing on opportunities in the new markets, the positions being taken are tiny compared to what is seen in the major currencies. 'At the moment, there just isn't the liquidity,' said a corporate dealer at a Swiss bank in London. 'If you try to do a $10 million order in these markets, particularly in central Europe, people do take notice. You must get more participants and then only those that will have a long-term commitment ... to make it worthwhile.'

Liquidity is hampered by underdeveloped operational and settlement processes as well as greater credit risk. Currency analysts say only those who have invested in building up local expertise will be able to negotiate the fundamental problems individual to each country. 'You have to look at the opportunity and what it is expected to return,' said Nigel Whittaker, head of local currency, fixed income, at Deutsche Morgan Grenfell in London. 'Then you have to work out how much it will cost to investigate the accounting, tax treatment, custody and credit process, and then you look at the bid offer spreads. Suddenly this great rosy idea doesn't look so good in the cold light of day.'

Liquidity constraints are also partly a by-product of restrictive exchange controls adopted by most emerging market central banks. James Montier, Latin American economist at Kleinwort Benson in London, does see opportunities in these markets but is cautious about the present trading environment. 'Many of these countries operate some form of capital control like fixed or pegged exchange rates, restrictions on shorting money or taxes on transactions, which could dampen some enthusiasm of the foreign exchange market.'

These controls are not likely to be altered to suit the foreign exchange market's appetite for new, exciting markets. Analysts in London and Asia say that Far Eastern central banks, ever wary of volatility, are likely to take a dim view of anything that begins to resemble the hectic European forex markets of the 1980s and early 1990s. Asian central banks are fully prepared to mount a ferocious defence of their currency regimes, which have been put in place to reduce exchange rate volatility, beat domestic inflation or increase international competitiveness, analysts say.

'These central banks are aware of the potential power of the markets if they let the markets get the upper hand,' said Chris Tinker, chief economist at Standard Chartered Bank in London. 'People will be looking at high-yield plays globally, in Latin America, Thailand, Malaysia and Indonesia, for example. But none of these are markets where central banks will be pleased to see their currencies pushed around by speculative yield players.'

One positive sign for the Asian exotic currency market was that brokers were aggressively expanding their presence in Singapore, said the proprietary trader at a U.S. bank. 'Electronic broking has taken away a lot of their (brokers') business. The euro will be no different and will almost certainly be largely traded electronically.' This 'would almost certainly be the final nail in the coffin for some brokers unless they look elsewhere – such as here.' The head of Treasury at the European bank agreed, noting, 'Foreign exchange brokers are putting more emphasis on the regionals, the currencies not covered by electronic broking.' But he added a note of caution for banks thinking of expanding in Singapore.'The regionals can be incredibly boring. Perhaps you ought to stick to trading the euro.'

Eastern European currencies

The Czech crown was eastern Europe's most actively traded currency, with an average daily turnover of about $3.4 billion in late 1996 — four times greater than a year earlier when the currency market was liberalised. Any foreign entity can trade on the Czech foreign exchange market through a licensed market maker. The main players are banks, but brokerages and larger foreign trade companies are also big participants. The currency is fully convertible in all current account transactions and most capital account deals, although some large capital flows still require central bank approval. From February 1996, the currency was allowed to float freely within a plus/minus 7.5 per cent band, widened from an earlier 0.5 per cent, and fixed daily within this corridor against a basket weighted 70 per cent to the mark and 30 per cent to the dollar.

The Polish zloty was actively traded by local entities, domestic and foreign-owned, in 1996, but foreign banks had to trade the currency indirectly though Treasury bills. The daily turnover on the forex market was about $500 million. The secondary T-bill market was gradually gaining in volume and foreign acess was practically unlimited. The zloty is convertible in all current account flows but restrictions were still in place in 1996 on the capital account, including direct positions by foreign banks or short-selling. The zloty floats in a 14 per cent band around the central parity rate, set daily by the central bank, the NBP, according to the value of a basket of Western currencies and a devaluation factor of one per cent per month. The basket weights are: 45 per cent dollar, 35 per cent mark, 10 per cent sterling, five per cent French franc, five per cent Swiss franc. The pre-announced devaluation is aimed at compensating for inflation at about 20 per cent, but it also makes the zloty less market-driven by allowing the authorities to speed up or slow down the peg. At the end of each daily session, the NBP sets one fixed rate for the zloty against the dollar and mark, according to the buy and sell orders it has received from commercial banks.

Hungary's forint is the least traded of the three currencies, at a daily turnover of some $250 million, and foreign access remained limited in 1996, with no capital account convertibility. The currency is convertible for all current account transactions. But foreign access to short-term treasury paper, the only vehicle for trading foreign exchange, was also limited: foreigners could only buy maturities longer than one year. Liquidity in that market is low. Like the zloty, the Hungarian unit is devalued monthly through a crawling peg of 1.2 per cent. The currency is allowed to float in a band of plus/minus 4.5 per cent around a parity rate against a basket weighted 30 per cent to the dollar. The remaining 70 per cent weighting was due to be switched to the mark from the Ecu from January 1, 1997. Apart from the interbank forex market, foreign currency futures are also traded at the Budapest Commodity Exchange, but foreigners are not allowed into that market.

Portfolio flows underdeveloped

Demand for exotic currencies will largely be driven by trade flows and portfolio flows. Analysts say trade flows are growing rapidly but portfolio flows will also have to increase to ensure higher currency volumes. 'None of the emerging markets has a highly developed capital market,' said UBS's von Maydell. 'Except for a few equity markets here and there, there are no liquid bond markets, no liquid money markets and these currencies are very trade dominated rather than from portfolio flows.'

Central European currencies, particularly the Czech koruna, are now attracting volumes of trade on a par with the relatively more mature Asian currencies. Analysts say this is due to the proximity of these countries to the European Union and the growth of trade flows with the EU as well as the aspirations of some Eastern and Central European countries to join the EU. As a result, trade in the euro against these currencies is expected to grow faster than against other exotic currencies.

If EMU happens, analysts note the process may turn into a non-event as far as foreign exchange is concerned. The latest forex survey by the Bank for International Settlements estimates that European cross trades, excluding mark/sterling, comprise only six per cent of total currency turnover in London, home of the world's biggest foreign exchange market. EMU is also coming at a time when the foreign exchange market is tightening its belt as technology advances and trading margins shrink. As a result, banks will be very selective on which currencies can support dealing operations.

'While banks are looking into other markets, dealing rooms are being pared back with only the largest of operations able to survive as market makers,' said the Swiss bank dealer. 'With or without EMU, I think it will be "goodbye" to a lot of traders and dealing rooms getting smaller.'

7

The battle for survival in the financial markets

By Stephen Nisbet and Rosemary Bennett in London, Catherine O'Mahony in Frankfurt and David Clarke in Paris

LONDON, PARIS OR FRANKFURT

As momentum towards EMU has increased, so has the battle for business. Futures exchanges have been some of the most vocal protagonists but politicians, monetary authorities and commercial bankers have all joined in the fray as vested interests in London, Frankfurt and Paris seek to ensure that their centre gets a big slice of the post-EMU pie. London, the world's top foreign exchange market, has dominated the European financial scene throughout the 20th century. Even though Britain has been sitting on the fence over EMU, it is widely expected to retain its heavyweight status. But with financial leaders in Frankfurt and Paris keeping up the pressure, few in London's venerable 'Square Mile' — colloquially known as the City — are complacent. The battle is on many fronts: from the speculative futures markets, to the clubby world of loans and Eurobond syndication, to the fiercely competitive arena of global banking where giant financial houses seek to attract institutional business and guide the capital flows that dominate trading.

What future for futures?

The advent of a single European currency will present Europe's flourishing futures and options exchanges with a severe test as much of their traditional business disappears. Diversity and volatility — the lifeblood of the industry — have spawned nearly 200 contracts in 13 different currencies. But a single currency is set to create one main set of interest rates and a unified government bond market. Exchange chiefs at the cutting edge of this dynamic industry say they face dwindling business volumes, defunct products and huge job losses after a decade of explosive growth.

Few underestimate the problem. 'When the euro arrives, we will lose all our interest rate products. It's as simple as that,' said Jos Schmitt, president of Belgian futures and options exchange Belfox. The fate of Europe's string of small domestic exchanges looks the most bleak, with Irish futures and options exchange IFOX already forced to close because of dwindling demand for its products.

The big exchanges are gloomy too. 'It is clearly more likely volumes will drop rather than rise in Europe after EMU, even though it is still a subject of debate about how stable it will be and how many countries will be involved,' said a spokesman for Frankfurt's DTB, one of Europe's three largest exchanges.

But the futures industry, one of the most innovative in financial markets, will not give up without a fight. The race for post-EMU supremacy among Europe's big three, Britain's LIFFE, France's Matif and the DTB, has already begun while small exchanges prepare to fight for their lives.

DERIVATIVES TRADING AND THE MAJOR EXCHANGES

LIFFE

LIFFE (the London International Financial Futures and Options Exchange) is the biggest European exchange by far and has the broadest range of interest rate and government bond contracts, including the only three-month German interest rate future and the most liquid Bund future. Once contracts have built up substantial liquidity, it is difficult to prise it away, so LIFFE is in a strong position to cling onto much of the business after EMU. The exchange has already changed the terms of some existing contracts to try to ensure a smooth transition after EMU.

'We are already trading the first euro instruments,' said LIFFE chairman Jack Wigglesworth. 'The euromark future is the biggest interest rate futures product in Europe and the bulk of liquidity is already here.' LIFFE has also altered the legal terms of the euromark future to accommodate all eventualities. If EMU starts on time in January 1999, euromark contracts will transfer to covering euro three-month rates and settle in euro. If EMU is delayed or reverses, they will change back to three-month German rates and settle in marks.

But if Britain is not included in the first wave of EMU entrants, it may not get automatic access to the full range of payment systems and liquidity so its position as Europe's main financial centre may be damaged. The Bank of England has insisted that any attempt to introduce differential terms for countries inside and outside EMU would be discriminatory and likely to contravene both the single market legislation and EU competition law. But elsewhere and notably in Germany, central bankers have been arguing that non-members should not have the same rights of access to the euro settlement system, known as TARGET.

The Deutsche Terminboerse

LIFFE is not the only exchange with a stake in what happens on TARGET. In Frankfurt, DTB officials believe if EMU's non-members have the same access to facilities as members, their exchange will be disadvantaged. 'If countries outside EMU have full access to the benefits other financial markets have, they will not be in any way disadvantaged and could in fact use their position to construct regulations to be a competitive factor,' a spokesman for the German exchange said.

But the DTB will benefit in other ways from being at the heart of EMU. The exchange will be the next door neighbour to the new European Central Bank. It offers a range of liquid contracts on German government debt, at five and 10 years, and it will compete for business in three-month euro futures as well. The exchange also intends to capitalise on its technological pre-eminence, with plans to colonise Europe with its remote trading terminals. More than 40 of nearly 150 members trade from workstations outside Germany. 'Our remote membership is growing at an impressive rate and our mission is to keep it that way,' said the DTB spokesman.

Even arch rival LIFFE does not predict the demise of its closest competitor. 'The DTB is in the next best position to survive. It has secured a decent share of Bund business and is bigger than Matif,' a spokesman said. Futures dealers suspect both exchanges will carve up EMU contracts between them, LIFFE keeping interest rate futures business, while DTB gets the bond business.

Matif

Matif also has plans to avoid being left out in the cold. Home to a huge domestic bond future and a three-month French interest rate contract, it is staking its claim on the franc's central position in the drive towards monetary union. The French government has been actively issuing Ecu-denominated debt since 1989 and is the leading sovereign borrower in Ecu, the forerunner of the euro. It plans to convert all its debt into the new currency at the start of EMU and analysts believe that where the active cash market resides, futures business is sure to follow. The Matif believes it is well placed to receive it. 'We will ensure that we offer the best market place to trade the future euro benchmarks,' said chairman Gerard Pfauwadel.

Even if the Matif loses interest rate contracts, it can fall back on its stock index future and commodities contracts.

The road ahead

When European bourse executives descended on Chicago, the heart of the US derivatives industry, for an industry conference in October 1996, they engaged in friendly, but slightly barbed point-scoring. Pfauwadel said Britain might have some advantages but that Paris would be the 'real' centre for activity. LIFFE's Wigglesworth countered that London was not connected as a financial services centre to the fortunes of the British economy or to any decision as to which currencies would be in EMU. 'London has always thrived from other people's restrictive practices,' he remarked. That prompted Jose-Luis Oller, general manager and chief executive of the Spanish Financial Futures and Options Exchange (MEFF) to charge LIFFE with scare tactics. 'The first thing you do in a battle is you try to frighten your adversaries to death,' he said.

But the exchanges may not have to bludgeon each other to divide up EMU business. A month after they were trading mild insults, two of the main EMU players, LIFFE and Matif, each separately linked up with the Chicago Mercantile Exchange, setting up arrangements for trade in each other's contracts. At first glance it looked like another round of competition. But the exchanges actually had carved up business between them. LIFFE set up a link with the CME for trading of its short-term interest rate contracts, while the Matif set up an accord for contracts of one year or more, and specifically for its popular 10-year French bond future.

Although tough times do lie ahead, futures exchanges also can look forward to several years of high volatility and turnover as speculation intensifies on the shape of monetary union. 'The transition period will be very interesting. As sentiment ebbs and flows over if it will happen and whichever currencies will be in and out, activity is bound to increase,' said Wigglesworth.

THE EUROBOND MARKET

In the more freewheeling world of offshore bond issuance, London has been the unquestionable leader since the 1960s, when the Eurobond market was born. London's aversion to stringent regulations suited Eurobond players well and has led steadily growing bond issuance.

The Euromarket's first bond transactions were launched as investment for dollar deposit holders who, for one reason or another, did not want their money held in the U.S. Business began to take off in the late 1970s and by the 1980s, issuance was picking up in Frankfurt and Paris. The dollar remained the dominant currency. 'The mark was only a small sub-section then. Nobody was interested in it,' said Tim Skeet, executive director of debt capital markets at Lehman Brothers International. Bankers said French franc issuance from Paris was partly cosmetic. In many instances, London branches of French banks actually did all the paperwork while the Paris headquarters took the credit in the industry league tables.

Life is hardly so simple in the 1990s, with scores of currencies and complicated bond deals running through the market regularly. More than half a trillion dollars moved through this market in 1996. Bankers see London staying as the Euromarket's 21st century base whether Britain joins EMU or not. Even German banks, which have been keen supporters of the DTB exchange, look set to keep their Eurobond flags flying in London. Dresdner Bank, one of the top three German banks, said in October 1996 that it would base its Eurobond operations in London. The announcement was in conjunction with its acquisition of boutique Eurobond firm Luthy Baillie Dowsett & Pethick.

Rival houses were hardly surprised. 'These days borrowers want to talk different structures, currencies, markets. You've got to have your sales and trading desks and syndicate departments all under the one roof if you want to compete in the future,' Skeet said. Merck Finck banking analyst Konrad Becker in Frankfurt was forthright: 'Germany is not where it's at in investment banking. If you want to be a global investment bank, you don't do it from Frankfurt.'

A bigger role for Frankfurt

Significant efforts are being made to liberalise Germany's markets in the runup to 1999, but Frankfurt has always played second fiddle to London as a financial centre and is generally seen as having little realistic chance of catching up. Nonetheless, the fact that it will host the European Central Bank has convinced many observers that Frankfurt has a good chance of playing a stronger role in Europe once the euro is launched, especially if the government takes a more active role in attracting debt business back to the centre.

Rigid market structures are perceived as one of the biggest problems but the Bundesbank appears to have taken on board the need for more liberalisation. In 1996, the central bank approved several crucial market improvements, most notably the introduction of short-term debt issuance and the removal in December of highly unpopular minimum reserve requirements on some securities repurchase business.

Foreign banks say they are placing their faith in efforts to improve trading conditions although many still bemoan the restrictions German law imposes on them.

While London remains the home for the bulk of trading in German cash bonds and futures, expectations are emerging that Bonn will intervene to bring Bund business back to Germany in the context of monetary union. Goldman Sachs economist Thomas Mayer says: 'I think there will be a return of the business that has been sitting so far in London to Frankfurt.' France, which demands that primary dealings in French bonds is done from Paris, will be the spur for the German government to intervene, Mayer predicts.

Although Mayer believes London has firm advantages over Frankfurt as a financial centre, he says: 'I do not think you can stay a global and European player without a very strong bridgehead in Frankfurt. You have to be able to observe monetary policy at close hand and trade debt in the place (of issue).'

By the end of 1996, after long deliberations, Germany had finally decided to convert its stock of mark denominated debt into euros to coincide with the planned launch of monetary union in 1999. Finance Minister Theo Waigel had been opposed to converting debt to euros prematurely, but he was understood to have been swayed by fears of ending up at a competitive disadvantage to France, whose debt will be converted to euros from the first trading day of 1999.

One of the most popular liberalisation moves has been the Bundesbank's decision in December 1996 to relax its reserve policy, a move for which banks had lobbied for years. The easing means banks no longer have to make reserve deposits (which are non-interest bearing) with the central bank to cover certain securities repurchase deals, although they still have to meet reserves to cover their sight and savings deposits.

Germany's minimum reserve system, established in 1948, is unique among developed European economies and a major thorn in the side of the banking industry. The Bundesbank itself said the step was directly designed to enhance Frankfurt's role under monetary union. 'The most important aspect of this move is that such a measure boosts the financial centre of Frankfurt without harming monetary policy,' said Hermann Remsperger, chief economist at BHF Bank.

Banks are now hoping that at least some of the securities repurchase business which had left Frankfurt for the more welcoming regime in London will now return, although some say the damage has already been done. Despite this easing gesture, the Bundesbank is determined to retain the bulk of reserve requirements and is keen to have them implemented by the future European Central Bank.

More vigorous equities culture

Lack of liquidity also hampers efforts in German financial circles to boost business, but here too action is being taken. Stock exchange holding company Deutsche Boerse AG is aggressively competing for a more vigorous equity culture and efficient stock market operations in Germany, supported by a raft of new financial market legislation. Bonn in November approved a bill aimed at increasing shareholder rights and reducing the power of the banks over corporations — long perceived as a disincentive for foreign investment.

The bill, which is expected to become law in 1998, will also simplify share buybacks, allowing companies to repurchase up to 10 per cent of their own capital in line with European Union norms.

Deutsche Boerse is expecting EMU to mean a boost for its business, and is preparing in a variety of ways, including setting up more user-friendly sector-based stock indices. The exchange views its technological sophistication as one of its main selling points — it has an advanced range of electronic trade options. Management board chairman Werner Seifert says the bourse wants to offer electronic access to German share dealings from London, Amsterdam, Zurich and Chicago by the time EMU is set to begin in January 1999.

There have also been further efforts to forge closer links between the regional bourses, which currrently compete for business with Frankfurt. Ultimately, Deutsche Boerse aims for price harmonisation between all eight exchanges, although the smallest exchanges are resistant to losing power to Frankfurt. Deutsche Boerse is also forming its own lobby group, a committee of leading industrialists, bankers and media representatives, to promote Frankfurt as EMU approaches. Founders of the group include Rolf Breuer, the future chief executive of Deutsche Bank AG, the country's most powerful bank.

Glimmers of light for Paris

London still has a stronghold on the bulk of international financial business, Frankfurt has the geographical pull of being home to the future European Central Bank, but what does the future hold for Paris? As one of EMU's great driving forces, France has shown no sign of wavering in its commitment to monetary union. But as EMU looks set to accelerate consolidation in the financial services industry, Paris is considered one of the more vulnerable centres.

According to Bank for International Settlements figures, France had a four per cent share of the market for foreign exchange turnover as of April 1995. That was on a par with Germany, which had five per cent, but paled in comparison with 30 per cent for Britain. Furthermore, Paris is far more heavily dependent than London on inter-European cross trading. Bankers in Paris have been nervous about the impact of EMU on their forex trading operations, with some saying they would have to cut their staff levels in half. Outside France, senior bankers talk of the determined efforts French authorities will make to retain as much business as possible going into EMU.

But with little chance of becoming a mecca for currency dealers, financial leaders in France are pinning their hopes on the capital markets and exchange-based business. In both the cash and futures markets, France has been making strides to grab and hold market share. The Matif, the French futures exchange, has been at the forefront of moves to make its contracts tradeable after EMU.

Deutsche board member Breuer says Paris and Frankfurt both will be competitive at the start of EMU, although he painted a gloomy picture across Europe for many financial centres. 'There are 31 cash markets and 23 futures markets in Europe — their existence is under threat,' he said. Breuer said no single centre would dominate in euro trading at the start, adding that Frankfurt and Paris are already well positioned to fight for post-EMU business. 'Both have tried to be very competitive. But the race has not taken place yet,' he said. 'I see these two competing at the start.'

CAPTURING THE FLOWS

Ultimately, the main issue at stake is which centre plays host to the enormous capital flows that drive international markets. The TARGET controversy will play a large role in determining how the post-EMU banking scene shapes up. Some analysts said the row over TARGET showed Britain to be vulnerable to political pressure from core EMU states which seek to deny access to it for countries outside the euro area. Others said this weapon could backfire against those who wield it because it would inconvenience mainland European and other foreign banks operating in London as well as casting EMU founder states in a negative light. However, as the fight for access to TARGET pans out, London is considered well placed to defend its primacy among European financial centres.

'We believe London will remain the top financial centre with or without the UK's participation in EMU,' said Rabbani Wahhab, managing director of GH

Asset Management. Graham McDevitt, senior bond strategist at Paribas Capital Markets, said LIFFE's launch of a one-month Euromark interest rate futures contract on November 21 was a pointer toward London retaining its status as the main financial centre. The fact that French bank Paribas and Germany's Deutsche Bank ran their main trading operations out of London also indicated the likelihood of London keeping its attraction, he said.

McDevitt said one the main factors influencing the intensity of competition between Europe's principal financial centres would be the post-EMU shape of European futures markets. 'Will we have one single 10-year future with different bonds being delivered by different countries or will there be different futures as now, one for France, one for Germany and so on?' McDevitt asked.

Competition between London, Paris and Frankfurt would be fiercest if there were lots of single futures — for one month, three months etc — and all exchanges were competing for the business. Mary Bloem, Ecu/EMU bond strategist at Paribas Capital Markets, said she was confident London would largely maintain its position — and it could even improve its stature relative to mainland centres, if the euro turned out to lack credibility.

Bloem said the TARGET controversy was unlikely to prompt any wholesale move of banks from London to mainland Europe. But she said there were unanswered questions about the impact of such unequal treatment on organisations like Paribas's London operation. If excluded from the payments system, Paribas might have to transfer its payments system to Paris, she added.

Wahhab said London had captured so much business at the expense of Frankfurt in many fields that it would be hard to dislodge the British capital, whatever happened on EMU in 1999 and beyond. He said mainland countries were using the TARGET row as a negotiating tool to try to persuade Britain to join EMU.

'At the end of the day full access for London will have to be provided because otherwise there would be so many hiccups in the banking system,' he added. Wahhab said that if Britain stayed out of EMU, there would be some repositioning of banks into core EMU countries. 'But like it or not, there will be some participation on matters relating to the euro coming out of London even though the UK may not be a fully-fledged EMU member,' he said.

Stephen Hannah, head of international research at IBJ International, predicted that London would still attract the main cross-border flows of banking business for the first two or three years after 1999, whether or not Britain had joined EMU. 'I doubt very much whether major banks would make significant diversions of resources (away from London) until they were clear the euro and the EMU institution was going to work in a stable and consistent fashion,' Hannah said.

'There will be a lot of uncertainty to begin with regarding taxation and regulatory aspects of EMU. Especially if Britain were out, there would be a strong incentive to leave things as they are till they see how these things develop.' Hannah said the TARGET dispute was important, but many of the banking institutions that would be affected had multinational operations. He wondered whether the protective barrier could work in practice when groups which had headquarters in London had subsidiaries in EMU member states.

A few years on, if the EMU experiment were successful and Britain appeared increasingly marginalised, London might start to lose some people who wanted to be nearer to EMU's centre of political power. But the exodus would not be huge and Britain might end up joining the monetary union after all. Hannah said continental Europeans, despite the TARGET dispute, could suffer themselves if action to alienate Britain led to an increased threat of competitive devaluations from sterling. Punitive action against a non-joiner would mean EMU giving an image of itself to the world as 'a closed shop full of regulations and restrictions' which would be anathema to Europe's 'real competition' in Asia and the U.S.

George Magnus, chief international economist at UBS, says factors working in London's favour even if it were outside EMU included its deregulated environment, international language, flexible labour market laws 'plus the fact that all the foreign banks that mean anything in the world are located here.' Magnus says there has been concern but no sense of panic about London's status.

8

Could euro bonds rival the U.S. market?

By Jacqueline Thorpe, Deepthi Wickremasinghe, Adam Cox, Kate Kelland, Dan Lalor, Jim Saft and Aline van Duyn in London; Myra MacDonald in Paris; and Tomasz Janowski in Warsaw

Betting on Hungary joining EMU could be the high-yielding government bond play of the next century. Investors will have to plumb more exotic territory as interest rate differentials shrink between the lynchpins of the current European bond scene. But many European bond analysts still see plenty of ways to make money. They believe that trading strategies based on which countries are fudging the EMU criteria and which countries will next make the grade will spur the growth of a euro government bond market that could eventually rival U.S. Treasuries in size and depth.

Many in New York and Washington are dubious. They say Europeans are deceiving themselves if they think the euro will be able to challenge the dollar's hold on global investors any time soon. They point out that what makes U.S. Treasuries the $3.5 trillion pivot of the global bond market is the fact that there is just one issuer of U.S. government debt. Where, they ask, will the euro find a benchmark creator to rival the U.S. Treasury, backed by the credit of some $7 trillion of annual GDP and capable of lining a 30-year yield curve with issues many times the size of any comparable European government bond? By late 1996, there was little sign that future EMU governments were making any firm plans to co-ordinate their debt issuance, much less that EU states would ever surrender enough sovereignty to issue through a single EMU government debt agency. Some Americans dismissed Europe's bond market ambitions with the retort that it had taken a civil war and a century of federal integration to create the Treasuries market.

European analysts acknowledge that Europe's vibrant government bond markets risk losing much of their excitement if monetary union succeeds. Post-EMU political plays would be unlikely to supply the drama of the 1990s, when every hawkish Bundesbank statement, every Italian budget cliffhanger, every Swedish vacillation on EMU and every hint of Franco-German tension has sent the adrenalin surging through European bond markets. Some fear that if EMU removes the added spice of currency plays and provides the market stability which governments crave, international investors will lose interest, finding little reward in playing off the differentials which will remain in credit risk.

There is also a danger that EMU might fragment markets further, at least at first, reducing rather than increasing the liquidity which is the lifeblood of any market. Each EMU entrant will issue new government debt in euros. France was quick to pledge to convert all its existing debt, too, into euros from January 1, 1999 — part of a French bid to grab European benchmark status from the now dominant German Bund market. Spurred on by the French challenge, other likely EMU governments were considering a quick national debt conversion to euros. But the private sector is under no obligation to convert outstanding debt in 1999 and it is unlikely to volunteer to spend time and money doing so. This means that corporate debt markets in marks, French francs and other currencies earmarked for extinction are likely to coexist for some time alongside national government bonds denominated in euros.

Even so, there is a consensus that the euro has the potential to generate new debt market business. The removal of currency risk could inspire big new corporate bond issues in euros, spur the growth of Europe's embryonic asset-backed debt market, and enable pension funds and risk-averse retail investors to do more bond trades across national borders. If EMU brings low interest rates, more investors might be willing to buy high-yielding debt from companies with weak credit-ratings, creating a euro junk bond market. And if national governments can be persuaded to supply the tax breaks that draw U.S. investors to municipal bonds, there is good scope for a euro muni market.

GOVERNMENT DEBT: SIZE AND LIQUIDITY

What's to become of the siesta spread?

The spectre of the euro has sent shivers down the spines of some government bond traders. Those who believe the euro government bond market could challenge Treasuries point out that the EU's total GDP rivals that of the U.S. and that the region has a bigger population to support the debt market. But others say government benchmark volumes would shrink, because countries honouring the EMU stability pact would need to issue less debt. National interest rate differentials, which fuel current bond trade, would evaporate along with the currency risk, leaving credit as the only trade determinant.

'The result is going to be very small differentials, perhaps 10 or 15 basis points,' said Adrian Owens, economist at Bank Julius Baer in London. If both Spain and Italy enter EMU successfully, Italy would probably still pay a credit risk premium on its much bigger debt burden, but the 'siesta spread,' the interest rate differential between Spanish and Italian bonds, would lose much of the volatility that has made it one of the favourite plays of the 1990s. Some fund managers, notably in the U.S., dispute this and expect EMU could add to debt market volatility. This is because after room for currency movements has been eliminated, the credit markets will feel the full force of any market tensions.

Mark Fox, chief European strategist in fixed income at Lehman Brothers in London, said there would still be enough volatility between core euro bonds to feed a healthy amount of trade. 'Unless countries follow absolutely identical policies, you have to let the stress of different policies out somehow. And if you can't do it through currencies, you have to do it through interest rate differentials,' he said. Andrew McCaffery, joint head of proprietary trading at Yamaichi International in London, said traders would be on the lookout for any signs of economic divergence. 'Will they fudge the criteria afterwards? That will cause tension and ramifications,' he added.

Short-term money markets would be no less immune to political, fiscal and supply and demand stresses, analysts said. 'Short-term bills of any particular country will still be bid for at local auctions run by the regional central banks of Europe,' said Fox. 'There's still a possibility some auctions will fail and rates will be bid up or down.'

Many European traders envision an environment akin to the U.S. municipal or Canadian provincial debt markets, where sovereign and regional authorities issue a whole range of debt. 'There are obvious differences between the (Canadian) provinces and so they trade at different spreads,' said Robin Baldwin, a director at London Bond Broking. 'But basically they are all in line.' Analysts expect the euro's effective removal of national boundaries to remove the blinkers from those European investors who now stick with paper denominated in their own currency. While Baldwin said many funds were already operating on a Europe-wide basis, Robin Monroe-Davies, managing director at the European credit-rating agency IBCA, said currency remained a formal barrier for many.

John Langton, Zurich-based chief executive of ISMA, said that for the euro market to thrive, there must be at least six or seven countries in the first round of EMU, the euro must be as serious a currency as the yen and the dollar, and a full yield curve must be developed. 'If these prerequisites are met, I believe we'll see a lot of investors come into the euro, and we'll see a proper liquid market,' Langton said.

Eastern Europe's euro aspirations

Hungary, Poland and the Czech Republic have all signalled that they will try to meet the Maastricht criteria as fast as possible, as part of their drive for admission to the EU. The three countries, which either fix or gradually devalue their currencies against baskets of foreign units, expect the euro to replace some currencies in these baskets or to serve by itself as a single yardstick.

- In Hungary, Gyorgy Szapary, deputy president of the Hungarian central bank, told Reuters that EMU should help the region's companies by limiting the exchange rate risk in trade with the EU, eastern Europe's main partner, and by reducing interest rates in western Europe, which would also ease eastern European borrowing costs.

  He said the euro could become a peg for the forint. 'If we can bring inflation ... to below 10 per cent, then we can shift towards a fixed exchange rate or flotation in a wider range. We are going in that direction.' Szapary said Hungary, which was aiming in 1996 for a budget deficit of four per cent of GDP and inflation of 23 to 24 per cent, hoped to join the EU by 2001 or 2002 and EMU soon after that. The finance ministry has been more cautious, putting a possible EMU entry date around 2005.

- Poland, which aims to meet two EMU criteria in 1997 with a budget deficit of 2.8 per cent and public debt below 60 per cent of GDP, must still grapple with inflation, running at about 19 per cent in 1996. Finance Minister Grzegorz Kolodko said he planned an initiative called Euro 2006 to trigger public debate on Poland's aspirations to enter the EU and later EMU. The plan's goals would include slashing inflation to two per cent by 2004. 'We have a long way to go when it comes to inflation, interest rates and the exchange rate .... We have an ambitious goal of slashing inflation to five per cent by 2000 but lowering it further will be harder,' Kolodko said.

- Czech central bank president Josef Tosovsky said that after EMU, the crown would be pegged to the euro instead of the present currency basket of marks and dollars.

- Slovenia was also upbeat about its chances of meeting all EMU criteria by 2001. In late 1996, Prime Minister Janez Drnovsek said the country stood a chance of cutting inflation to three per cent from the current nine per cent within the next two to three years.

- In Russia, pursuing a policy of keeping the rouble in an exchange rate corridor which is gradually devalued against the dollar, the euro seemed too distant in late 1996 to provoke serious debate. This was still more true for Bulgaria and Romania. The first was struggling with hyperinflation and the second expected inflation to rebound to 45 per cent after it loosened fiscal and monetary policy.

TRADING STRATEGIES IN AND OUT OF THE EURO BLOC

New plays for old

But analysts said one major focus of trade would switch to bonds issued by countries outside the EMU core. The great European bond play of the mid-1990s has been the convergence trade, anticipating a sharp narrowing of yield spreads between Bunds and bonds issued by countries with less stable economies. Politically-astute investors have also made plenty of money from divergence trades, anticipating a sudden widening of spreads on fears the weaker economies might not make it into EMU after all.

If the Spanish bono loses its convergence/divergence appeal after EMU, that play could be switched to trading euro benchmarks against the bonds of Poland and Hungary, analysts said. 'Investors will be looking to pick up yield by looking outside the core markets into emerging markets, ie eastern Europe,' said Owens at Julius Baer. This would protect bonds of those countries left outside EMU — including gilts if the British government does not join — from being seriously undermined. 'It's going to be a two-way process: an evaluation of the EMU core and individual countries outside as well,' said Yamaichi's McCaffery. 'If it is successful, then you do start talking about Poland and Hungary converging also.'

Since the EU would watch such convergence to test whether east European countries were ready to join their community, east European sovereign borrowers could make it simple by using the international bond market to issue in euros. 'European Union candidates from eastern and central Europe can demonstrate their readiness (to join the EU) by having bonds in euros at yield spreads little different from EU governments,' said Graham Bishop, EU advisor at Salomon Brothers International in London.

Debt futures markets will throw up a host of possibilities for bond trades in 2000, analysts said. The futures markets in London, Paris and Frankfurt, all hustling to become the main centre of trade, must decide whether there will be one bond future on the various cash bonds or individual futures on each euro cash bond. 'If there is one futures contract, you're going to have bonds of different governments with different credit ratings all deliverable into the same futures contract,' said Fox. This would fuel basis trading, the arbitrage between the cash and futures markets which plays on the price differences between a variety of bonds that can all be used to honour the same futures market commitment. 'That means that there is potential for far more complex basis trading … than there is today,' Fox added. 'There's lots and lots of room to make money.'

Much will depend on which countries qualify for EMU in 1999. Steve Major, head of bond research at Credit Lyonnais in Paris, estimated the total amount of national government debt in Europe would be around 70 to 75 per cent of the size of the U.S. Treasuries market. 'European total debt of around $2.0 trillion would need to be issued. It is an absolutely awesome number, which creates the second biggest market in (the) world, bigger than Japan,' Major said. 'It's more or less one bond market with a bit of credit and liquidity spread.' Bishop at Salomon Brothers said that based on Salomon's world index of government bonds, the euro market would total about the same size or slightly larger than U.S. Treasuries. 'That will be the tradeable universe for clients.'

The need to cover all areas of the curve would inevitably lead to an increase in the number of debt products. 'EMU will lead to a greater variety of instruments for government debt. Availability of all instruments on all points of the yield curve will be crucial. There will be fierce competition between the various issuers,' said Werner Becker, senior economist at Deutsche Bank in Frankfurt. 'The volume of single bonds and notes will be much bigger than now because the most liquid instruments will become benchmarks, and benchmarking means lower costs for governments.'

Major at Credit Lyonnais expects Germany to provide the benchmarks, with Germany and France being the biggest issuers of new paper and Belgium also a leading player once existing debt was converted. 'The credit spreads and main liquidity will be in the markets of Germany and France,' he said. The conversion of existing debt would create some secondary market trading along with the refinancing of maturing debt that had been rolled over. 'There will be a big pool of tradable bonds pretty quickly,' he said.

The data, which includes regional and municipal government issuance,
shows debt outstanding for 1995.

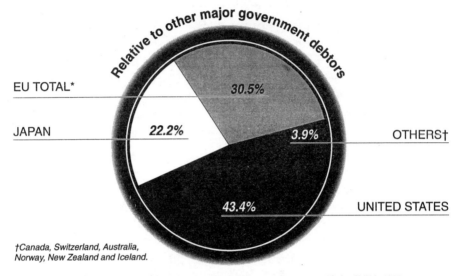

†Canada, Switzerland, Australia,
Norway, New Zealand and Iceland.

*EU total excludes Greece, which is the one EU state certain not to qualify for EMU in 1999;
and Luxembourg, which has negligible government debt.

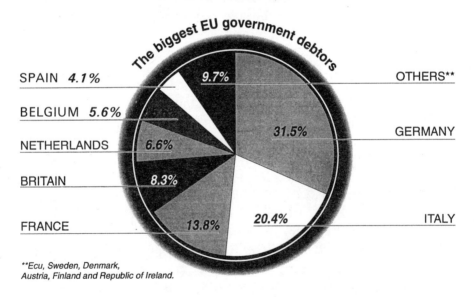

**Ecu, Sweden, Denmark,
Austria, Finland and Republic of Ireland.

Figure 8.1: *Scale of EU government debt*

Source: Merrill Lynch, 'Size and Structure of the World Bond Market: 1996'

Supply risks

Decisions about maturities and sizes of issues will probably be made at a national level, analysts say. Stephen King, international economist at HSBC James Capel in London, said in the short term there would be nothing to prevent countries borrowing as much as they wanted. 'The restraint will be via the stability pact when it is up and running,' King added. He likened it to local authorities or individual states in the U.S. which are, theoretically, free to issue as much as they want.

Bishop agreed. 'At the moment, if a government borrows too much, the risk is either interest rates have to rise quite quickly or the exchange rate starts to suffer, or possibly a combination of both,' he said. 'The incentive to become a fiscal free rider is much greater (under EMU) because you can borrow more, and there is no exchange rate risk associated with that. The problem would be if everyone decided to do that at the same time, a huge deficit would build up. Hence the stability pact.' Credit Lyonnais's Major said the pact would provide a shrinking basis for debt. 'The three per cent (EMU entry deficit) target can be hit by anyone on a cosmetic basis, but what is important to financial markets and longer-term credibility is a sustainable reduction in the deficit.'

EMU may also encourage governments to standardise auction techniques. Candidate states currently use three, a primary dealer system, tenders and consortium procedures. Becker in Frankfurt said the consortium procedure, used in Germany, was not particularly profitable or efficient, so he expected to see a primary dealer system and a tender procedure in nearly all national markets. Bishop said it would probably be an evolutionary process as countries found the most efficient system with the minimum yield spreads in order to reduce government costs. 'Each country will do its own thing as they always have. There will be no currency question. It will simply be what is the credit quality, and that is measured in basis points of yield,' Bishop said.

But he noted the French approach was being widely adopted world wide. Major agreed. 'In European government bond markets, the role model of how to create transparency and liquidity has been created by the French. The only other country that is as good as France is Spain because they have literally copied the French system. Portugal is going the same way,' he added.

CONVERTING NATIONAL DEBT TO EUROS

Fixing European exchange rates may be the most visible move in creating a single currency, but the conversion of debt into euro paper is meant to set it in stone. Plans to convert quickly a large part of the stock of outstanding European debt into euros were gathering momentum in late 1996, going beyond a 1995 agreement that participating governments' bonds will be issued in the single currency from 1999.

France has led the drive to get government debt issued in euros, which it sees as one way of ensuring there will be no turning back on EMU. 'It's a sign of confidence. It's a signal of irreversibility,' said Stefan Collignon, director of research at the Association for the Monetary Union of Europe. After conversion, the practical and technical problems in unravelling a Europe-wide, euro-denominated bond market would mean that only a very serious crisis could prompt a reversal of the move.

For France, settling the debt question was important enough to be considered a reasonable trade-off for dropping its opposition to naming the new currency the euro at the 1995 Madrid summit. In return, it wrested a compromise whereby all new issues from 1999 must be in euros, while individual countries can choose to convert their existing stock of debt any time up to 2002.

France said it would convert all its debt in 1999. Germany finally bowed to pressure from commercial banks in late 1996 and agreed to follow suit, recognising the need to stay competitive as a debt market centre. Belgium said that it too would convert all of its existing main bond issues from Belgian francs into euros from the start of monetary union. Most other countries had yet to announce their plans.

Technicians in national capitals getting ready for EMU are keen to make sure their own markets are as liquid as possible, to attract business and keep the cost of funding low.

France's banking and government officials are trying to get a head start by working out exactly how debt should be converted. They believe French debt should be among the easiest to convert. It is fully dematerialised — there are no more bearer bond certificates — standardised and easily negotiable. But how will France convert franc bonds, traded in round numbers, to euros?

Rounding up the euros

The franc/euro exchange rate, expected to run to five decimal places, would create paper in unmanageable numbers. The French Treasury is looking at various methods, including fragmenting its OAT bonds, which currently have a minimum denomination of 2,000 francs, into 2,000 holdings with a denomination of one franc, official sources say. Once converted, the issues could be rebundled into round euro numbers although there might be initial difficulties as operators tried to match up their bits and pieces of debt. 'It might create a bit of indigestion at the beginning,' Credit Lyonnais bond analyst Iain Lindsay said. Governments may have to repay some of the odds and ends, though French official sources say this is likely to represent a small amount of outstanding debt. Retail investors could retain bond holdings at awkward numbers, while big market players who want round numbers would be dealing in such large quantities that bundling will be easier.

Europe's governments may also use the switch to euros as an excuse to scrap minimum denominations altogether, allowing trading in theory down to the last euro. 'One could decide to use the change to have tranches of one euro. It would improve the flexibility of trading on the market, particularly for derivatives products,' one French Treasury source said. Already BTANs, medium-term French notes, have no minimum denomination but trade in large amounts. That too would probably be the case for euros, and operators would discourage trading in smaller sizes by charging a higher price. 'Economic discipline forces an unwritten denomination on the market,' Lindsay said.

The absence of a minimum denomination would boost liquidity in the strip market, where coupon repayments are stripped from the bond itself and traded separately. At the moment stripped coupons carry a denomination derived from the original bond. Without this restraint, they would be more interchangeable. France, with the leading strip market outside the United States, is keen to make sure it keeps this position after EMU, and has a clear incentive to scrap denominations. Britain, keen to build a strip market of its own, was also looking at the possibility of scrapping denominations, bond analysts said.

Another option is to step up issues in ecus ahead of EMU to smooth the transition to the euro. Ecus will be converted one-for-one for euros on January 1, 1999. France and Britain are the only countries to have regular Ecu issuance. France was considering adding Ecu Treasury bill issues to its existing programme and French banks and back-offices were likely to be ready by the middle of 1997 to deal with such issues. 'One of the paths worth exploring is to use the Ecu market in the preceding months,' one French Treasury source said. A 1996 report by bankers and the Bank of France earlier this year, meant to provide a basis for debate rather than official proposal, recommended that the Treasury issue 'a sufficient volume of Treasury bills and negotiable debt' in Ecus from 1998 onward with a maturity after January 1, 1999. But the Ecu market is still starved of liquidity and has shown little sign of a real pick-up ahead of the launch of EMU. As a result, countries which borrow in Ecus run the risk that when they repay the debt, it will be in a stronger currency — the euro. 'We have to be pragmatic. We are not going to go against our own inter-ests,' one French source said.

THREAT TO NATIONAL CREDIT RATINGS

If the euro achieves one of its main objectives, it will eliminate costly and dis-turbing currency fluctuations. But it would also eliminate a country's ability to print money, the method of last resort in paying back debt. That, say analysts, raises a big question: which EMU member countries would be able to maintain their current debt ratings? Rating agencies such as Standard & Poor's, Moody's Investors Service and IBCA will need to look even more closely at countries' fis-cal health. Apart from debt, deficits and budgets, broader issues like labour markets, tax structure, and pension funding will come under closer scrutiny. 'Credit is going to be the number one issue in terms of European bonds,' said Michael Lewis, economist at Deutsche Morgan Grenfell in London.

IBCA, the European credit rating agency, and Standard & Poor's have both said the credit quality of sovereign countries joining EMU would likely remain strong. Moody's co-head of sovereign ratings David Levey said: 'If you form a European monetary union there would be a single ceiling for that entire area which would likely be AAA, given the membership and the strength of the overall economic area.'

Foreign and local debt issued by Germany, France, the Netherlands, Austria and Luxembourg, likely candidates for EMU in the first wave, are all rated top notch AAA by the major rating agencies and that is unlikely to change. But the ratings of three other frontline candidates, Belgium, Ireland and Finland, could be eroded. They all currently have AAA local currency ratings but lower ratings for their foreign currency debt. IBCA has said without the ability to print money, the ratings of these countries would likely drift down to the level of their foreign currency ratings.

Lewis at Deutsche Morgan Grenfell said ratings for both Ireland and Finland would be at risk because their two main trading partners, Britain and Sweden respectively, would likely remain outside the EMU bloc at the beginning, increasing the risk of secession. Belgium could suffer because it has a huge amount of debt set to be converted into euros, he said. Analysts said credit risk of sovereign debt, minus currency risk, can be assessed by looking at yields of sovereign Eurobonds over benchmark Bunds. Yields on mark Eurobonds issued by countries such as Belgium, Finland and Italy currently trade a few basis points over benchmark Bunds. 'This is credit risk only, with currency risk stripped out,' said Deutsche's Lewis. 'And you can see the differences.'

The 'outs'

Countries that stayed outside EMU, at least initially, should be able to hang onto their existing credit ratings. 'Britain won't be at risk of a downgrade,' said Bronwyn Curtis, chief economist at Nomura Research Institute in London. 'They have done a lot more than other countries in terms of deregulation, pensions and getting their fiscal situation under control.' If Italy and Spain do not make it into the first wave, they should also be able to retain high ratings as they struggle to get into shape for the second round — 'unless of course they abandon all hope and start pursuing irresponsible policies,' said Phyllis Reed, European bond strategist at BZW in London. 'And that very is unlikely.' However, those countries would be in the unusual position of having a higher local currency rating outside EMU than their foreign currency rating inside EMU.

Analysts and rating agencies said that whether ratings stand or fall, agencies will need to look deeper at the mechanics of a country's economy to assess credit risk after EMU. While the whole process of EMU has been broadly positive for ratings as countries slash spending and deficits to meet the entry criteria, it has had unpleasant side effects. High unemployment has put pressure on deficits as governments pay out more in welfare benefits. Whether countries can maintain austere economic policies after EMU will be crucial. Levey at Moody's said the rating agency would be looking closely at the consequences of giving up the adjustment mechanism offered by a national exchange rate and the ECB's role in setting monetary policy. 'What degree of flexibility would (nations) lose and what would they gain?' said Levey. 'Printing money — was it anything more than a theoretical possibility?'

Economist Lewis said tax structure would be a major focus for agencies as taxation replaces printing money as means of raising funds to repay obligations.

Countries can raise taxes but there will come a point where corporations will shirk high duties for more tax-friendly climates. 'It's going to be a competition as to which country sets the lowest taxes in Europe,' Lewis said.

Investors may be pleasantly surprised by the effect of EMU on corporate ratings, agencies and analysts said. S&P says EMU should be broadly positive for credit trends within European countries without triggering substantial changes for corporate ratings. 'The most straightforward benefits of a single currency stem from the reduction in cross-border financial transaction costs within the EMU zone, via the elimination of foreign exchange risks and costs,' Rupert Atkinson, director of corporate ratings for S&P, said in a 1996 report.

While one-off costs of switching to the euro may depress profitability initially, the cost of capital should be reduced by low interest and inflation rates. A fiscally sound corporation could even be in the unusual position of having a higher credit rating than its base country, as an AAA euro rating becomes its ceiling, analysts said. 'Corporates will be nearly as important as sovereigns,' said Nomura's Curtis.

COORDINATING ISSUANCE

The kinks in the curve

If debt issuing bodies in potential EMU front-runners don't start to talk soon about coordinating bond issuance, some analysts say the euro market's competitive edge may be eroded. The danger is that a future euro yield curve will be lumpy and illiquid in parts, potentially discouraging investors wanting to get in and out of the market quickly and making the ECB's monetary policy-making more tricky.

'There should be more standardised issuance,' said Fox at Lehman Brothers. But in late 1996, there were few signs that central banks and issuers were working together, or even talking about working together, to ensure euro-denominated debt under EMU is distributed in relatively equal amounts along the curve. 'Quite the opposite,' Fox said. 'In fact, a number of central banks still seem to be very anxious to preserve their independence in the bond issuing process.'

Currently, Germany issues paper through the Bundesbank which sells it on to a consortium of banks, while France holds a relatively transparent monthly auction of government bonds, with the timetable and overall issuance plans laid out well in advance. In Britain, the Bank of England produces a quarterly statement setting dates for auctions, and reveals maturities and amounts to be offered a week before the sale. In Italy, bi-monthly auctions of medium- and long-term paper are well publicised, with the Treasury announcing both maturities and amounts at set times. Spain too has monthly auctions and gives notice of how much paper and which maturities it will sell.

But while individual auction processes are reasonably transparent, a bigger problem lies in putting them together and spreading euro government debt across all maturities. Europe is a long way, for example, from producing a rival to the U.S. 30-year 'long bond' which provides the global litmus test for bond market sentiment. All the EMU contenders have had to build up a 10-year benchmark, if only to satisfy the entrance criteria which measures long-term yield spreads. France has made the most serious attempt to establish benchmarks across a full, 30-year range of maturities. But few countries venture out that far along the curve with anything like the size and regularity of issuance that would be needed to build a liquid market in 30-year euro bond issues.

Countries such as Belgium and Italy currently borrow largely though short-dated issues, a legacy of the heavy debt burdens which made investors loath to lend money to them for too long. Both countries seek to extend maturities, but that will take time. The Bundesbank is reluctant for Germany to issue much in the way of short-term products, while at the other end of the German curve, years go by between new 30-year Bund issues. The Dutch government has a stated policy of extending the average life of the national debt. Britain's funding is spread across a wide range of maturities to meet a keen appetite among London's pension funds and life assurance companies for gilts with maturities of 15 years and more, but some long-dated areas remain illiquid.

Monetary policy dangers

Michael O'Hanlon, chief international economist at PaineWebber in London, said the ideal scenario for both issuers and investors would be for EMU governments to set out a clear debt issuance calendar at the beginning of each year. Without such co-ordination, the ECB will find itself tiptoeing along a fine line in its monetary policy decisions, risking damage to some EMU members' economies while helping others — perhaps unfairly.

The way things stand, Belgian debt is much more sensitive to short-term rates, the German economy is far more susceptible to 10-year rate movements, and the two-to-five year area is the most tender part of the curve for France. Unless major structural changes are made, analysts say a monetary policy conflict will prevail long after 1999. 'The ECB will have to judge monetary conditions across the union, and its job won't be helped by these kinds of distortions in the curve,' said O'Hanlon. 'You may for instance have a situation where the market became concerned that short rates may rise, putting Belgian euro-debt under pressure and pushing euro yields higher at the short end of the curve, but the ECB might actually have its eye on France, seeing France as a weak country.'

Lehman's Fox agreed the lack of coordination could present problems, emphasising credit differentials between individual EMU members and hence recreating the disharmony that the single currency was meant to iron out. Fox said one of the major problems arising from patchy bond issuance from a number of different sources would be increased discrepancy between market interest rates. 'The differences will be there already because of credit differentials,' he said. 'But having localised auction processes will just exacerbate that risk because it highlights localised supply and demand situations.'

Effective coordination would be no mean feat. 'Governments under EMU will still have the demand to issue much the same quantity of paper as they do now,' said Fox. 'That is already a hugely complex task: choosing maturities, coordinating the auction process, getting feedback and so on. To try to do it on a Europe-wide scale will be an enormous job.' Some small efforts are being made by individual countries, Germany and Belgium for example, to spread their funding a little more across the curve, but analysts said this goes only a short way towards a full euro debt issuance programme. 'It is hard to see how it would be worked out in the initial stages,' said O'Hanlon. 'You have a huge amount of debt already in existence in Europe and it will come up for refinancing at different times and in different magnitudes. What countries will have to do is smooth out debt issuing calendars over a long period of time.'

That period could stretch 10 years or more beyond 1999. Bishop at Salomon Brothers also saw no sign of coordination yet among European authorities. But he said the process would be natural. 'If it didn't come about it would pose a problem for the market, but I'm pretty confident it will come about, purely as a result of market forces,' he said.

Some analysts say the effort needed to achieve Europe-wide coordination would not be worth it. Chris Golden, head of fixed income research at Nomura International in London, said any moves towards coordination of funding would be made only if governments were convinced such a process would be efficient. 'Until you can make a compelling case that coordination would have the consistent effect over time of lowering the cost of borrowing for governments, you're not going to get too many people spending too much energy on trying to do it,' he said.

An unwieldy euro curve, where there may be a glut of 10-year paper but little at three and seven years, would merely mimic the current situation in European debt markets as a whole, Golden said. And that did not seem to bother investors now. Ironing out differences in the issuing process may create a beautifully transparent, smooth and liquid euro-denominated market, but the wealth of time and effort involved in doing so was unlikely to offer sufficient rewards. 'Far too much is made of the idea that transparency is necessarily a good thing, either for investors or for the issuers,' Golden said.

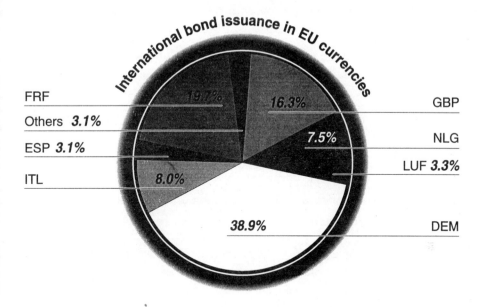

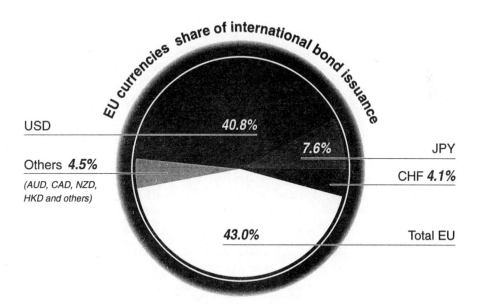

Figure 8.2: *International bond issuance*
Data for January to mid-November 1996.
Source: Capital DATA Bondware

Euro Eurobonds

In the fast-paced Eurobond markets, EMU will revolutionise thinking as credit risk takes centre stage and the importance of relative market value diminishes. New issues specialists, believing the euro has an assured position as the world's alternative reserve currency, say it would inevitably draw in many more investors than the sum of its component currencies, sending euro-denominated international bond issuance soaring. Most analysts believe euro Bunds would be the benchmark against which all other deals would be priced.

At the moment investors looking at a new Eurobond issue ask two questions. First, 'Do we like the market?' then 'Do we like the credit?' The answer to the first question primarily involves making a judgement on the currency. High coupon bonds can prove a poor investment if the currency weakens over the life of the deal. 'With a single currency domestic markets will disappear, relative market value goes out the window and the answer to the first question must be yes,' said Tim Skeet, executive director of debt capital markets at Lehman Brothers International. 'Then we have a credit spread market and the answer to the second question becomes all important.'

Robin Monroe-Davies at ratings agency IBCA agrees. He says that credit risk would be the only real differential for investors. 'Of course, say, unrated German firms will still be able to get cheap funding from German banks on name recognition. But if they want to broaden their base the first thing an investor will ask is "What is the rating?"' Ratings would be the key to opening up cross-border investment by funds and individuals who now focus on debt denominated in their national currency, analysts say. 'Patriotism won't last long once investors see they can get a much better deal elsewhere,' said Skeet.

Those better deals may well be large, liquid transactions which smaller, weaker credits would not be able to issue. So borrowers from particular sectors may group together, first nationally and later on a pan-European scale, to issue on the scale the market demands and reap the benefits of cheaper funding.

Seven German states launched the first such jumbo deal in 1996, a four billion mark 10-year issue. Some years ago several small British breweries combined to launch a sterling bond which has been increased by small amounts since. A treasury manager at one of Britain's largest building societies said: 'It's an obvious idea for smaller societies to consider if EMU means a bigger entry level size for bond issues. They will certainly respond to what the market wants. (Longer term) it may also be a route for the bigger societies if they have an increased demand for funds.'

The same forces could also mean a big consolidation in the Eurobond industry. 'No longer will European banks have protected home markets. (Investor) flows will overcome patriotism,' said Skeet at Lehman. Monetary union could accelerate existing trends, for companies to bypass the banking system and go directly to central markets, and for financial institutions to securitise their assets. 'Many innovations will be rearrangements of existing credit currently provided by the banking system or the insurance industry through direct loans or private placements,' said one U.S. banker. 'I can see all these coming into the public market because the borrowers will feel they can get the best price there.'

EUROBONDS AND THE SWAPS MARKET

Dealers in the swaps market, which thrives on interest rate uncertainty, will be faced with the possibility that volumes in the multi-trillion dollar sector will be eroded. 'EMU may be a golden opportunity due to increased volatility, but in the long term (when EMU works smoothly), it may be a real depressant of swap volumes,' said David Gelber, managing director at derivatives broker Intercapital.

The technical path to EMU has been going smoothly, dealers said, because most of the legal issues are being resolved. But in terms of trading during the transition to EMU, the swaps market is wary. There could be tremendous volatility and yield changes, both among currencies that will be in and those that will be out of the euro, dealers said. 'This could lead to a lot more hedging, but it is not happening yet,' said a senior derivatives trader at SBC Warburg. 'People do not yet have a good enough feel for what will actually happen.'

What is certain is that the volume of currency swaps, in which currencies are exchanged with an agreement to switch back at the same rate at the end of the contract, would fall if EMU succeeds, dealers said. But currency swaps totalled only $1.2 trillion against more than $12 trillion of interest rate swaps outstanding at the end of 1995, according to ISDA, the International Swaps and Derivatives Association. Most interest rate swaps are a 'plain vanilla' exchange of fixed- and floating rate interest payments, allowing firms to minimise funding costs by issuing in whichever form is cheaper for them to use to raise funds. A typical swap enables one side of the deal to reduce risk, for example by locking in fixed rates while interest rates are low, while the other side takes on a desired interest rate exposure.

'Players are obviously very worried about the amount of business we will have after EMU,' said the SBC Warburg trader. 'But I think the euro will be of similar size to the dollar market, and volumes in dollar interest rate swaps alone are far greater than trades involving European currencies.'

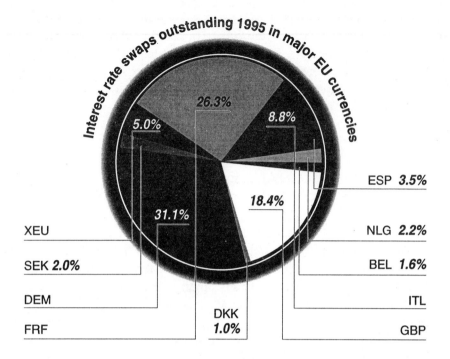

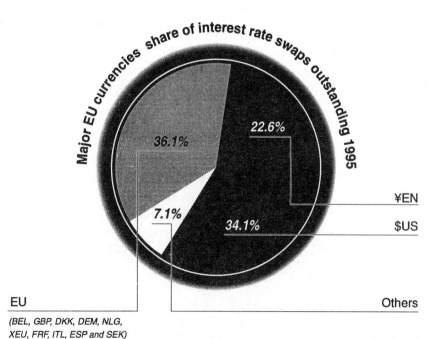

Figure 8.3: *Interest rate swaps*
Source: International Swaps and Derivatives Association. Percentages rounded

'There is no reason why euro interest rate swaps should not also be big business. There is a strong likelihood the euro will become another reserve currency like the dollar and yen,' said Clifford Dammers, secretary general of the International Primary Markets Association (IPMA). At the end of 1995, the ISDA figures showed dollar interest rate swaps accounted for 34 per cent of outstanding deals, while those denominated in the main EU currencies totalled 36 per cent.

A MARKET FOR EURO-MUNIS?

When the fat lady sings ...

Europe's municipalities have a wealth of history and grand tradition behind them but they are poor at attracting funds from international investors. City and regional bond issues are sporadic and there is no European market with the depth of interest and homogeneity as the U.S. municipal bond market. The euro's advent could change all that, although analysts said there would still be plenty of obstacles, both practical and cultural.

'Given the cloak of a single currency, there's a chance that (a European muni bond market) could happen,' said ISMA's John Langton. 'The market needs that. The sort of funding that's been done at a local level could certainly be done on an international basis.'

So far, moves towards European muni issuance have been patchy, although they are gaining momentum. In March 1996, Italy authorised city administrations to issue municipal bonds abroad in foreign currencies. Italrating, an Italian credit agency, said in July that there were some 240 potential issuers which could tap the market. Rome launched 100 billion lire of munibonds in July to pay for a fleet of new trams. In the same month, Milan said it would issue a foreign currency bond valued at 150 billion lire to help pay for projects such as renovating La Scala opera house.

Michael Maguire, managing director of bond guarantors MBIA/AMBAC International in Armonk, New York, said that in the U.S. virtually 100 per cent of such funding goes to the capital markets. 'In Europe you've probably got somewhere between five and 10 per cent of the financing being done in the capital markets.' That could quickly jump to about 20 per cent, he said, but growth after that would be slower. In 1995, estimated U.S. municipal bond issuance was nearly $160 billion. That compared with some $465 billion worth of international bonds issued through the Eurobond market in that year, according to Euromoney Bondware data.

The first, and most important, issue to resolve is tax. The muni bond market in the U.S. has thrived on the tax breaks investors receive. Aside from gaining a sense of civic pride, U.S. muni bond investors avoid paying various taxes in return for funding local projects. But in Europe, tax regimes vary as widely as the cultures in each country.

'My gut feeling is that if the single currency goes ahead — I still say if, I don't think it's a given — then the second phase would mean far closer consolidation of all tax and fiscal policies,' Langton said. Fox at Lehman Brothers said EMU's impact on muni bond markets in Europe would be modest unless tax matters became a priority. 'Yes, EMU will help the muni market grow. But no, it will get to nowhere like the U.S. unless tax breaks are introduced.'

Once the currency risks were eliminated and tax implications were determined, investors would still have to grapple with name recognition, a factor that does not affect the more homogeneous U.S. market so greatly. Credit rating agencies will be one key to overcoming this obstacle, analysts said. 'It will be much more focused on actual credit and less on the advantage of name recognition,' said Konrad Reuss, director of the sovereign group at Standard & Poor's in London. 'It will just be a much bigger and more transparent market than the domestic markets are right now.' He said that by removing currency risk, EMU would enlarge the pool of potential muni bond investors.

'Going forward, whether you invest in a Swedish municipality or German Länder or a French region, this issue isn't there anymore,' Reuss said. Lehman's Fox added: 'the potential range of buyers for any specific city changes dramatically. There's no reason why an Italian mutual fund shouldn't buy a bond issued by a UK city.' These prospects, of course, hinge on whether countries such as Britain and Sweden take part in EMU.

Maguire said there were other reasons, apart from tax and currency risks, why muni bond issuance has been slower to get going in Europe than the U.S. For one thing, he said, competition among European banks is that much fiercer, making it easy for local entities to borrow directly from the banks. For another, the investment base for muni issues is different. 'In Europe the primary buyers of capital issuance are institutional investors. In the U.S. you have retail, or funds directed at retail investors,' Maguire said. He estimated about 75 per cent of U.S. munis went to retail investors or their proxy. 'It will grow but it will grow relatively slowly. Clearly Italy has made a big push to put laws in place. There has been issuance in Spain. There's some level of issuance in France.'

BANK LENDING AND SYNDICATION

The European syndicated loan market has been lending money hand over fist, but strong volume hides a structural weakness. EMU could be the catalyst for change. More than $200 billion in syndicated loans have been made in the Euromarket so far this year, but rates of return are worrying. Monetary union would raise new threats to competitiveness and force banks to look long and hard at the economics of lending.

If, as widely expected, bank income from currency exchange and swaps ebbed after monetary union, banks would be forced to cast a cold eye on loan book earnings. Banks have been lending money to European corporations at crushingly low rates of interest, 'at margins which are not covering the capital costs of anyone,' as one banker said. Banks do this because they view syndicated loans as the handshake agreement that opens the door to other, more profitable, business with clients. In effect, banks subsidise corporate lending with profits from currency exchange, swaps and other product lines.

For many corporations, monetary union will remove the need for some of the ancillary business which cheap syndicated loans are meant to attract. 'If you have a bank that is very heavily exposed to a Deutschmark/French franc swap business, then they are in big trouble,' said Mark Hoge, banking analyst at CSFB. 'There will be no market any more for that swap.' This loss of ancillary income could come at a bad time for bank portfolio managers. Driven down by banks awash in liquidity, margins and fees in the European syndicated loan market have been in a three year swoon. At the end of 1996, British corporations in the AA credit rating range were paying just 0.14 point over LIBOR on average, according to a study by Standard & Poor's and Loan Pricing Corporation. For BBB-type companies, it was 0.25 point.

'Banks realise they are losing money on syndicated lending,' said Hoge. 'In terms of return on capital it has got to be appalling. Banks are getting a better understanding of where they are making money and where they are not. With fee income declining, loans will have to pay their own way.' In theory, this should push up borrowing rates. Remove some of the income that used to subsidise loan rates, and those rates will have to rise, many bankers say.

Though the logic might seem compelling, not all market players agree. Thomas Wolfe, associate director of loan syndications at Deutsche Morgan Grenfell, is not convinced that EMU will mean higher borrowing costs for corporations. 'In the long run banks will cede their home field advantage,' he said, taking the fight for market share into each other's regions. German borrowers, for instance, which now meet much of their financing needs through bilateral agreements, may be the subject of a bidding war of sorts as banks compete to offer services. In short, this competition will keep banks keen to lend.

The consensus among bankers is that monetary union will quicken the pace of consolidation. Tim Ritchie, head of syndications at BZW, thinks this could follow the pattern of the U.S., where changes in banking laws led regional banks to expand and buy into other regional markets. The effect of consolidation on loan costs is unclear. While in the long run fewer market participants should lead to more rational lending rates, observers caution that in the few years following EMU competition could get ugly. 'If you are no longer competing on currencies you will have to compete on know-how and distribution,' said Dietmar Stuhrmann, head of syndications at Dresdner Bank. 'There will be more pressure on capital market players to be among the top three or four in Europe.'

EMU may open the door to a world in which banks, strange to say, have more important issues to grapple with than the rate at which money is lent. 'Banks need to prepare themselves for a time when lending money is not done in the way it was in the past, meaning out of their own resources. They may have to become more of an intermediary,' said Stuhrmann. In taking away with one hand some advantages that banks have always enjoyed, EMU may with the other push banks towards a new role in the capital markets. Because monetary union will reduce the need for multi-currency services, banks are faced with a real threat of disintermediation, the process whereby borrowers bypass them to head directly for investment institutions.

For instance, one of the traditional selling points of syndicated loans is that they can be issued in several currencies. To the extent that European currencies disappear, this advantage diminishes and the threat of disintermediation increases. Banks may be able to turn this misfortune to their advantage. Taking currency out of the equation opens up a whole new group of investors for banks to sell to. Ritchie of BZW thinks that EMU may open up the syndicated loan market for pension funds and other investors. Europe could see the development of a high-yield market along the lines of the one already thriving in the U.S., where banks are active in selling junk bonds and high-yield syndicated loans to institutional investors.

'The bank's job of collecting deposits and making loans may transform into taking liquidity risk,' said Stuhrmann. He envisions a European market in which banks both provide liquidity backstops that ensure availability of credit and also help clients find funded debt through a variety of instruments, be they bonds, commercial paper or medium term notes. 'Banks are being taken out of the equation of collecting liquidity. They will be there to take risk and structure products,' Stuhrmann added.

9

Legal headaches, IT traumas

By Aline van Duyn, Lisa Wilson, Hayley Pienaar and Ruth Pitchford in London and David Clarke in Paris

Sharing a currency may be the grand ideal of EU leaders, but those who negotiate private financial market contracts have more practical concerns. What happens in 1999 to a deal involving marks, French francs, guilders or Ecus? Did the financial institution which drew up the contract warn its client that the currency might disappear, along with the national interest rate used to calculate payments? Is it time to call in the lawyers?

ENSURING THE VALIDITY OF OTC CONTRACTS

As EMU started to look more like a probability than a possibility, financial market organisations began beating a path to the European Commission. They spent more than a year explaining just how much detailed certainty was needed to prepare for EMU in the vast over-the-counter (OTC) markets where most currency and debt deals are done. By the end of 1996, they were cautiously optimistic that the Commission had listened. Even so, disappearing currencies are likely to be good for legal business.

The EU responded to the market pleas with proposals for two regulations aimed at settling as many potential disputes as possible. One regulation cannot be finalised before the 1998 decision on who joins EMU, because it can be endorsed only by the countries which adopt the euro as their currency. Nor can it take effect until the euro's birth on January 1, 1999. But the other regulation was due to be enacted in early 1997, using the powers which the EU gave itself in the Maastricht Treaty.

'The proposals clearly reduce legal uncertainty and legal risk,' said Cliff Dammers, secretary general of the International Primary Market Association (IPMA). 'We would have liked them to be a bit more robust but we got the best we could.'

Kit Farrow, director general of the London Investment Banking Association (LIBA), agreed. 'On all these things, I would never rule out the ingenuity of lawyers in thinking that they can find cases that it didn't cover,' Farrow said. 'But by and large I think people have set out to draft a widely effective instrument.'

Main points of the regulation due to be enacted in early 1997

- Any contracts referring to the Ecu, however loosely defined, will be taken to refer to the official Ecu currency, which will be converted one-for-one into euros.

- The euro's introduction will not in itself give either party to a contract the right to terminate or alter it unilaterally.

- This provision, and all the others in the regulation, are 'subject to anything which the parties may have agreed' — in other words, the regulation can be overridden if the contract states explicitly that both parties have agreed something different.

- Euro conversion rates will be expressed as one euro per number or part of each national currency unit within EMU, accurate to six figures, excluding initial zeros. These rates cannot be rounded or truncated when making conversions.

- Inverse calculations cannot be used for conversions. To convert from one EMU national currency to another, people must convert the first currency into euros, rounded to at least three decimal places, then convert it into the other currency.

- Once calculated, the euro amounts can be rounded up or down to the nearest cent, with a rounding up if the conversion figure ends in a five.

The regulations should cover nearly all the individual contracts due to be settled after EMU, the financial market associations said. This includes most of the derivatives deals, which are based on standard currency, bond or equity instruments but involve intricate calculations about the changing value of these basic building blocks.

Main points of the draft regulation due to take effect in 1999

- The euro becomes the legal currency of each EMU state from January 1, 1999 and will be substituted for national currencies at the official conversion rate. The ECB and the EMU national central banks will use the euro as their accounting unit.

- During the three-year transition period, when national currencies will still be in circulation, a contract which refers to a national currency unit will be interpreted as referring to that currency's value in euros at the official conversion rate.

- Contracts in national EMU currencies will not have to be physically redrafted in order to change the currency denomination.

- EMU governments can convert their existing national currency debt to euros. The EU was still working on regulations to cover sovereign debt denominated in other EMU currencies and private sector debt. It planned to announce these in mid-1997.

- EMU governments can make arrangements for their financial markets to use the euro instead of their national currencies.

- Financial institutions can use EMU national currencies and euros interchangeably when netting, setting receivables off against payables to reduce their exposure to credit and settlement risk and making it easier for them to observe rules on capital adequacy.

- From 2002, when national currencies are due to disappear altogether, contracts referring to them will be read as meaning euros at the set conversion rate.

One party has usually sought such a contract aiming to reduce a risk, such as the currency risk which a multinational corporation runs in its everyday business. The other party may offer to take on the risk to offset another obligation, or to take a stand on which way the market is moving in the hope of making a profit, or to get a fee at a minimal risk.

What many such contracts have in common is that they are likely to refer to a national currency or an interest rate based on the currency, such as PIBOR or FIBOR, the Paris or Frankfurt Interbank Offered Rates which act as the benchmark for French and German short-term interest rate contracts traded in the wholesale financial markets.

These rates are set to disappear under EMU. Disappearing short-term interest rates would be replaced by a single euro rate agreed by national regulators or trade associations. Although national long-term bond yields would probably still vary quite a lot under EMU, reflecting differences in national debt burdens, economic growth and fiscal policies, most people in the markets expect short-term euro rates to be identical in all EMU financial centres.

LEGAL QUESTIONS AND ANSWERS

IPMA and LIBA are in the forefront of market efforts to prepare for EMU. Following are Dammers' and Farrow's views on some of the main legal concerns about the validity of financial market contracts after EMU.

Have you resolved the question of references to national interest rates?

Dammers: 'We want to make sure the successor rate is introduced smoothly from a legal and economic point of view. This is not a legal debate. The markets will decide.'

During the transition period from 1999–2002, national currencies will still circulate. Do the EU regulations resolve the legal problems presented by this transition period?

Farrow: 'The old national currencies will continue in existence, but they won't be separate currencies.' He suggests an analogy with the British pound and the guinea, worth a pound and a shilling in Britain's pre-decimal coinage and equal to 1.05 pounds today. 'They coexisted for a long time in Britain and you could express a sum as a pound and a shilling or as a guinea. They were simply alternative words that conveyed exactly the same sense, and the intention is that from January 1, 1999 the same will be true of the relationship between the euro and national currencies. The two will be interchangeable in most respects from the start, at least in principle.'

There is some residual risk over the legal status of the euro, which cannot be formalised until 1998. 'However much agreement there has been beforehand, you can never be sure there isn't a possibility of someone having second thoughts.'

Do the regulations cover the EMU 'out' countries?

Farrow: 'The regulation on continuity is designed to cover all contracts that are subject to the law of EU member states, whether they're EMU "ins" or EMU in the future or possibly EMU never countries. So in terms of jurisdiction, that's as wide as it could be. The EU can't make a law for non-EU countries so the question of what a New York judge will make of it has to be perceived separately.'

It is common practice in London to agree contracts under U.S. law. LIBA made an estimate based on 1993 figures and concluded that such contracts amounted to a face value of roughly $1.5 trillion. Is this a major problem?

Dammers: 'There is a general provision under international law called *lex monetae*, which says that each state will recognise what other states do with their own currency. That general principle will take care of 99 per cent of contracts.

'But when you get more complicated situations, it is less clear. For example, with a French franc/mark swap, a New York court could say that two legs of the swap become euro/euro and it does not look like a swap anymore, but an annuity. The purpose of the swap was to hedge or speculate and it no longer fulfils that purpose. The court may or may not say you need to terminate the contract, or rewrite it, because it no longer serves the original function.

'We need legislation in the EU to make sure in that case, no one can make that argument. We would like to have legislation in New York and anywhere else it is necessary, such as Japan, Canada, Australia and Switzerland. But in the vast majority of cases there is no problem.'

Does this raise tax issues?

Farrow: 'There are accounting rules which essentially spread the cost of a hedge over the period of the hedge (such as a transaction in marks and French francs, aimed at neutralising exchange rate risk, which should disappear with EMU). You can argue that once complete certainty has arrived, you are no longer entitled to spread the cost of the hedge, so you should take it into the profit and loss account, and therefore your tax payments, as soon as it's crystallised ... .

'Oversimplifying, our preferred argument would be that, say you took on a two-year hedge, it's still a two-year hedge even if there wasn't any uncertainty for the last 18 months or so, and it remains appropriate to amortise the cost over the original two-year period.' The issue would have to be argued out at a national level. The EU authorities 'don't have the power to change national taxes except by unanimity among member states, and that's pretty difficult to come by.'

Could retail market clients claim no-one warned them about EMU?

Dammers: 'German law has *lex monetea*, but if one party is stronger and smarter than another, if the big smart guy did not warn you (about the impact of EMU), there may be a risk that he could be liable. German banks have expressed some concern about this.'

Farrow: 'The regulation attempts to answer the question, "If I'm due a currency that's going to disappear and it disappears before my contract has expired, can I say, for example, that my contract has been frustrated, that it's impossible to perform because you said I was going to get marks and I'm getting these new euros instead?" It essentially says that the mere substitution of the euro for a national currency is not in itself grounds to terminate a contract. That's the kernel of it and it's drafted with great generality.'

Do the EU regulations strike the right balance between providing greater certainty without negating contracts that already address the issues explicitly?

Farrow: 'If you and I have agreed that on the introduction of EMU our contract comes to an end, then the regulation says, "That's fine, you agreed it, you knew what you were doing, carry on." It's really trying to deal with the circumstances in which it's not at all evident that either of the parties has thought about what to do. To save them then litigating in uncertainty, it provides some general priciples about how you decide the questions.'

'I think (the Commission) has made a good shot at achieving that. As a group of firms (LIBA) that are counterparties to very, very large numbers (of contracts), uncertainty about what those contracts might mean in the future would be a very, very troublesome situation. Nothing's ever perfect in life, but by and large our objective has been achieved.'

ECU BONDS

The EU's draft legislation would also clear away one of the major clouds which have hung over the Ecu bond market. This clarifies that the vast majority of private contracts referring to the Ecu should be interpreted in law as meaning the official Ecu, a basket of 12 EU currencies, which is destined to be converted one-for-one with the euro.

IPMA's Dammers says there are four broad types of private Ecu contracts. Three of these will convert straightforwardly, one for one, to euros: those defined as the official Ecu; those where no definition has been given; and those where the contract is unclear. A fourth category of contracts — possibly theoretical, Dammers said, since he had yet to find an existing example — might say explicitly that the parties did not want to track the official Ecu, in which case they would be free to do whatever they had agreed.

On the face of it, Ecu government bonds seem like the perfect route to invest in the new single currency. The bonds are likely to be worth more after EMU because the euro is likely to exclude some of the weaker currencies in the Ecu basket.

But the Ecu bond market has never recovered its liquidity after the 1992 crisis of confidence in EMU. Analysts said it would take a hefty injection of new Ecu government bond issuance, preferably from Germany, to revive the market. Since the second world war, Germany has eschewed debt issuance in any foreign currency, including Ecu, at the behest of the Bundesbank. It is not impossible that Germany might take a political decision to support the Ecu bond market in the final run-up to EMU, but it is highly unlikely.

Meanwhile, the market has been kept alive by France, Italy and Eurosceptical Britain. However, even the French Ecu bond market, which enjoys whole-hearted government support, has lacked enough issues to give efficient pricing along the yield curve. The conversion pledge meant that any pricing benefits for the issuers would be undercut by the prospect of borrowing in a weak Ecu and repaying in a potentially strong euro — unless they could hedge the risk in the swaps market, where there was some reluctance to take on the exposure. The pledge is an even bigger worry for Italy: if it did not qualify for a successful, hard core EMU launch, it would be saddled with euro debt and a lira weakened by the country's failure to enter monetary union.

So in late 1996, Ecu paper seemed destined to retain a yield premium over Bunds, unless and until a credible final line-up for EMU emerges in 1998.

The Ecu attained the height of bond market fashion in 1991 and early 1992. The bar chart overleaf shows how investors rushed to buy Ecu bonds, almost completely eroding the Ecu's yield premium over Bunds, and how issuers rushed to quench their thirst for the paper. In 1991, the Ecu was second only to the dollar as a source of debt market funding.

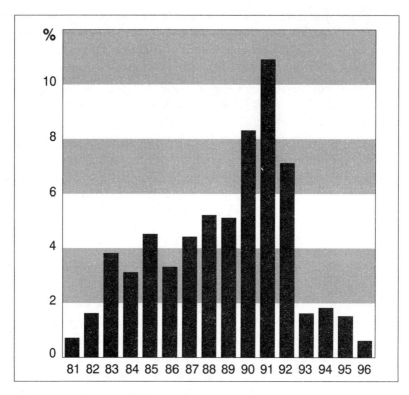

Figure 9.1:   *Ecu bond supply as a percentage of total international bond issuance 1981–1996*

Source: Capital DATA Bondware

The Ecu market touted the bonds as offering a one-stop shop for buying a stake in EMU, saving investors the trouble of putting together their own basket of bonds. The calculation of the day was the actual/theoretical spread. Market analysts devised their own weighted selections of bonds from EU countries to derive a theoretical value for what the Ecu basket should yield, and compared that with the interest rate which the market was demanding for investing in Ecus. From 1989, these calculations showed Ecu bonds were commanding higher prices that the synthetic values. Analysts argued that the bonds were still trading at fair value, because investors were saving themselves the transaction costs of buying parcels of bonds from different EU countries.

This 'Maastricht premium' disappeared when the Danes voted against monetary union in 1992. Investors remained haunted by memories of the morning after the Danish 'no' vote, when Ecu market-makers traded allegations of failure to honour their obligation to quote firm bid prices. Over the years since 1992, fair value sales talk based on the actual/theoretical spread has fallen largely on deaf ears and some analysts now question the value of the calculation.

They say that it is just not worth trying to assess the probability of EMU entry, how much yield can be picked up and the potential currency gains or losses for each of the 12 countries which make up the Ecu basket. They now favour self-made baskets on the grounds that investors can make sure their purchases are weighted towards the most liquid markets and what they think are the best-value convergence trades. The EU froze the Ecu basket before Austria, Finland and Sweden entered the EU, so the basket excludes these stronger economies but includes Greece, the one country certain not to qualify in 1999.

The one Ecu trade which attracted some interest in 1996 was arbitrage between the French government's franc and Ecu bonds. The French commitment to convert all its outstanding debt to euros at the start of EMU, combined with the one-for-one Ecu conversion pledge, drew domestic institutions to buy Ecu OATs to cover future euro payments. The Ecu OATs were more attractive because they offered a higher nominal yield than the standard French franc OATs, which had already priced in EMU. Since both types of bond carried the French AAA credit rating, this was a simple and relatively risk-free transaction.

The French government has tried hard to boost the Ecu market, with the ulterior motive of cornering the market in euro-denominated bonds for Paris after 1999. But as the bar chart shows, Ecu issuance by non-sovereign borrowers has all but dried up since 1992. Derivatives markets reflected the Ecu drought, too. ISDA figures showed just $223 billion in Ecu interest-rate swaps outstanding at the end of 1995, just 1.7 per cent of the global total. The Ecu market gets some support from supra-national issuers such as the European Investment and the European Bank for Research and Development. But with Ecu interest confined largely to individual, retail investors, there is little motivation for even the biggest organisations to bring deals of more than 50 to 100 million Ecus, a fraction of what they can raise in a single dollar, mark or yen offering. The EU legislation may come too late restore the Ecu bond market to its former glory.

A turbulent transition?

Europe's leaders did much to reassure financial markets that they were serious about monetary union when they set a firm timetable in late 1995 for introducing the euro. However, that left Europe's financial industry just three years in which to undertake the technological transformation that EMU demands. It took Britain more than three years to prepare to make the pound a decimal currency in 1971 — and that involved just one currency and only three new coins. In the case of EMU, banks and securities houses will not know until April 1998 which currencies are set to merge in the euro eight months later.

Many banks were willing to make the assumption early in 1996 that monetary union would happen and to start making some generic arrangements. But it took them most of that year to acquire basic guidelines, such as how many digits computer systems should allow for euro conversions.

Banking associations were also uneasy about the EU's decision to rule out the 'big bang' option of enforcing a complete switch to euros at the start of 1999. The EU has opted instead to launch the euro only in the wholesale market. By comparison with clearing banks, the wholesale market handles a small number of transactions in very large amounts, so in theory the back offices of investment banks and securities houses should be better placed to sort out any transitional problems individually. However, the phased transition also means that these institutions will have to be able simultaneously to do business in euros among themselves and to deal with their clients using the old national currencies.

These retail clients will still be buying and selling their goods and services using the notes and coins of the old national currencies. But these notes and coins will each be worth a fixed euro amount, and retail clients will have the option of switching their book-keeping and their bank accounts to euros at any point between 1999 and 2002. No one can tell how many will choose to do so. If the euro establishes its credibility early on, many big corporations will rush to switch their accounts to the single currency. That could pressure their suppliers to make an early switch, too, with a knock-on effect right down the business ladder. Or major companies might seek to pay their employees in euros, or their dividends in euros, which would spread the currency to tens of thousands of retail bank accounts. The EU might welcome that, but it would put heavy logistical pressure on clearing banks, which could only handle the demand if their information technology systems were fully prepared for it.

What they say about the risk of delay

'It will be difficult to win this race against time even if modern management methods are applied and all participants cooperate unbureaucratically.' Bundesbank council member Helmut Schieber, March 1996.

'The currency union, once set in motion, cannot be allowed to derail. If necessary, a delay is less problematic that a later derailment.' Bundesbank President Hans Tietmeyer, February 1996.

'A postponement of the introduction of the euro would be the safest way to doom it to failure.' EU Commissioner Yves-Thibault de Silguy, February 1996.

'A start date on January 1, 1999, is not a question of war or peace; to threaten an end to currency union, or disastrous consequences for European integration, if there is a delay is a crass exaggeration.' Bundesbank council member Reimut Jochimsen, November 1996.

'Anyone who demands a delay in the start of the project is clearly not aware of the consequences.' Bundesbank council member Hans-Juergen Krupp, November 1996.

'For the Bank of France things are simple. There is a treaty which imposes a timetable. We will apply it.' Bank of France governor Jean-Claude Trichet, January 1996.

Time for second thoughts?

If the euro has a more traumatic birth, non-financial companies will prefer to stick to the old currencies for as long as possible. That might help to preserve what many analysts regard as a rather artificial divide between wholesale and retail participants in the financial markets. But some analysts fear that the three-year transition period would prolong and intensify any doubts about the irreversibility of monetary union. The Maastricht Treaty says the conversion rates between national currencies and the euro will be 'irrevocably fixed' at the start of EMU. However, during the transition period investors would still be able, for instance, to buy corporate bonds denominated in marks and to sell bonds denominated in the currency of an EMU country whose voters were finding their fixed conversion rate painful. At that point a pension fund that held debt denominated in the suspect currency would start to fear that the bonds might not, after all, be worth the fixed amount of euros which the fund needed to cover payouts in another EMU national currency. Such anxieties could generate great pressure on the banking system.

IPMA's Dammers said legislation cannot entirely rule out the risk that an EMU country will fail to sustain the exchange rate that it fixed for its national currency against the euro. 'There is no provision for changing an exchange rate if they got it wrong,' Dammers said. 'Regulations alone are not going to determine whether or not a conversion rate sticks. It's mostly a matter of psychology and whether the central banks will be willing to convert (national currencies) at no cost. If the market decides exchange rates are wrong, legislation will not be enough to enforce them.'

Farrow at LIBA said the regulations should prove adequate to protect financial market professionals against undue risk. 'If we had a sudden panic over one member state, then that might cause problems for its central bank. But I do not expect that we'll finish up with a system in which a commercial bank is worried that it's got a mismatch between its assets and liabilities in national currency and euros. I think it'll have sufficient freedom to shift its assets around to be able to cope with that.'

A few case studies:

Deutsche Bank/Deutsche Morgan Grenfell was viewed as having one of the more ambitious and transparent strategies in place by late 1996. It had made plans to centralise business in London and Frankfurt, expecting trading, pricing and origination to be centralised and sales to be decentralised in order to be closer to clients. Deutsche Morgan Grenfell had required every head of staff to analyse the implications of EMU on their business and had produced a booklet on EMU for all staff, to enable anyone from the chief economist to a retail bank tiller to answer customer questions. Deutsche Bank was planning to overhaul systems and procedures for the retail banking side and had set plans to offer clients accounts in euros from day one. It sees more jobs for credit analysts and fewer jobs for macroeconomists after EMU, because there will be less central bank watching.

A major U.S. investment bank said it had set up an EMU taskforce of 30 people, to organise the collection of information, formalise planning processes, establish working groups, assess the impact of the changeover, set a defined strategy, calendar and budget, and establish communication and training. 'As we progress, we'll have to get a project specialist to work full-time on this,' the bank's EMU-team leader said. The bank saw trading teams centralised and an increase in the number of sales staff spread out across Europe.

A large French bank had set up an internal EMU steering committee of 10 people. Most of the group was made up of staff from the custody and securities department. The bank was participating in all the EMU working groups in France and London which were trying to tackle technical issues. It also had a special EMU research team. It said it may relocate some traders from London to either Paris or Frankfurt, and it was working at preventing non-Continental London-based banks from running any active business in euro bonds in continental Europe.

INFORMATION TECHNOLOGY: DEADLINES, COSTS AND OBSTACLES

Commercial banks stand to make — or lose — the most from EMU, but there is mounting concern many will find themselves unprepared for the biggest event to hit financial markets this century. The British Bankers Association (BBA) said it estimated the necessary information technology changes would take about three years.

That means any bank intending to be ready at the start-date of EMU should already have its plans in hand, so it would be easy to assume that banking groups are busily installing trading teams and defining internal strategies for 'E-day' on January 1, 1999. Yet research by Reuters into at least 15 major banks in late 1996 showed operational strategies varying from the super-organised to those who had only just begun to assess the implications.

At one end of the spectrum, there was talk of relocating dealers out of London to centres such as Frankfurt and Paris, briefing booklets were being produced, training was on the agenda, and working groups and taskforces were all the rage. At the other end, preparations were still in their infancy.

Plans at many British banks were noticeably less developed than in Germany and France, where political will to be at the forefront of EMU is strong. Analysts said British banks' planning is complicated by the wait-and-see attitude of British policy makers towards EMU.

John Gubert, chairman of the EMU settlement committee of the London Investment Banking Association (LIBA) and also a senior manager at HSBC Holdings, said the British banking industry must get ready for EMU anyway in order to deal with countries that do adopt the single currency. But some of those questioned by Reuters were vague about internal operational strategy and preferred to take the line favoured by British politicians, saying that decisions on EMU should be put off to the last moment because of multiple uncertainties. One British bank EMU-spokesman was reluctant to talk about EMU, calling it 'a sensitive topic inextricably linked to politics.' Many Japanese banks, too, were still in the fledgling stages of EMU-strategy, saying flexibility was the key. 'It is only now that most people realise something is going to happen and they had better take their heads out of the sand and do something about it,' a banker at a major U.S. house said.

'People who have ignored EMU have found to their cost that it has affected the markets,' Deutsche Morgan Grenfell chief economist Stephen Bell said. 'If EMU happens, it will be one of the most dramatic financial changes of this century.' In continental Europe, Bell added, 'They believe it is going to happen. In

London, until very recently, people didn't believe it was going to happen ... . But now they do, and it's getting closer. We've put an enormous amount of work and effort into the EMU process, and it really affects us at all levels.'

Lehman Brothers managing director Philip Howard said the U.S. firm had set up a working group of a dozen people which he co-chairs. 'Banks in Britain are a mixture of people (ranging from those) who haven't woken up at all, to people who are taking EMU quite seriously,' he said. Major systems changes are needed and Howard said Lehman was addressing this 'so that we can process things on day one.'

The euro timetable

1998

April: European Union political leaders due to decide which countries qualify to launch monetary union, using 1997 economic data which will already have been analysed for them by the Commission, the EMI and ECOFIN.

Next: ECOFIN legislates to confirm details of the ECB's mandate. The political leaders appoint the new central bank's executive board in time for the ESCB and ECB to start work in July. The ECB's governing council lays down the final details of how it will operate. The central banks test the systems they will use to manage the euro. The EU sets a date for introducing euro notes and coins. Mints and printing presses start rolling out the new currency.

1999

January 1: Irrevocably fixed exchange rates take effect between the euro and participating currencies and between these old national currencies. The old Ecu basket of EU currencies is replaced by the euro, at a rate of one euro for one Ecu.
From January 1: ESCB uses only the euro in its money market and foreign exchange operations; the TARGET system operates for making cross-border euro payments; EMU governments issue new debt only in euros; the private sector is neither obliged to nor barred from using euros.

2002, possibly earlier

At latest from January 1: national currencies are withdrawn as euro notes and coins are introduced as legal tender.
At latest by July 1: old national currencies are no longer legal tender.

Whatever their state of preparedness, a cross-section of investment banks agreed there was uncertainty about details, timing and customer demand. They also fear the potentially large transition costs. One test run of an EMU scenario on software at a French bank revealed that of one million programming lines, 8,000 were directly affected and a further 15,000 were indirectly affected. However, 'it is a difficult climate in which to be very precise,' an EMU spokesman at the French bank said. 'The practical rules of convention concerning stocks, bonds and securities have not been made,' said another French banker. An economist at a U.S. bank agreed. 'No one has a blueprint on EMU. There are still a lot of twists and turns ahead.'

Bull market for computer experts

Ready or not, most London-based banks were at least starting to expand their in-house IT staff by late 1996. 'Many organisations have taken the view that they have got to get prepared come what may,' said Stewart MacKinnon, head of European affairs at Britain's Association for Payment Clearing Services (APACS). 'The investment decisions may have to be taken before we have the political decision.'

Computer experts will be well-placed to bid for big bonuses for solving EMU problems. Banks will be recruiting them to bring the euro on line at precisely the time when companies in all sectors are seeking urgent help in reprogramming older 'legacy systems' to recognise the year 2000. Because older computers use only the last two digits of a year, they will misinterpret 2000, in many cases thinking the year 1900 has dawned. That could mean electronically held records will be deleted and automated cash transfers will cease to work. The British government-sponsored group Taskforce 2000 has estimated that up to 80 per cent of computers will be affected, and that there may not be enough experts to tackle both EMU and the year 2000 at the same time. Alec Nacamuli, head of payments at computer giant IBM's consultancy group based in London, said core European countries were relatively well advanced in planning but would not start implementing changes until early 1997.

'Most banks realise they must also review their strategic and business planning to face the new competitive Euro-landscape,' he said. 'They don't always have the necessary resources to do everything in-house and are calling on external consultancies for help.' Since many systems are already running at or near full capacity, banks were likely to outsource testing of new software and platforms. He said many were taking this opportunity to upgrade and revamp all their computer systems.

How long is a euro bond year?

One major problem in adapting computer systems for EMU is that industry standards for the transformation have been slow to emerge. A senior manager at a major British bank said it was difficult for individual banks to progress beyond the planning stage. 'Put it this way, we're not ready to start writing code tomorrow,' he said. 'The continentals are in the same position. There are no design details available and the state of readiness ranges from black alert to red alert.'

In Germany, commercial banks made an agreement in 1996 with the Bundesbank to operate their systems in both euros and marks from the beginning of 1999. 'German banks have made exemplary progress,' said Dr Stefan Collignon, director of research at the Association for the Monetary Union of Europe in France. He also pointed out that the Italian Banking Association was planning EMU training for all of the country's 330,000 banking employees. But what industry sources say they lack are agreements on the nuts-and-bolts rules on which existing bond markets rely. Problems for bond-trading systems include how many days there will be in a bond year for the new euro-denominated bonds — the British 365 days or the German 360 days — and which rounding algorithms will be used to convert historic values into euro debt issues.

'One example is interest rate calculation convention and rate sources. Harmonisation of interest rate calculation would be helpful, and maintenance of quote sources until all relevant contracts had expired would aid in preventing windfall gains or losses,' said Gay Evans, chairman of ISDA.

Dammers at IPMA said 'Lots of people are working on it. IPMA wants to have a standardised approach, but whether you standardise or not, you will not get complete harmonisation.' If there were a new standard convention for bonds in euros, that would differ from the conventions for outstanding bonds. If each country decided to keep the same conventions before and after conversion, then conventions would still differ between national markets. 'There will be discontinuity, either temporal or geographical,' he said, adding that it should be up to the markets, not the authorities, to work it out.

Farrow at LIBA said the markets might get a lead from organisations operating in the EMU 'in' countries, or from a recommendation by the EU authorities. 'It may be we'll finish up without harmonisation — there's nothing unthinkable about that,' he said. 'It may be more efficient to standardise but at the end of the day it's "just tell us so we can programme the machines". I think it's more likely than not there will be a degree of convergence.'

The cost of the euro

It is a relatively simple task to add a new bond from an existing country to current computer systems. But euro instruments are due to come into existence over a three-year period, during which bonds in the national currencies of EMU entrants will still be trading. During this migration period, bonds could be issued in both the euro and domestic currencies and settled by investors who do not necessarily have euro accounts. 'It's now generally expected that the technological costs of a phased-in introduction of EMU will be higher than the big bang method,' said Roger Brown, director of statistics and economics at the BBA.

Banks will need to keep dual entry records of all their transactions during the migration period, effectively doubling the capacity needed for data storage. 'Trades will have to be done at a time when people are at different stages of developing their IT and using equivalent currencies,' said LIBA's Gubert. 'The core standard information — the things banks don't need to check, things we rely on — will change.'

All this may preoccupy the back offices, but it is unlikely to distract traders from the latest swing of sentiment on whether EMU is on or off. 'The answers to the specification questions are more pressing for the IT specialist who's got to get the corporate system or the national settlement system singing and dancing rather than for the trader,' said one investment banker. 'Traders trade, if it's cucumbers or gold bars they'll quote you a price, and they're pretty agile at it.'

10

The European Central Bank

By Janet Northcote in Frankfurt, Henry Engler in Brussels and Mariam Isa and Michael Peacock in London

THE MOST INDEPENDENT CENTRAL BANK IN THE WORLD

In the United States, Fed-watching is something of an industry. Reputations have been made in the markets for those who can pick up on the tiniest nuances of the Federal Reserve's actions, or its inaction. The dominance of U.S. policy in global markets reinforced the need for astute interpretations of every little move by the Fed's policy makers. Europe too has a history of central bank scrutiny, albeit a shorter and more fragmented history. There are those who know the ins and outs at the Bundesbank, and experts on Britain's 'Old Lady,' the Bank of England. But what happens when the European Central Bank suddenly appears on the scene? It is designed to be fully independent from the political sphere. So how will markets know how to glean the right interpretations from an unfamiliar institution which has no time-honoured traditions? More immediately, what will its role be and what sort of information will it use in making decisions? These questions have begun to come to the forefront for market professionals as EMU approaches.

HOW WILL THE ECB WORK?

Operations at the European Central Bank and of the European System of Central Banks (ESCB), which would group the ECB and the national central banks, are defined in a protocol to the Maastricht Treaty. The central bank, set to be up and running in mid-1998, will be guided by an Executive Board composed of the president, vice-president and four others. This 'directorate,' together with the heads of national central banks within the EMU bloc, will form a governing council. That council will decide policy at the ECB, notably its monetary policies.

There are also plans for a third body, the General Council, to be established. This will comprise the president and vice-president of the ECB and the governors of all the EU national central banks, not just those within EMU. This body will allow discussion and coordination of policies within the EU but will not be the sovereign decision-making body of the ECB.

Monetary policy decisions will be made on a one-person, one-vote basis within the governing council. Only those actually present at a meeting can vote. The statutes do allow for exceptional participation through a teleconference and for the transfer of voting powers to a deputy. At least two-thirds of the council must be present for the meeting to be quorate. Apart from decisions on some financial matters (which must be made by weighted voting in line with capital holdings of central banks in the ECB), decisions are to be taken by a simple majority. In the event of a tie, the president has a casting vote.

While it is impossible to say with certainty what policies the ECB will pursue, many in the markets and official circles feel they have a pretty good idea already. The ECB governors, like the council members of the Bundesbank, will be unflinching in the defence of price stability, they say. 'This is a brotherhood which only wants one thing – for the value of money to be stable,' said one source familiar with the workings at the European Monetary Institute, the ECB's forerunner.

Any political opposition is likely to hold little sway over ECB decision-makers. Even the fiercely-independent German central bank says the ECB statutes are sound and should give it even more freedom from political pressure than the German central bank itself enjoys. The statutes state clearly that 'neither the ECB, nor a national central bank, nor any member of their decision-making bodies shall seek or take instructions from Community institutions or bodies, from any Government of a Member State or from any other body.'

The single eight-year period of office for the directorate members also promotes independence. 'Because members of the Executive Board cannot be reappointed, they should not feel the need to please politicians,' wrote EMU expert Peter Kenen of Princeton University, in *Economic and Monetary Union within Europe*.

The EMI is charged with paving the way for the central bank in terms of researching and proposing details of planned monetary instruments. Some decisions can only actually be made once the central bank exists, but progress on the framework for monetary policy tools has been steady.

The view from Frankfurt's Eurotower

The ECB has to meet at least 10 times a year. Its ultimate size and precise location will depend on a number of factors — not least on how it shares out responsibilities with national central banks.

What is clear is that there will not be a geographical division of tasks, under which, for example, one central bank could take responsibility for open market operations and another for economic forecasting. But the national central banks as a group could play a larger or smaller role in each of these activities, and the extent to which the tasks are decentralised will dictate the size of the ECB itself.

This uncertainty alone means that the ECB is likely to start its life in the Eurotower in Frankfurt which currently houses the EMI. 'We will almost certainly start here,' one source close to the EMI said, adding that a new building may ultimately have to be built to house one of the world's top monetary authorities.

Kenen said that the structure of the ECB may point to sharing out the workload with national central banks. 'The governors of the national central banks will have a voting majority in the Governing Council and can be expected to favour decentralisation so as to preserve the roles of their own institutions,' he said.

How will the ECB know when to raise interest rates?

In determining monetary policy for Europe, the ECB will have a large hand in guiding the EMU-bloc's economy. But what information will it use to set policy? Financial leaders will have to come up with a coherent set of cross-country economic indicators if a unified European economy is to work smoothly, economists say. What's more, many of the problems on the statistics front have yet to be addressed, they say.

The EMI has taken on the mammoth task of harmonising economic indicators in time for the launch of a single currency in January 1999. In a report the EMI said some revised statistics would be needed from mid-1998. But time is running short and concrete proposals are still thin on the ground.

'The work of implementing changes ... must start now to make the necessary statistics available in time for ... 1999,' EMI President Alexandre Lamfalussy said. Nothing was more important for monetary policy under a single currency than good statistics, particularly monetary, financial and balance of payments figures, he said.

Michael Lewis, economist at Deutsche Morgan Grenfell, said at least 12 months of harmonised statistics would be needed prior to the introduction of the euro to provide a base year. That could be cutting things fine and even lead to a small delay for the launch of EMU, he noted.

The EMI has said the transition process for monetary data would be difficult, particularly since the initial line-up moving to a single currency would not be known until 1998. But to address data problems only then would be too late. Paul Horne, chief international economist at Smith Barney in Paris, said most pressing was a Europe-wide inflation measure, applicable to all EMU members.

Under the Maastricht treaty, countries wishing to sign up for the single currency must have reduced their inflation rates to no more than 1.5 percentage points above the rates of the best three performing nations by 1997. But they will have to maintain that sort of parity ad infinitum after the euro comes into being, otherwise the whole structure of the single currency could be wrecked.

'The Commission has a Europe-wide CPI index, which is a start, but inadequate,' Horne said. 'Presumably, the EMI will produce a combined basket for the EU as a whole.' That basket will comprise a set number of goods to be monitored and stand as the definition for inflation in all member nations.

Creating a basket for one country is already difficult. In Britain, for instance, authorities tend to revise the goods and services they monitor each year to ensure that changing consumer trends are caught by the data. Economists said EMU must also swiftly be followed by a single monetary policy otherwise the conflicting tensions of divergent national policies could tear the system apart.

Yet European countries have very different measures of money supply growth and the EMI has yet to specify which aggregate it may target. Germany uses M3 to measure money supply. This includes notes and coins in circulation, time deposits of less than four years and certain savings deposits. Britain prefers to monitor M0 which basically measures only notes and coins in circulation.

'There is no agreement yet on a monetary target but the German model will probably be the blueprint,' Horne said. Lewis agreed. 'The financial markets would want EMU monetary policy to have the same sort of flavour as the Bundesbank.'

The problems will not end there though, as different European economies have differing correlations between price stability and money supply growth. 'With the same interest rates and similar inflation rates under a single currency, that problem should disappear over time but it will be difficult initially,' Horne said. The EMI recognises those concerns. 'In some cases there are genuine differences in financial systems of which the harmonisation work should take account,' it said.

Balance of payments data will also be crucial for the ECB to keep a pan-European economy on the rails. The EMI report said it would need trade figures from member countries with changes to isolate and report transactions with countries outside EMU — another huge batch of data for member countries to take on board.

To see just how laborious harmonisation of statistics could be, one has only to look at the efforts of Eurostat, the statistics agency of the European Community. Eurostat publishes monthly figures for the major economic indicators in European Union nations, but it produces some glaring anomalies with data given by the countries themselves.

For instance, Germany's Labour Office measured Germany unemployment at 10.2 per cent in July 1996 while the Eurostat figures came up with 8.9 per cent. And Belgium said 14.5 per cent of its workforce was out of work while Eurostat said just 9.8 per cent were unemployed.

Michael O'Hanlon, chief international economist at PaineWebber in London, said those anomalies would have to be ironed out under a single currency. 'In many cases, the EU numbers include some things that the national figures don't and vice versa,' he said.

MONETARY POLICY

Out of the monetary frying pan, into the inflationary fire

Assuming there are good data covering the EMU bloc for the ECB to look at, the next question is whether it should choose money supply or inflation as intermediate targets for price stability. This ties in with the complex problem of harmonising monetary and inflation indicators, but bankers say there is little dissent among those countries most likely to join EMU in 1999: Germany, France, the Netherlands, Austria and Belgium.

Countries which have an inflation target include Canada, Finland, New Zealand, Spain, Sweden and Britain. This involves predicting where inflation will be in the future based on a large range of indicators, including money supply.

Dutch Central Bank President Wim Duisenberg, who has been tipped as a future head of the ECB, has made clear which approach he prefers. 'For a direct inflation objective, it is not clear beforehand on which information policy decisions are based. The direct inflation strategy therefore, does not score very high in respect of transparency and possibility to justify decisions,' he said.

The Bank of England opposes using money supply as a target because the indicator has proved unreliable across Europe at times, growing above target levels despite subdued inflation. Changes in techniques of money transmission were partly responsible, and it would be unwise to focus on such an untested aggregate at the start of EMU, the Bank maintains.

Issing of the Bundesbank has said that a combination of both targets is on the cards. Adopting a money supply target would help to pass on some of the Bundesbank's inflation-fighting credibility to the ECB, but there would be considerable uncertainty in the early stages of monetary union for the empirical basis of this method, he said. 'A middle road worth thinking about would therefore be to supplement money supply control with an inflation forecast. During the transition period, until we have sufficient knowledge about actual money demand behaviour in EMU, the advantage of greater flexibility for the central bank should outweigh the disadvantage of a certain loss of public transparency.'

The EMI has been doing intensive research into monetary indices to resolve the pros and cons. 'The conclusions suggest that the EU-wide demand for money actually has been more stable in the past than the individual demand functions in the separate economies,' said economist Paul Mortimer-Lee of Paribas Capital Markets.

Currency tensions may have led to flows which boosted money supply in one country and lessened it in another, but one could not then assume the whole would be more stable than its parts because not all EU countries would be in EMU, he said. Greater competition between European banks could make interest rates on monetary assets behave more like those on non-monetary assets, which would make it more difficult for the ECB to influence the difference through interest rates, he said.

BIS research has identified another problem: a given change in official interest rates does not have a uniform effect on money market and loan rates in different countries. There was a very full and rapid pass through rate in Britain and the Netherlands, with slower rates in France, Germany and Spain, Mortimer-Lee said. But he said volatility in interest rates was likely to decrease for those countries in EMU allowing differences in pass through rates to decline over time.

As for exchange rate policy, Duisenberg has sought to dampen speculation that there would be any formal currency agreement between EMU countries and non-EU countries. 'The ECB will probably not pursue an exchange rate objective ... within the framework of keeping inflation in check, it would be useless to peg the euro to the dollar or the yen.' He said this was because monetary union would span a large and relatively closed area where the level of inflation would be determined by internal rather than external developments.

The tools of the trade

By the time the ECB knows whether it wants to turn the screws on the European economy or loosen things up a bit, it will need to have a set of monetary tools to use. Senior bankers on the continent said there was agreement on several key features. A German-style sale and repurchase system (repo) was seen as the main tool for adjusting liquidity and interest rates, with open market operations as a key method of controlling monetary policy.

The ECB will also probably use a combination of money supply and inflation targets as the route to its ultimate goal of price stability. In other words, Europe's top financial authorities are likely to aim for inflation as close to zero as possible. The term 'price stability' was coined by Federal Reserve governor Alan Greenspan but quickly found favour at the Bundesbank, which prides itself on being the scourge of inflation. In central banking circles, the term is frequently interpreted to mean inflation of two per cent or less.

One thorny issue was still dividing the countries most likely to take part in the first wave of EMU, minimum reserve requirements. 'This is the main bone of contention ... the Bundesbank clearly favours such an instrument and wants it in the toolbox of the ECB,' said Werner Becker, senior economist at Deutsche Bank in Frankfurt.

Minimum reserve requirements, if non-interest bearing, would enable the ECB to invest the money at a return that would pay for its own operation, according to research from Mortimer-Lee at Paribas Capital Markets. Some central bankers also believe growth in money supply can be fine-tuned through adjustments in reserves, although others think this method is too simplistic for modern financial markets.

The Bundesbank is the only central bank in Europe to insist on significant non-interest bearing reserve requirements, which restrict credit in its domestic market.

Central banks in Austria, Belgium, Finland, France, Germany, Ireland, Italy, Luxembourg, the Netherlands, Spain and Britain have only token requirements. The EMI has prepared plans for reserve requirements despite the uncertainty. Paul Mercier, head of financial markets at the EMI, said in 1996 that if used, central reserves would not be held in addition to national systems. 'We must have uniform rules through the region,' he said.

Commercial banks outside Germany have hardly been warm to the idea. 'German banks have become used to reserve requirements so they would profit the most,' said Carlo Demeyer, senior Treasury economist at ABN AMRO in Amsterdam. 'It will put us at a disadvantage, especially if they (any requirements) are non-interest bearing.'

German banks must hold between 1.5 and two per cent of the short-term money they borrow from foreign banks and domestic non-banks in non-interest bearing deposits at the Bundesbank. German banks have lobbied hard for the requirements, which have been pared sharply in recent years, to be scaled down even further ahead of EMU to give them a competitive edge.

But some Bundesbank officials strongly disagree. 'It would be legitimate to ask whether one would not run the risk of completely sabotaging the concept of minimum reserves if Germany were to cut its own again,' council member Hans-Juergen Koebnick said. 'The founding fathers of Europe's planned currency union have intended that there should be a minimum reserve requirement and the Bundesbank has already taken a set of steps to ready its own reserve requirements for Europe.'

Bundesbank President Hans Tietmeyer held out hope of a compromise in November 1996. 'We do not rule out the fact that small changes can be made to the German system but we do think that our system is acceptable for Europe,' he told foreign bankers in Frankfurt. By the end of the year, the Bundesbank had followed through on Tietmeyer's words, with the announcement that it would exempt securities repurchase agreements from the reserve requirement. German finance minister Theo Waigel hailed the move, saying it would boost Frankfurt as a financial centre.

Back in Britain, the Bank of England, which attracted large numbers of foreign banks to London by ditching its reserve requirements years ago, was fighting hard against reinstating them under EMU. The BOE says they are effectively a tax on banks and distort the relationship between broad money growth and inflation.

BANK REGULATION

Money market operations

Far less contentious but more complex is the issue of how the ECB will operate in its unified money market. 'Everyone agrees there should be an interest rate band with a Lombard or penal lending rate at the top and a deposit rate at the bottom,' one European central banker said. 'Local market operations would be conducted between those two bands, and there could be both a long- and a short-term repo,' he said.

Bundesbank chief economist Otmar Issing has said the ECB would focus on open market operations to influence monetary policy, and would supply funds to banks through three-month and shorter-term repos. There was also good reason to allow banks to use private sector securities as collateral for central bank credit, as well as government securities, he said.

Mortimer Lee points out that a number of European central banks already take private sector collateral in their money market operations. 'The EMI has indicated that the ECB is likely to accept both private and public collateral,' he said. Bankers say that in addition to open market facilities, which are at the initiative of the central bank, the ECB is likely to have 'standing facilities.' This would comprise a marginal lending facility at rates slightly above market rates and a deposit facility at rates normally below market levels. But Issing has poured cold water on hopes that a German-style discount window (which gives banks privileged access to cheap funds), might be passed on to the ECB. 'It is not exportable for Europe,' he said.

Normally, the Bundesbank uses a fortnightly repo on a weekly basis to adjust liquidity in its money markets, setting either a fixed or variable interest rate to signal direction. It intervenes with a repo of shorter duration if this is warranted. The French, Dutch, Irish and British central banks all operate more frequently in their money markets, and some European banks are hoping the ECB will follow suit.

'I would prefer the ECB to be active in the money market every day in order to know where the liquidity is. But for the time being, we don't have a clear answer,' said Philippe Ithurbide, chief economist at Societe Generale in Paris.

So what else will central banks do?

Central banks do more than set monetary policy. They often have vital roles in overseeing entire banking systems, whether that involves the conduct of banks, the efficiency of their networks, or the level of understanding by senior staff of financial products. Events such as the collapse of British merchant bank Barings or the string of derivatives-based corporate disasters throughout the 1990s have underlined the need for market-savvy regulators.

But the regulation and safeguarding of banks under EMU is an unresolved issue. Unlike the Federal Reserve, which has wide authority over banks, the ECB's mandate will give it more of an advisory role. Its diminished authority stems largely from the Maastricht treaty, which gives greater weight to national monetary authorities and finance ministers.

The treaty says EU finance ministers have authority:

'acting unanimously on a proposal from the Commission and after consulting the ECB and after receiving the assent of the European Parliament, (to) confer upon the ECB specific tasks concerning policies relating to the prudential supervision of credit institutions and other financial institutions.'

This heavily hedged statement is complicated further by EU rules. A bank in one country may establish subsidiaries and branches in other EU countries. However, each bank will be subject to home-country supervision. Some see this arrangement as a potential source of trouble. 'In a system of segmented financial markets, differences in bank regulation can be tolerated. In integrated markets they cannot,' says Princeton University's Kenen.

SETTLEMENT SYSTEMS

Lender of last resort

The market needs clarification over the role national central banks and the ECB would have as lenders of last resort during a crisis. Dirk Schoenmaker, an economist at the Bank of England, says two questions need to be answered: will national central banks continue their lender of last resort operations at their own choice and on their own account, and is there a need for the ECB to preserve European-wide systemic stability?

'When responsibility is not clearly allocated, there is a risk that a crisis will be exacerbated by delays in the provision of assistance,' says Schoenmaker. 'Such delays may be due to misunderstandings and disputes among potential lenders of last resort about who is responsible,' he added.

Schoenmaker suggests the hypothetical case of a large French company that issues commercial paper in London which is bought by the London branch of a Portuguese bank. Suppose the French company faces financial problems and cannot repay its debt at maturity. The implications include uncertainty in the London market and doubts about the solvency of the Portuguese bank. The question then becomes which central bank — the Bank of England, the Banque de France or the Banco de Portugal — should intervene.

Most analysts have concluded that official intervention should depend on the scale of the problem. Support for individual banks can still be given at the local level by national central banks on their own account. But problems affecting EMU-wide markets will require ECB intervention. The primary worry is what happens when local problems become cross-border headaches.

In terms of regulation, the Maastricht Treaty provides greater powers to national authorities. At present, 10 of the 15 national central banks in the EU are directly responsible for banking supervision. The remaining five are indirectly involved.

Studies have suggested a variety of approaches toward supervision, with some focusing on the distinction between small and large international banks. A report by the Brussels-based Centre for European Policy Studies argues for a two-tier structure, with national authorities responsible for smaller and medium-sized banks and the ECB in control of big multinationals. Alternatively, EU finance ministers could be given greater powers to oversee banks, particularly since EMU would probably prompt consolidation in the financial industry.

Targeting TARGET

Meanwhile there has been controversy over the future payments system for the euro currency. By the start of 1997, negotiations over access to the planned cross-border system, TARGET, were at a stalemate. European monetary officials say public debate on TARGET has been so acrimonious there is little chance of a compromise between EMU 'ins' and 'outs' before the ECB is actually formed.

If the impasse lasts, only countries launching the euro in January 1999 would be able to decide who can have intra-day credit in euros under TARGET. In theory banks in all EU countries will be able to access TARGET for payments, but without this facility they must hold a credit balance covering the amount with their own central bank. If access to intra-day credit is denied or restricted it means that banks may not get the funds they need as quickly or as cheaply as their EMU competitors. Alternatives will be available but bankers say they may not be as efficient.

'If you want to know how they compare there is a range of imponderables. No-one knows yet what the pricing of TARGET will be, so there is no definite answer,' said Roger Brown, head of statistics and economics at the British Banking Association. Banks in Germany have made clear they do not favour equal credit treatment for 'ins' and 'outs.' The Bundesbank has taken pains to point out this is because of fears that granting credit to countries outside EMU will disrupt the ECB's attempts to control monetary policy by enlarging money supply outside of its area.

'It is not just or sensible to treat unlikes alike,' Bundesbank President Tietmeyer said. 'A central bank which does not take part in the currency union, and thus retains monetary policy sovereignty for its own national currency, cannot create liquidity in euros from nothing,' he told a political forum in Bonn.

The Bank of England argues that wider use of TARGET will enhance use of the single currency and ensure its success. It also says euro liquidity would be affected only if intra-day credit spilled over into overnight funding, which could be prevented by stiff interest rate penalties. 'No other measures are necessary or could be justified on monetary policy grounds,' the BOE said in a report. 'Any attempts to introduce differential terms for "outs" compared to "ins" would be discriminatory and likely to contravene both single market legislation and the EU competition law.'

The BOE has pledged to smooth over any inconveniences for banks in London. 'When it comes to it banks will be able to make payments one way or another. If there's going to be a problem we will try to find a way around it,' a BOE spokesman said. If need be, the BOE would take on additional exchange rate risk and hedge it to provide euros for London-based banks, banking sources say. But the costs would have to be passed on, which could make this route unappealing. Other routes for 'out' banks in any country would include receiving payments through a subsidiary, branch or correspondent bank based in an EMU state which had access to TARGET there. Although this is currently the most attractive alternative, it may be slow, bankers say. Another route would be via what is now the Ecu clearing system, which is being upgraded by the Paris-based Ecu Banking Association (EBA) to become its future euro payment system.

Bankers say the issue which has to be settled before they can see whether the alternatives to TARGET are really viable is how much it costs to access the system. Put simply, TARGET as a whole will comprise the national RTGS (real time gross settlement) systems for large-value financial trades in each EU member state, plus an interlinking network which will join them together. The problem is that RTGS is a fairly new concept and each country's system has to be made compatible with the linking component.

Some countries are building entirely new RTGS systems to comply. Consequently, costs for use of each domestic system differ widely and countries with a cheap, efficient network could underprice their component to attract more business.

The Bank of England says it wants common pricing to extend only to the interlinking component of TARGET, leaving the rest of the charge to differ reflecting costs of national systems. EMU 'ins' want the common charge to cover the whole of TARGET to create a level playing field.

A symbolic war?

If Britain opts out of EMU, London looks vulnerable but banks in other 'out' countries may be hit even harder. 'For the City as a whole, it probably doesn't amount to much, although it would be a nuisance for any clearing bank,' said Graham Bishop, European financial affairs advisor for Salomon Brothers. 'The ones which could be most damaged could be banks outside of Britain which lose a significant part of commercial business.'

Protest has been heard from banks in both Denmark and Sweden, who are now clearly worried that payments business will migrate to their European counterparts. 'What is at stake is potential conflict between the EU's member states and their respective financial systems, entirely contrary to the overriding purpose of the European process,' Sweden's central Bank governor Urban Backstrom said.

Even Switzerland, which is not an EU member but is home to some of the most prestigious banks in the world, has complained bitterly of unfair discrimination.

'A war among financial centres within the EU is not to be ruled out,' Jean-Pierre Roth, vice-President of the Swiss National Bank said in October 1996.

Many bankers hope a peaceful settlement can be reached in time for EMU. 'I think at the end of the day we are reasonably optimistic a sensible solution will be reached. The twin imperatives of avoiding discrimination and ensuring the efficiency of monetary policy in the euro area should help,' the BBA's Brown said.

The Bank of England, which is playing a significant role in developing the TARGET system, has said it will continue to provide expertise regardless of whether credit access to 'outs' is restricted or not. Both private and central bankers agree that the most worrying aspect about the dispute is the symbolic importance it has for relations between EMU 'ins' and 'outs.'

'TARGET is important for what it stands for rather than for detail ... it's one of what I expect to be a whole series of attempts at discrimination if Britain seeks to aggressively exercise its opt-out from EMU,' Michael Cassidy, policy chairman of the Corporation of London said.

11

The euro: a force to be reckoned with

By Mike Dolan and Stephen Nisbet in London, Rich Miller in Washington, Christopher Pizzey in Singapore, Henry Engler in Brussels and Myra MacDonald in Paris

European economists have discerned some auspicious omens for the euro's future. Many predict that the currency's birth will act as a catalyst for a multi-billion dollar adjustment in central bank reserves, presenting the biggest challenge to the dollar's dominance as a benchmark currency since World War Two.

They say EMU entrants will be left with surplus dollar reserves, which could help to cushion the euro through any early uncertainties by offsetting any flight of private capital to dollars. EMU member states could also use a large reserves windfall to reduce government debt, easing concerns about fiscal strains within the new euro bloc. Private banks and investment houses backed the theory, citing studies including a U.S. Federal Reserve report.

'The impact of EMU on demand for reserves comes against a backdrop of a steady accumulation of dollar reserves by EU countries in recent years,' said Joe Prendergast, foreign exchange strategist at Merrill Lynch in London. 'After EMU, these dollars will become increasingly surplus to requirements.'

A THREAT TO THE DOLLAR?

Studies estimate the drop in demand for dollar reserves within the European Union (EU) could be as much as $200 billion around or after EMU. 'It is argued that official dollar holdings could decline on the order of 35 per cent or more from current dollar holdings, although the range of uncertainty is quite large,' said one report written in 1994 by Michael Leahy, staff economist at the Board of Governors of the U.S. Federal Reserve.

Collectively, EMU entrants will have far more foreign exchange reserves, mostly stored in dollars, than is typically needed for a single currency area or a single central bank. In 1996, estimates put total foreign exchange reserves in a possible eight-country euro area of Germany, France, the Netherlands, Belgium, Luxembourg, Austria, Ireland and Finland at about $200 billion worth. Of this total, these countries hold as much as $50 billion worth in each other's currencies and that money would cease to count as foreign exchange after EMU.

That would still leave the euro zone with $150 billion of reserves, almost entirely in dollars. By most measures, this is far more than they would need under EMU. The Maastricht Treaty only requires 50 billion Ecus, about $63 billion, to be transferred to the ECB at the start of EMU. That still leaves a surplus of about $90 billion in EU coffers. Alternatively, the ECB might look at the ratio of imports to reserves in the likely euro area. If the ECB adopted the average for this ratio in industrial countries at present, it would need about $80 billion in reserves. That corresponds to estimated imports of about $700 billion from outside the likely euro area.

Even if the European central banks decided to hold $100 billion worth of reserves in the initial days of the euro to bolster confidence in the new currency, it would still have about $50 billion of excess dollars. The total excess reserves in the euro zone would then be about $100 billion.

Potential for debt reduction

'Excess reserves represent an economic loss,' said Avinash Persaud, head of European currency research at JP Morgan, who wrote an influential report on the subject in 1996. 'Here is capital that fiscally hard-pressed goverments will want to put to other more productive uses.' This extra cash could then be used either to reduce debt levels or relieve the burden on spending and deficits. Belgian central bank governor Alfons Verplaetse, for instance, has said that the proceeds of Belgian gold sales in recent years might be used to reduce the country's debt to GDP ratio, the highest in the EU.

JP Morgan estimates that if the windfall were used to reduce the budget deficits of the eight countries listed as likely EMU candidates, it would bring down the average deficit to two per cent of GDP, comfortably below the target ceiling of three per cent set at Maastricht. Goldman Sachs economist Martin Brookes said he expected that surplus reserves in the euro zone would be between 45 and 75 billion Ecu ($55 to $95 billion) and would be run down gradually.

'This surplus is too large to be run down abruptly without causing disruption to financial markets,' said Brookes. He said using reserves to redeem foreign currency debt would help to minimise the market impact of winding down the surplus and could have a bullish effect on European bond markets by reducing public sector debt. However, using the surplus to finance government spending would mean selling dollars for euros.

The euro could also gain in stature against the dollar from the use of the euro for trade invoicing and investment, analysts said. After EMU, JP Morgan estimates 17 per cent of the world's exports will originate in the European core, slightly more than the U.S. share and twice that of Japan. Economists say that trade in smaller, less liquid currencies could also be denominated in euros, increasing the new currency's share of world trade to as much as 25 per cent. That would create an estimated $400 billion of extra demand for euros; and that, in turn, could create additional euro demand from non-core, non-European central banks of more than $100 billion.

Even if the total demand for euros — the excess EU core reserves, the $100 billion demand from non-EU central banks and the $400 billion demand from exporters and importers — was spread out evenly over 10 years, it would come to about $60 billion extra a year, Persaud said.

Some economists believe this process would sharply accelerate the already steady decline in the dollar's reserve dominance. At the end of 1994, the dollar accounted for about 63.3 per cent of world currency reserves against 79 per cent 20 years earlier. After EMU, the euro's share of world reserves could rise to as high as 30 per cent of world reserves, twice the mark's current share, Germany's Dresdner Bank estimates.

ECONOMIC CHALLENGES: EUROPEAN, ASIAN AND U.S. VIEWS

Cold water from overseas

The view from overseas was sceptical. Desmond Supple, senior emerging markets economist at IDEA in Singapore, said there was no certainty that Asian central banks, for instance, would rush to stock up their foreign exchange reserves with euros. He said there was a rival theory that non-European central banks would buy dollars to replace their mark reserves.

'The fact is, a euro does not equal a mark,' Supple said. 'It's extremely contentious whether (the euro) will be a positive or a negative for the dollar.'

U.S. officials and private economists do not see EMU central banks dumping excess reserve dollars onto the market. 'It is not in the interest of any governments to sell some or all in such a way that the value they receive in exchange for their dollars would suddenly decrease,' said Karen Johnson, an assistant director at the Federal Reserve. She argued that the U.S. central bank has nothing to fear from EMU, so long as it continues to hew to an anti-inflation policy that fosters confidence in the dollar.

The dollar has been gradually losing influence for some time, without having any serious impact on the United States, Johnson said. The introduction of the euro — especially if it is accompanied by a deepening of Europe's financial markets — may contribute to that trend. 'There is no reason for the Federal Reserve to be unduly concerned about the implications of EMU,' she said. 'The international fate of the dollar still remains largely in our own hands.'

Economists and officials generally dismiss fears that the euro will quickly and seriously damage the dollar's role as the world's key reserve currency. 'Such predictions seem excessively optimistic if not wholly out of touch with reality,' said Benjamin Cohen, professor at the University of California at Santa Barbara. 'They remind me of the standard definition of second marriages: the triumph of hope over experience.'

Cohen said the dollar will remain the overwhelming favourite in Latin America and East Asia, where economic ties to the U.S. are at least as strong as to Europe. 'Once people start using a currency it's costly to switch to another currency,' said Ramon Moreno, a senior economist at the Federal Reserve Bank of San Francisco. 'If we go back to what happened with sterling, there was a basic shift in the relative importance of the UK economy and a couple of World Wars before its status changed,' he added.

In Europe, commodities traders and analysts expect the dollar to remain the dominant denominator in their key contracts. Few envisage a euro challenge to the dollar as the currency in which items like gold, grains, oil or base metals are valued in worldwide trade, not least because Europe's role in commodity markets is shrinking.

Many in the United States believe that the launch of the euro can only strengthen the dollar as investors flee to an established safe haven while Europe struggles with EMU. 'The biggest danger for the U.S. is not that monetary union succeeds,' said Robert Hormats, vice chairman of Goldman Sachs International. 'The biggest danger is that it falters or that the birthing pains are so painful it causes the European economy to suffer.'

U.S. economists say they are more worried that, at least initially, EMU may strengthen the dollar too much. 'A strong dollar is good for the United States up to a point,' said Jeffrey Garten, Dean of the Yale School of Management and former senior U.S. official. 'But a super-strong dollar will clearly have some competitive implications.'

To head off wild currency swings after the onset of the euro, the U.S. and its partners should let markets know what they think an appropriate value for the new currency should be, American University Professor Randall Henning said. 'There is a strong possibility of precipitous inflows and outflows of capital and of currency volatility,' he said. 'It is those kind of extreme swings governments should head off.'

U.S. questions Europe's dash for EMU

One senior U.S. official likened America's view of the drive towards EMU to living next door to a couple having a fight. 'You don't want to get involved. You certainly don't want to tell them what to do,' said White House economic adviser Robert Kyle. 'You just hope they settle their differences. But if they don't and they crash through the wall, you certainly don't want them to hurt your apartment.'

Privately, that's exactly what some U.S. officials are afraid might happen. Although Washington insiders have become less sceptical about the chances of EMU going ahead, they worry that the run-up to, and aftermath of, the launch could prove turbulent economically and politically.

'If I had to distil what I've heard around Washington from people, there is head-scratching about is this really a sensible thing for the Europeans to do,' said Princeton University professor and former U.S. Treasury Department adviser Peter Kenen. 'On the other hand, it's none of our business to say so.'

U.S. officials and private economists worry that Europe's headlong drive to slash budget deficits for the launch of EMU could prove counter-productive at a time when economic growth on the continent is meagre and unemployment is sky-high. 'They're trying to show that they can take pain,' Federal Reserve Governor Lawrence Lindsey said. Along with much of American academia, many in Washington also question the economic reasoning behind EMU. 'The notion of European monetary union is fundamentally driven by politics,' said Garten at Yale. 'The economic rationale is exceedingly thin.'

European companies will gain from being able to do business in a single currency, cutting down or eliminating transaction costs. But those benefits pale against what many U.S. economists see as the social and financial risks of monetary union in Europe.

The ECB would not cut interest rates to spur growth if only one country in the monetary union enters a recession. That is the stance that the Fed takes when one American state suffers a downturn. But U.S. workers have proved to be much more ready than Europeans to move to another state within the union to seek jobs. Europeans face real barriers to job mobility, notably language; and by late 1996 the EU had made little progress in reforming tax and pensions rules to help workers cross national borders.

Above all, there is no central government in Europe that can shift money from one region to another, as Washington does by doling out jobless and other benefits. 'They're going to have real problems dealing with asymmetric shocks to their economies,' said Benjamin Cohen, professor at the University of California at Santa Barbara.

What they say about the EU's drive to cut fiscal deficits

'Our strategy has been to get the deficit down and by getting the deficit down to get interest rates down. The problem is that you've got to phase this in in the right way. If you go too quickly on the deficit reduction, you have so much of a drag you can overwhelm the interest effect ... that's something they (EU leaders) have got to be very focused on.' US Treasury Secretary Robert Rubin, Reuters interview, August 1996.

'It is important to avoid aggravating a difficult (economic) situation through unduly procyclical (tight) fiscal policies.' IMF's World Economic Outlook, September 1996.

'The stability pact is a credible signal that the euro will be a hard currency.' German Finance Minister Theo Waigel, December 1996.

DISSENT IN EUROPE

There are doubts in Europe, too, about the strong euro theory. Some London-based fund managers believe that EMU is being forced ahead before economies have converged properly. They say the risks which this creates challenge the conventional wisdom that the ECB would stamp out inflation with hawkish monetary policy. Instead, they say, the dash for EMU could generate instability and, ultimately, soaring prices.

The three-year transition period between the euro's launch and the demise of national currencies could exacerbate the risk of EMU coming unglued, some analysts say. They believe that the continued existence of national currencies, albeit locked at legally 'irrevocable' exchange rates to the euro, could help to undermine confidence in EMU if an economic shock hits the region or the markets are sceptical about the choice of candidates or conversion rates.

Finland, whose forestry industry accounts for roughly 30 per cent of total exports, is a frequently cited example. If the industry hit a major downturn, analysts say it might threaten the government's ability to honour the stability pact, putting pressure on EMU central banks to maintain the markka/euro exchange rate and adding to Finland's troubles by putting an extra risk premium on its borrowing rates.

Aside from the provisions already made in the stability pact, one way around such potential trouble spots would be for the EU to adopt a fiscal transfer system based on the U.S. model. If a state such as California suffers an unanticipated shock, its citizens' federal tax payments fall and they receive more transfer payments from the federal government. Without such a system, an EMU state could suffer enormous financial losses which could jeopardise its credit ratings.

Under most monetary unions, a central budget plays an important role through redistributing taxes. But the EU's common budget is relatively small and in 1996 the fiscal transfer idea was not under formal consideration. Some analysts doubted the usefulness of such a mechanism. 'Fiscal policy would not be the appropriate adjustment instrument,' says Daniel Gros, economist at the Centre for European Policy Studies in Brussels. 'It alleviates some symptoms but not the lack of demand. The adjustment channel always has to be through the labour market.'

With Europe's labour markets notorious for their lack of flexibility, greater labour mobility cannot be the sole mechanism. So Gros argues that if governments under EMU run prudent budget policies, aimed at deficits close to zero of GDP, they would have enough scope through increased borrowing to handle the adverse effects of severe recessions. But many question the effectiveness of such an accord during times of economic stress, particulary if there is no fiscal transfer mechanism. The Maastricht Treaty offers only a limited provision for granting EU aid to a member state 'seriously threatened with severe difficulties caused by exceptional circumstances beyond its control.'

The euro's strength would depend heavily on which states were chosen to found EMU. If markets believed a state had been chosen purely on political grounds, investors might well start ditching that country's assets and switching their funds into stronger EMU economies, or out of the euro bloc altogether. How would the monetary authorities cope?

Kenen at Princeton University reckons that much would depend on how integrated the euro-denominated debt market was and on the reserves available to the ECB. If EMU states had been quick to convert their outstanding debt to euros, the liquidity of the debt market would be deeper and better able to handle the capital flight.

However, the Maastricht Treaty's efforts to entrench the independence of the ECB mean that the central bank would not be able to grant credit facilities to a troubled member state or to buy its debt directly. Some believe this 'no bail-out' clause could deepen uncertainty in a crisis, sending the stricken country's risk premium even higher and pushing a solution to its fiscal problems ever further beyond its reach.

Rumblings in France

Some European analysts also question how whole-heartedly Germany's partners back its drive to make the euro at least as strong as the mark. 'I suspect potential participants will arrange to devalue a lot in the run-up to EMU so that when they freeze they have an ultra-competitive currency,' said Nigel Morgan, European economist at Old Mutual International Asset Managers in London.

His views were supported by an outburst of dissent in France in late 1996. Two Bank of France members and former president Valery Giscard d'Estaing joined other prominent public figures in challenging the 'franc fort' policy, pursued for a decade with EMU as the promised destination. The strong franc had required dogged adherence to German monetary policy and dogged endurance of economic pain.

Economists and officials in Paris said the debate, couched largely in terms of the mark/franc rate, was really about the relative strength of the euro. 'We are having the beginnings of a debate of what will happen after the European single currency comes together,' UBS economist Darren Williams said.

There was no immediate sign that the dissidents were gaining the upper hand. But their latest adherents were hard to ignore. Giscard d'Estaing is an elder statesman of European unity. The comments from central bankers Jean-Pierre Gerard and Paul Marchelli were the first public sign that Bank of France governor Jean-Claude Trichet, nicknamed the Ayatollah of the strong franc, faced any internecine conflict within the nine-member policy council.

Trichet's antagonists were tapping into a long-standing vein of tension between Germany and France over the shape of EMU. France has long advocated a political dimension to monetary union to balance the German-designed

ECB. The dispute over the future euro/dollar rate symbolises a deep-rooted conflict between German fear of inflation and French fear of economic depression.

'I don't think that what we have now is a debate about whether we want to link our future to Germany or not. The thing now is a problem of how strong the euro will be,' Daiwa Institute of Research economist Bernard Godement said. 'I have the feeling that there is a major policy conflict with Germany.'

The government and Trichet were prompt to issue official rebukes, defending the mark/franc rate and the strong euro concept. The official French line is that exchange rates will matter much less after EMU because the vast bulk of trade will be within the euro zone. 'Our commercial transactions will be sheltered from currency fluctuations,' a senior finance ministry source said. 'What is very urgent is to switch to the euro.' And, the theory goes, as the euro becomes a rival reserve currency to the dollar, the U.S. will find it harder to get away with a weak currency without paying the price in terms of higher interest rates.

Lining up against that view, however, was an increasingly vocal minority arguing that France desperately needs a change of policy to cut unemployment, already running at a record 12.6 per cent in late 1996 and expected to keep rising. 'The way things are going the present conservative majority could very well lose the (1998 parliamentary) election,' Daiwa's Godement said.

Prime Minister Alain Juppe intervened in formal defence of the franc fort. But he made plain that conflict over the stability pact had revived the fundamental Franco-German conflict over politicians' role in EMU. 'Our German friends say they do not want a "soft euro". Neither do I. Neither a soft euro, nor soft economic growth. I want a "fair euro" in order to have strong employment,' he said in a book on public policy. 'I insist that these questions must not be left to the judgement of central bank governors alone ... . It is essential this vital question is clarified before 1999 and entry to the European currency.'

What they say about the euro and the franc fort

'People today are asking questions, because they fear a Europe of the unemployed ... . We are seeing the start of a big debate on what the dollar-euro parity will be ... . It would be a mistake to try to have a euro which was as strong as possible from the start.' Paul Marchelli, Bank of France council member, November 1996.

'If the government lets its intention be known to fix a parity of seven francs for one euro, corresponding to 5.50 francs per dollar, we would have within six to nine months a significant acceleration of growth.' Former French president

Valery Giscard d'Estaing, November 1996. The franc was then trading at around 5.08 per dollar.

'Valery Giscard d'Estaing has hit the nail on the head by stating that employment is the absolute priority, evoking the crucial issue of the relationship between the euro and the dollar and indirectly the franc-mark relationship.' French National Assembly speaker Philippe Seguin, November 1996.

'Thanks to the stability and growth pact, the euro can be as solid, credible and strong as the franc today, as the guilder today, as the mark today ... . A large majority of (French) public opinion supports the current monetary policy of a stable, strong and credible franc.' Bank of France governor Jean-Claude Trichet, December 1996.

'No-one can honestly say whether the euro will be strong or weak ... . The value of currencies is not established by decree.' European Commissioner Yves-Thibault de Silguy, November 1996.

FINDING YOUR WAY WITHOUT A MAP

Chartists seek euro map

For technical analysts, the start of EMU may be a journey without maps — unless a synthetic euro comes to the rescue. Chartists have begun to ponder how they will predict price movements of the new currency in its early days when the euro has no record of its own from which to draw historical data. Some banks have experimented with ways of creating a version of the euro, and the help of market mathematicians has been enlisted to evaluate whether such a synthetic currency is possible or even useful. But analysts said it was a hazy question how far mathematicians could second guess a synthetic euro until they knew which currencies were to merge in the euro and what exchange rates they would join at.

Analysts are also looking to the Ecu or the mark to provide substitute information, but are wary of overstating the usefulness of any of the techniques in a new monetary era. 'We are not trying to build up a synthetic history for the euro because the result we got would be wrong,' said Dominique Barbet, senior bond analyst at Banque Paribas in Paris. 'To date the behaviour of the market depends on how we perceive EMU — will it happen and if so with whom? From the day the euro appears, all that uncertainty will disappear and behaviour will be different from anything that can be described as a weighted average of a monetary zone.'

He said Paribas was 'building systems that allow us to follow the future single currency zone from an economic, financial and capital market point of view.' Paribas was using the traditional method of calculating the Ecu theoretical yield, using a weighted basket of existing bonds from EU countries, to derive what it thinks should be the fair value for euro bonds, choosing what it sees as the likeliest combinations of countries to launch the single currency. But Barbet said that even when markets know all they can in advance of the euro's birth, 'we will still not know people's reactions to the actual appearance of the euro. Will they like it? Will they be keen to invest? Which part of the yield curve will they prefer?'

'All you can do at the moment is plot the Ecu against other currencies,' said Anne Whitby, head of technical analysis at 4CAST agency and chairman of Britain's Society of Technical Analysts. 'There is so much volatility that to try to construct anything synthetic would not work very well. Possibly something could be done nearer its introduction. You won't get great precision but certainly areas where (price movements) might be expected to stop would show up.' Whitby said the lack of exact historical data would be a headache, but not a serious worry. 'It's just something we'll have to deal with — stock market indices get changed all the time,' she said. Whitby said she expected the euro in its early life to be more volatile than individual European currencies against the dollar. 'Not just technical analysts but a lot of other people won't know where the levels are. There will be a lot of worry whether levels countries went in on were right,' she said.

Another technical analyst drew a parallel between the birth of the euro and the switch of LIFFE's gilt contract to an eight per cent coupon from 12 per cent in 1988. He said attempts then to plot back past movements of a synthetic eight per cent contract had produced no useful guidance on future actual behaviour. Dominique George, managing director at JP Morgan in Paris, said the best makeshift guide to how the euro would have performed pre-EMU might simply be to use a mark chart. This could be done, he said, if EMU's founders were to comprise a stable core group of Germany, France, the Benelux states and Austria. But the result would be less meaningful if EMU kicked off with a wider group, George said.

A fixed income strategist for a U.S. bank in London doubted whether any attempt at a synthetic euro would work. 'When you get a Russian revolution you don't just look at the term structure and data from before,' said the strategist. 'There will be an entirely new central bank — not an average of the Banque de France, Bank of Italy and Bundesbank — and it will have totally new instructions.'

However, Barbet at Banque Paribas said the dearth of data about the infant euro was unlikely to leave technical analysts idle. At present markets rapidly digest a huge amount of data on individual European currencies because they were so familiar with the subjects. 'Even if we have less information than today we will still feel we have more because it will take longer to read,' he said. 'And I have never seen any technical analyst with nothing to say.'

Moving on

After the currency crises of 1992 and 1993, markets were surprised by just how much European leaders were prepared to redouble their efforts to forge a single currency. But that is what the movement towards a single currency has all been about: the will of policymakers set against the ebbs and flows of market sentiment and the ups and downs of economic reality. After banks made bumper profits by selling the British pound, against the explicit desires of the government and the Bank of England, market professionals became convinced that it was they and not the politicians who called the shots. After all, what central bank could fight against the tide of tens of billions of dollars? The Bank of England tried and lost billions of pounds of taxpayers' money. What's more, the funds that flowed through the market did not move on a whim. They were based on the collective view of investors, analysts, economists and dealers, who all believed that lower interest rates were what many European economies needed. So, with economic evidence on their side, they were prepared to take on the politicians at any time.

But after the turmoil of 1992–93 died down, politicians and central bankers, including the often-sceptical Bundesbank, set to work at convincing banks and investors that they meant business. The Bundesbank's collusion was vital. It had slowly gained the respect of the markets after decades of strict and coherent policies, so its words and actions were listened to. Now, if the momentum can be maintained, EMU in some form will become a reality.

Then what? The political leaders will have achieved their cherished goal and linked European nations after centuries of discord. But for the markets, the euro will be a currency just like any other, bought and sold as investors see fit. So after years of financial struggle, it will be back in the market's hands.

Appendix 1: Extracts from the Treaty on European Union ('the Maastricht Treaty')

Source: Official Journal of the European Communities, C 191, 29.7.1992, pp 1–67

TITLE II: ARTICLE G

B — Article 2

The Community shall have as its task, by establishing a common market and an economic and monetary union and by implementing the common policies or activities referred to in Articles 3 and 3a, to promote throughout the Community a harmonious and balanced development of economic activities, sustainable and non-inflationary growth respecting the environment, a high degree of convergence of economic performance, a high level of employment and of social protection, the raising of the standard of living and quality of life, and economic and social cohesion and solidarity among Member States ... .

Article 3a

1. For the purposes set out in Article 2, the activities of the Member States and the Community shall include, as provided in this Treaty and in accordance with the timetable set out therein, the adoption of an economic policy which is based on the close coordination of Member States' economic policies, on the internal market and on the definition of common objectives, and conducted in

accordance with the principle of an open market economy with free competition.

2. Concurrently with the foregoing, and as provided in this Treaty and in accordance with the timetable and the procedures set out therein, these activities shall include the irrevocable fixing of exchange rates leading to the introduction of a single currency, the Ecu, and the definition and conduct of a single monetary policy and exchange rate policy the primary objective of both of which shall be to maintain price stability and, without prejudice to this objective, to support the general economic policies in the Community, in accordance with the principle of an open market economy with free competition.

3. These activities of the Member States and the Community shall entail compliance with the following guiding principles: stable prices, sound public finances and monetary conditions and a sustainable balance of payments.

TITLE VI: ECONOMIC AND MONETARY POLICY

Chapter 1: Economic policy

Article 102a

Member States shall conduct their economic policies with a view to contributing to the achievement of the objectives of the Community, as defined in Article 2, and in the context of the broad guidelines referred to in Article 103(2). The Member States and the Community shall act in accordance with the principle of an open market economy with free competition, favouring an efficient allocation of resources, and in compliance with the principles set out in Article 3a.

Article 103

1. Member States shall regard their economic policies as a matter of common concern and shall coordinate them within the Council, in accordance with the provisions of Article 102a ... .

3. In order to ensure closer coordination of economic policies and sustained convergence of the economic performances of the Member States, the Council shall, on the basis of reports submitted by the Commission, monitor economic developments in each of the Member States and in the Community as well as the consistency of economic policies with the broad guidelines referred to in paragraph 2, and regularly carry out an overall assessment.

For the purpose of this multilateral surveillance, Member States shall forward information to the Commission about important measures taken by them in the field of their economic policy and other information as they deem necessary.

4. Where it is established, under the procedure referred in paragraph 3, that the economic policies of a Member State are not consistent with the broad guidelines referred to in paragraph 2 or that they risk jeopardizing the proper functioning of economic and monetary union, the Council may, acting by a qualified majority on a recommendation from the Commission, make the necessary recommendations to the Member State concerned. The Council may, acting by a qualified majority on a proposal from the Commission, decide to make its recommendations public.

The President of the Council and the Commission shall report to the European Parliament on the result of multilateral surveillance. The President of the Council may be invited to appear before the competent Committee of the European Parliament if the Council has made its recommendations public.

5. The Council, acting in accordance with the procedure referred to in Article 189c, may adopt detailed rules for the multilateral surveillance procedure referred to in paragraphs 3 and 4 of this Article.

Article 103a

1. Without prejudice to any other procedures provided for in this Treaty, the Council may, acting unanimously on a proposal from the Commission, decide upon the measures appropriate to the economic situation, in particular if severe difficulties arise in the supply of certain products.

2. Where a Member State is in difficulties or is seriously threatened with severe difficulties caused by exceptional occurrences beyond its control, the Council may, acting unanimously on a proposal from the Commission, grant, under certain conditions, Community financial assistance to the Member State concerned. Where the severe difficulties are caused by natural disasters, the Council shall act by qualified majority. The President of the Council shall inform the European Parliament of the decision taken.

Article 104

1. Overdraft facilities or any other type of credit facility with the ECB or with the central banks of the Member States (hereinafter referred to as 'national

central banks') in favour of Community institutions or bodies, central governments, regional, local or other public authorities, other bodies governed by public law, or public undertakings of Member States shall be prohibited, as shall the purchase directly from them by the ECB or national central banks of debt instruments ... .

Article 104b

1. The Community shall not be liable for or assume the commitments of central governments, regional, local or other public authorities, other bodies governed by public law, or public undertakings of any Member State, without prejudice to mutual financial guarantees for the joint execution of a specific project. A Member State shall not be liable for or assume the commitments of central governments, regional, local or other public authorities, other bodies governed by public law or public undertakings of another Member State, without prejudice to mutual financial guarantees for the joint execution of a specific project ... .

Article 104c

1. Member States shall avoid excessive government deficits.

2. The Commission shall monitor the development of the budgetary situation and of the stock of government debt in the Member States with a view to identifying gross errors. In particular it shall examine compliance with budgetary discipline on the basis of the following two criteria:
   (a) whether the ratio of the planned or actual government deficit to gross domestic product exceeds a reference value, unless:
   — either the ratio has declined substantially and continuously and reached a level that comes close to the reference value;
   — or, alternatively, the excess over the reference value is only exceptional and temporary and the ratio remains close to the reference value;
   (b) whether the ratio of government debt to gross domestic product exceeds a reference value, unless the ratio is sufficiently diminishing and approaching the reference value at a satisfactory pace.
   The reference values are specified in the Protocol on the excessive deficit procedure annexed to this Treaty.

3. If a Member State does not fulfil the requirements under one or both of these criteria, the Commission shall prepare a report. The report of the Commission shall also take into account whether the government deficit

exceeds government investment expenditure and take into account all other relevant factors, including the medium term economic and budgetary position of the Member State.

The Commission may also prepare a report if, notwithstanding the fulfillment of the requirement under the criteria, it is of the opinion that there is a risk of an excessive deficit in a Member State.

4. The Committee provided for in Article 109c shall formulate an opinion on the report of the Commission.

5. If the Commission considers that an excessive deficit in a Member State exists or may occur, the Commission shall address an opinion to the Council.

6. The Council shall, acting by a qualified majority on a recommendation from the Commission, and having considered any observations which the Member State concerned may wish to make, decide after an overall assessment whether an excessive deficit exists.

7. Where the existence of an excessive deficit is decided according to paragraph 6, the Council shall make recommendations to the Member State concerned with a view to bringing that situation to an end within a given period. Subject to the provisions of paragraph 8, these recommendations shall not be made public.

8. Where it establishes that there has been no effective action in response to its recommendations within the period laid down, the Council may make its recommendations public.

9. If a Member State persists in failing to put into practice the recommendations of the Council, the Council may decide to give notice to the Member State to take, within a specified time limit, measures for the deficit reduction which is judged necessary by the Council in order to remedy the situation.

In such a case, the Council may request the Member State concerned to submit reports in accordance with a specific timetable in order to examine the adjustment efforts of that Member State.

10. The right to bring actions provided for in Articles 169 and 170 may not be exercised within the framework of paragraphs 1 to 9 of this Article.

11. As long as a Member State fails to comply with a decision taken in accordance with paragraph 9, the Council may decide to apply or, as the case may be, intensify one or more of the following measures:

— to require the Member State concerned to publish additional information, to be specified by the Council, before issuing bonds and securities;

— to invite the European Investment Bank to reconsider its lending policy towards the Member State concerned;

— to require the Member State concerned to make a non-interest-bearing deposit of an appropriate size with the Community until the excessive deficit has, in the view of the Council, been corrected;

— to impose fines of an appropriate size.

The President of the Council shall inform the European Parliament of the decisions taken.

12. The Council shall abrogate some or all of its decisions referred to in paragraphs 6 to 9 and 11 to the extent that the excessive deficit in the Member State concerned has, in the view of the Council, been corrected. If the Council has previously made public recommendations, it shall, as soon as the decision under paragraph 8 has been abrogated, make a public statement that an excessive deficit in the Member State concerned no longer exists.

13. When taking the decisions referred to in paragraphs 7 to 9, 11 and 12, the Council shall act on a recommendation from the Commission by a majority of two thirds of the votes of its members weighted in accordance with Article 148(2), excluding the votes of the representative of the Member State concerned.

14. Further provisions relating to the implementation of the procedure described in this Article are set out in the Protocol on the excessive deficit procedure annexed to this Treaty.

The Council shall, acting unanimously on a proposal from the Commission and after consulting the European Parliament and the ECB, adopt the appropriate provisions which shall then replace the said Protocol.

Subject to the other provisions of this paragraph the Council shall, before 1 January 1994, acting by a qualified majority on a proposal from the Commission and after consulting the European Parliament, lay down detailed rules and definitions for the application of the provisions of the said Protocol.

Chapter 2: Monetary policy

Article 105

1. The primary objective of the ESCB shall be to maintain price stability. Without prejudice to the objective of price stability, the ESCB shall support the general economic policies in the Community with a view to contributing to the achievement of the objectives of the Community as laid down in Article 2. The

ESCB shall act in accordance with the principle of an open market economy with free competition, favouring an efficient allocation of resources, and in compliance with the principles set out in Article 3a.

2. The basic tasks to be carried out through the ESCB shall be:
— to define and implement the monetary policy of the Community;
— to conduct foreign exchange operations ...;
— to hold and manage the official foreign reserves of the Member States;
— to promote the smooth operation of payment systems.

3. The third indent of paragraph 2 shall be without prejudice to the holding and management by the government of Member States of foreign exchange working balances.

4. The ECB shall be consulted:
— on any proposed Community act in its fields of competence;
— by national authorities regarding any draft legislative provision in its fields of competence, but within the limits and under the conditions set out by the Council in accordances with the procedure laid down in Article 106(6) ... .

5. The ESCB shall contribute to the smooth conduct of policies pursued by the competent authorities relating to the prudential supervision of credit institutions and the stability of the financial system.

6. The Council may, acting unanimously on a proposal from the Commission and after consulting the ECB and after receiving the assent of the European Parliament, confer upon the ECB specific tasks concerning policies relating to the prudential supervision of credit institutions and other financial institutions with the exception of insurance undertakings.

Article 105a

1. The ECB shall have the exclusive right to authorise the issue of bank notes within the Community. The ECB and the national central banks may issue such notes ... .

Article 106

1. The ESCB shall be composed of the ECB and of the national central banks.

2. The ECB shall have legal personality.

3. The ESCB shall be governed by the decision-making bodies of the ECB which shall be the Governing Council and the Executive Board ... .

Article 107

When exercising the powers and carrying out the tasks and duties conferred upon them by this Treaty and the Statute of the ESCB, neither the ECB, nor a national central bank, nor any member of their decision-making bodies shall seek or take instructions from Community institutions or bodies, from any government of a Member State or from any other body. The Community institutions and bodies and the governments of the Member States undertake to respect this principle and not to seek to influence the members of the decision-making bodies of the ECB or of the national central banks in the performance of their tasks.

Article 108

Each Member State shall ensure, at the latest at the date of the establishment of the ESCB, that its national legislation including the statutes of its national central bank is compatible with this Treaty and the Statute of the ESCB ... .

Article 109

1. By way of derogation from Article 228, the Council may, acting unanimously on a recommendation from the ECB or from the Commission, and after consulting the ECB in an endeavour to reach a consensus consistent with the objective of price stability, after consulting the European Parliament, in accordance with the procedure in paragraph 3 for determining the arrangements, conclude formal agreements on an exchange rate system for the Ecu in relation to non-Community currencies. The Council may, acting by a qualified majority on a recommendation from the ECB or from the Commission, and after consulting the ECB in an endeavour to reach a consensus consistent with the objective of price stability, adopt, adjust or abandon the central rates of the Ecu within the exchange rate system. The President of the Council shall inform the European Parliament of the adoption, adjustment or abandonment of the Ecu central rates.

2. In the absence of an exchange rate system in relation to one or more non-Community currencies ... the Council, acting by a qualified majority either on a recommendation from the Commission and after consulting the ECB or on a recommendation from the ECB, may formulate general orientations for

exchange-rate policy in relation to these currencies ... without prejudice to the primary objective of the ESCB to maintain price stability.

3. By way of derogation from Article 228, where agreements concerning monetary or foreign exchange regime matters need to be negotiated by the Community with one or more States or international organizations, the Council, acting by a qualified majority on a recommendation from the Commission and after consulting the ECB, shall decide the arrangements for the negotiation and for the conclusion of such agreements. These arrangements shall ensure that the Community expresses a single position. The Commission shall be fully associated with the negotiations.

Agreements concluded in accordance with this paragraph shall be binding on the institutions of the Community, on the ECB and on Member States.

4. Subject to paragraph 1, the Council shall, on a proposal from the Commission and after consulting the ECB, acting by a qualified majority decide on the position of the Community at international level as regards issues of particular relevance to economic and monetary union and, acting unanimously, decide its representation in compliance with the allocation of powers laid down in Articles 103 and 105.

5. Without prejudice to Community competence and Community agreements as regards economic and monetary union, Member States may negotiate in international bodies and conclude international agreements.

Chapter 3: Institutional provisions

Article 109a

1. The Governing Council of the ECB shall comprise the members of the Executive Board of the ECB and the Governors of the national central banks.

2 (a) The Executive Board shall comprise the President, the Vice-President and four other members.

(b) The President, the Vice-President and the other members of the Executive Board shall be appointed from among the persons of recognized standing and professional experience in monetary or banking matters by common accord of the governments of the Member States at the level of Heads of State or Government, on a recommendation from the Council, after it has consulted the European Parliament and the Governing Council of the ECB.

Their term of office shall be eight years and shall not be renewable.

Only nationals of Member States may be members of the Executive Board.

Article 109b

1. The President of the Council and a member of the Commission may participate, without having the right to vote, in meetings of the Governing Council of the ECB.

The President of the Council may submit a motion for deliberation to the Governing Council of the ECB.

2. The President of the ECB shall be invited to participate in Council meetings when the Council is discussing matters relating to the objectives and tasks of the ESCB.

3. The ECB shall address an annual report on the activities of the ESCB and on the monetary policy of both the previous and current year to the European Parliament, the Council and the Commission, and also to the European Council. The President of the ECB shall present this report to the Council and to the European Parliament, which may hold a general debate on that basis.

The President of the ECB and the other members of the Executive Board may, at the request of the European Parliament or on their own initiative, be heard by the competent Committees of the European Parliament ... .

Article 109c

2. At the start of the third stage, an Economic and Financial Committee shall be set up ... (it) shall have the following tasks:
— to deliver opinions at the request of the Council or of the Commission, or on its own initiative for submission to those institutions;
— to keep under review the economic and financial situation of the Member States and of the Community and to report regularly thereon to the Council and to the Commission, in particular on financial relations with third countries and international institutions ...
— to examine, at least once a year, the situation regarding the movement of capital and the freedom of payments ... the Committee shall report to the Commission and to the Council on the outcome of this examination.

The Member States, the Commission and the ECB shall each appoint no more than two members of the Committee ... .

4. ... if and as long as there are Member States with a derogation as referred to in Articles 109k and 109l, the Committee shall keep under review the monetary and financial situation and the general payments system of those Member States and report regularly thereon to the Council and to the Commission ... .

Chapter 4: Transitional provisions

Article 109f

1. At the start of the second stage, a European Monetary Institute (hereinafter referred to as 'EMI') shall be established and take up its duties; it shall have legal personality and be directed and managed by a Council, consisting of a President and the Governors of the national central banks, one of whom shall be Vice-President.

The President shall be appointed by common accord of the governments of the Member States at the level of Heads of State or Government, on a recommendation from, as the case may be, the Committee of Governors of the central banks of the Member States (hereinafter referred to as 'Committee of Governors') or the Council of the EMI, and after consulting the European Parliament and the Council. The President shall be selected from among persons of recognised standing and professional experience in monetary or banking matters. Only nationals of Member States may be President of the EMI. The Council of the EMI shall appoint the Vice-President.

The Statute of the EMI is laid down in a Protocol annexed to this Treaty.

The Committee of Governors shall be dissolved at the start of the second stage.

2. The EMI shall:
— strengthen cooperation between the national central banks;
— strengthen the coordination of the monetary policies of the Member States, with the aim of ensuring price stability;
— monitor the functioning of the European Monetary System;
— hold consultations concerning issues falling within the competence of the national central banks and affecting the stability of financial institutions and markets;
— take over the tasks of the European Monetary Cooperation Fund, which shall be dissolved; the modalities of dissolution are laid down in the Statute of the EMI;
— facilitate the use of the Ecu and oversee its development, including the smooth functioning of the Ecu clearing system.

3. For the preparation of the third stage, the EMI shall:
– prepare the instruments and procedures necessary for carrying out a single monetary policy in the third stage;
— promote the harmonization, where necessary, of the rules and practices governing the collection, compilation and distribution of statistics in the areas within its field of competence;

— prepare the rules for operations to be undertaken by the national central banks within the framework of the ESCB;

— promote the efficiency of cross-border payments;

— supervise the technical preparation of Ecu banknotes.

At the latest by 31 December 1996, the EMI shall specify the regulatory, organizational and logistical framework necessary for the ESCB to perform its tasks in the third stage. This framework shall be submitted for decision to the ECB at the date of its establishment.

4. The EMI, acting by a majority of two thirds of the members of its Council, may:

— formulate opinions or recommendations on the overall orientation of monetary policy and exchange rate policy as well as on related measures introduced in each Member State;

— submit opinions or recommendations to Governments and to the Council on policies which might affect the internal or external monetary situation in the Community and, in particular, the functioning of the European Monetary System;

— make recommendations to the monetary authorities of the Member States concerning the conduct of their monetary policy.

5. The EMI, acting unanimously, may decided to publish its opinions and its recommendations.

6. The EMI shall be consulted by the Council regarding any proposed Community act within its field of competence.

Within the limits and under the conditions set out by the Council, acting by a qualified majority on a proposal from the Commission and after consulting the European Parliament and the EMI, the EMI shall be consulted by the authorities of the Member States on any draft legislative provision within its field of competence.

7. The Council may, acting unanimously on a proposal from the Commission and after consulting the European Parliament and the EMI, confer upon the EMI other tasks for the preparation of the third stage.

8. Where this Treaty provides for a consultative role for the ECB, references to the ECB shall be read as referring to the EMI before the establishment of the ECB ... .

9. During the second stage, the term 'ECB' used in Articles 173, 175, 176, 177, 180 and 215 shall be read as referring to the EMI.

Article 109g

The currency composition of the Ecu basket shall not be changed. From the start of the third stage, the value of the Ecu shall be irrevocably fixed in accordance with Article 109l(4).

Article 109j

1. The Commission and the EMI shall report to the Council on the progress made in the fulfilment by the Member States of their obligations regarding the achievement of economic and monetary union. These reports shall include an examination of the compatibility between each Member State's national legislation, including the statutes of its national central bank, and Articles 107 and 108 of this Treaty and the Statute of the ESCB. The report shall also examine the achievement of a high degree of sustainable convergence by reference to the fulfilment by each Member State of the following criteria:

— the achievement of a high degree of price stability; this will be apparent from a rate of inflation which is close to that of, at most, the three best performing Member States in terms of price stability;

— the sustainability of the government financial position; this will be apparent from having achieved a government budgetary position without a deficit that is excessive as determined in accordance with Article 104c(6);

— the observance of the normal fluctuation margins provided for by the Exchange Rate Mechanism of the European Monetary System, for at least two years, without devaluing against the currency of any other Member State.

The durability of convergence achieved by the Member State and of its participation in the Exchange Rate Mechanism of the European Monetary System being reflected in the long-term interest rate levels.

The four criteria mentioned in this paragraph and the relevant periods over which they are to be respected are developed further in a Protocol annexed to this Treaty. The reports of the Commission and the EMI shall also take account of the development of the Ecu, the results of the integration of markets, the situation and development of the balances of payments on current account and an examination of the development of unit labour costs and other price indices.

2. On the basis of these reports, the Council, acting by a qualified majority on a recommendation from the Commission, shall assess:

— for each Member State, whether it fulfils the necessary conditions for the adoption of a single currency; ...

— and recommend its findings to the Council, meeting in the composition of the Heads of State or Government. The European Parliament shall be consulted and forward its opinion to the Council, meeting in the composition of the Heads of State or Government ... .

4. If by the end of 1997 the date for the beginning of the third stage has not been set, the third stage shall start on 1 January 1999. Before 1 July 1998, the Council, meeting in the composition of Heads of State or Government, after a repetition of the procedure provided for in paragraphs 1 and 2 ... taking into account the reports referred to in paragraph 1 and the opinion of the European parliament, shall, acting by a qualified majority and on the basis of the recommendations of the Council referred to in paragraph 2, confirm which Member States fulfil the necessary conditions for the adoption of a single currency.

Article 109k

1. ... If the Council has confirmed which Member States fulfil the necessary conditions for the adoption of a single currency ... those Member States which do not fulfil the conditions shall have a derogation as defined in paragraph 3 of this Article ... .

2. At least once every two years, or at the request of a Member State with a derogation, the Commission and the ECB shall report to the Council in accordance with the procedure laid down in Article 109j(1). After consulting the European Parliament and after discussion in the Council, meeting in the composition of the Heads of State or Government, the Council shall, acting by a qualified majority on a proposal from the Commission, decide which Member States with a derogation fulfil the necessary conditions ... and abrogate the derogations of the Member States concerned.

3. A derogation referred to in paragraph 1 shall entail that the following Articles do not apply to the Member State concerned: Articles 104c(9) and (11), 105(1), (2), (3) and (5), 105a, 108a, 109, 109a(2)(b). The exclusion of such a Member State and its national central bank from rights and obligations within the ESCB is laid down in Chapter IX of the Statute of the ESCB ... .

5. The voting rights of Member States with a derogation shall be suspended for the Council decisions referred to in the Articles of this Treaty mentioned in paragraph 3 ... .

6. Articles 109h and 109i shall continue to apply to a Member State with a derogation.

Article 109l

1. Immediately after the decision on the date for the beginning of the third stage has been taken in accordance with Article 109j(3), or, as the case may be, immediately after 1 July 1998:
— the Council shall adopt the provisions referred to in Article 106(6);
— the governments of the Member States without a derogation shall appoint, in accordance with the procedure set out in Article 50 of the Statute of the ESCB, the President, the Vice-President and the other members of the Executive Board of the ECB. If there are Member States with a derogation, the number of members of the Executive Board may be smaller than provided for in Article 11.1 of the Statute of the ESCB, but in no circumstances shall it be less than four.

As soon as the Executive Board is appointed, the ESCB and the ECB shall be established and shall prepare for their full operation ... . The full exercise of their powers shall start from the first day of the third stage.

2. As soon as the ECB is established, it shall, if necessary, take over tasks of the EMI ... .

3. If and as long as there are Member States with a derogation, and without prejudice to Article 106(3) of this Treaty, the General Council of the ECB ... shall be constituted as a third decision-making body of the ECB.

4. At the starting date of the third stage, the Council shall, acting with the unanimity of the Member States without a derogation, on a proposal from the Commission and after consulting the ECB, adopt the conversion rates at which their currencies shall be irrevocably fixed and at which irrevocably fixed rate the Ecu shall be substituted for these currencies, and the Ecu will become a currency in its own right. This measure shall by itself not modify the external value of the Ecu. The Council shall, acting according to the same procedure, also take the other measures necessary for the rapid introduction of the Ecu as the single currency of those Member States.

5. If it is decided, according to the procedure set out in Article 109k(2), to abrogate a derogation, the Council shall, acting with the unanimity of the Member States without a derogation and the Member State concerned, on a proposal from the Commission and after consulting the ECB, adopt the rate at which the Ecu shall be substituted for the currency of the Member State concerned, and take the other measures necessary for the introduction of the Ecu as the single currency in the Member State concerned.

Appendix 2: Selected protocols annexed to the Maastricht Treaty

Source: Official Journal of the European Communities, C 191, 29.7.1992, pp 84–85, 87–89.

Protocol on the excessive deficit procedure

Article 1

The reference values referred to in Article 104c(2) of this Treaty are:
— Three per cent for the ratio of the planned or actual government deficit to gross domestic product at market prices;
— 60 per cent for the ratio of government debt to gross domestic product at market prices.

Article 2

In Article 104c of this Treaty and in this Protocol:
— government means general government, that is central government, regional or local government and social security funds, to the exclusion of commercial operations, as defined in the European System of Integrated Economic Accounts;
— deficit means net borrowing as defined in the European System of Integrated Economic Accounts;
— investment means gross fixed capital formation as defined in the European System of Integrated Economic Accounts;

— debt means total gross debt at nominal value outstanding at the end of the year and consolidated between and within the sectors of general government as defined in the first indent.

Article 3

In order to ensure the effectiveness of the excessive deficit procedure, the governments of the Member States shall be responsible under this procedure for the deficits of general government as defined in the first indent of Article 2. The Member States shall ensure that national procedures in the Budgetary area enable them to meet their obligations in this area deriving from this Treaty. The Member States shall report their planned and actual deficits and the levels of their debt promptly and regularly to the Commission.

Article 4

The statistical data to be used for the application of this Protocol shall be provided by the Commission.

Protocol on the convergence criteria

Article 1

The criterion on price stability referred to in the first indent of Article 109j(1) of this Treaty shall mean that a Member State has a price performance that is sustainable and an average rate of inflation, observed over a period of one year before the examination, that does not exceed by more than 1 1/2 percentage points that of, at most, the three best performing Member States in terms of price stability. Inflation shall be measured by means of the consumer price index on a comparable basis, taking into account differences in national definitions.

Article 2

The criterion on the government budgetary position referred to in the second indent of Article 109j(1) of this treaty shall mean that at the time of the examination the Member State is not the subject of a Council decision under Article 104c(6) of this Treaty that an excessive deficit exists.

Article 3

The criterion on participation in the Exchange Rate Mechanism of the European Monetary System referred to in the third indent of Article 109j(1) of this Treaty shall mean that a Member State has respected the normal fluctuation margins provided for by the Exchange Rate Mechanism of the European Monetary System without severe tensions for at least the last two years before the examination. In particular, the Member State shall not have devalued its currency's bilateral central rate against any other Member State's currency on its own initiative for the same period.

Article 4

The criterion on the convergence of interest rates referred to in the fourth indent of Article 109j(1) of this Treaty shall mean that, observed over a period of one year before the examination, a Member State has had an average nominal long-term interest rate that does not exceed by more than two percentage points that of, at most, the three best performing Member States in terms of price stability. Interest rates shall be measured on the basis of long term government bonds or comparable securities, taking into account differences in national definitions.

Article 5

The statistical data to be used for the application of this protocol shall be provided by the Commission.

Article 6

The Council shall, acting unanimously on a proposal from the Commission and after consulting the European Parliament, the EMI or the ECB as the case may be, and the Committee referred to in Article 109c, adopt appropriate provisions to lay down the details of the convergence criteria referred to Article 109j of this Treaty, which shall then replace this Protocol.

Protocol on the transition to the third stage of EMU

The High Contracting Parties

Declare the irreversible character of the Community's movement to the third stage of Economic and Monetary Union by signing the new Treaty provisions on Economic and Monetary Union.

Therefore all Member States shall, whether they fulfil the necessary conditions for the adoption of a single currency or not, respect the will for the Community to enter swiftly into the third stage, and therefore no Member State shall prevent the entering into the third stage.

If by the end of 1997 the date of the beginning of the third stage has not been set, the Member States concerned, the Community institutions and other bodies involved shall expedite all preparatory work during 1998, in order to enable the Community to enter the third stage irrevocably on 1 January 1999 and to enable the ECB and ESCB to start their full functioning from this date ... .

Protocol on certain provisions related to the United Kingdom

The High Contracting Parties

RECOGNIZING that the United Kingdom shall not be obliged or committed to move to the third stage of economic and monetary union without a separate decision to do so by its government and Parliament,

NOTING the practice of the government of the United Kingdom to fund its borrowing requirement by the sale of debt to the private sector,

HAVE AGREED the following provisions, which shall be annexed to the Treaty establishing the European Community:

1. The United Kingdom shall notify the Council whether it intends to move to the third stage before the Council makes its assessment under Article 109j(2) of this Treaty;

Unless the United Kingdom notifies the Council that it intends to move to the third stage, it shall be under no obligation to do so ... .

2. Paragraphs 3 to 9 shall have effect if the United Kingdom notifies the Council that it does not intend to move to the third stage.

3. The United Kingdom shall not be included among the majority of Member States which fulfil the necessary conditions referred to in the second indent of Article 109j(2) and the first indent of Article 109j(3) of this Treaty.

4. The United Kingdom shall retain its powers in the field of monetary policy according to national law.

5. Articles 3a(2), 104c(1), (9) and (11), 105(1) to (5), 105a, 107, 108, 108a, 109, 109a(1) and (2)(b) and 109l(4) and (5) of this Treaty shall not apply to the United Kingdom. In these provisions references to the Community or the Member States shall not include the United Kingdom and references to national central banks shall not include the Bank of England.

6. Articles 109e(4) and 109h and i of this Treaty shall continue to apply to the United Kingdom. Articles 109c(4) and 109m shall apply to the United Kingdom as if it had a derogation.

7. The voting rights of the United Kingdom shall be suspended in respect of acts of the Council referred to in Articles listed in paragraph 5. For this purpose the weighted votes of the United Kingdom shall be excluded from any calculation of a qualified majority under Article 109k(5) of this Treaty.

The United Kingdom shall also have no right to participate in the appointment of the President, the Vice-President and the other members of the Executive Board of the ECB under Articles 109a(2)(b) and 109l(1) of this Treaty.

8. Articles 3, 4, 6, 7, 9.2, 10.1, 10.3, 11.2, 12.1, 14, 16, 18 to 20, 22, 23, 26, 27, 30 to 34, 50 and 52 of the Protocol on the Statute of the European System of Central Banks and of the European Central Bank ('the Statute') shall not apply to the United Kingdom.

In those Articles, references to the Community or the Member States shall not include the United Kingdom and references to national central banks or shareholders shall not include the Bank of England.

References in Articles 10.3 and 30.2 of the Statute to 'subscribed capital of the ECB' shall not include capital subscribed by the Bank of England.

9. Article 109l(3) of this Treaty and Articles 44 to 48 of the Statute shall have effect, whether or not there is any Member State with a derogation, subject to the following amendments:

(a) References in Article 44 to the tasks of the ECB and the EMI shall include those tasks that still need to be performed in the third stage owing to any decision of the United Kingdom not to move to that Stage.

(b) In addition to the tasks referred to in Article 47 the ECB shall also give advice in relation to and contribute to the preparation of any decision of the Council with regard to the United Kingdom taken in accordance with paragraphs 10(a) and 10(c).

(c) The Bank of England shall pay up its subscription to the capital of the ECB as a contribution to its operational costs on the same basis as national central banks of Member States with a derogation.

10. If the United Kingdom does not move to the third stage, it may change its notification at any time after the beginning of that stage. In that event:

(a) The United Kingdom shall have the right to move to the third stage provided only that it satisfies the necessary conditions. The Council, acting at the request of the United Kingdom and under the conditions and in accordance with the procedure laid down in Article 109k(2) of this Treaty, shall decide whether it fulfills the necessary conditions.

(b) The Bank of England shall pay up its subscribed capital, transfer to the ECB foreign reserve assets and contribute to its reserves on the same basis as the national central bank of a Member State whose derogation has been abrogated.

(c) The Council, acting under the conditions and in accordance with the procedure laid down in Article 109l(5) of this Treaty, shall take all other necessary decisions to enable the United Kingdom to move to the third stage.

If the United Kingdom moves to the third stage pursuant to the provisions of this protocol, paragraphs 3 to 9 shall cease to have effect.

11. Notwithstanding Articles 104 and 109e(3) of this Treaty and Article 21.1 of the Statute, the government of the United Kingdom may maintain its 'ways and means' facility with the Bank of England if and so long as the United Kingdom does not move to the third stage.

Protocol on certain provisions relating to Denmark

The High Contracting Parties

DESIRING to settle, in accordance with the general objectives of the Treaty establishing the European Community, certain particular problems existing at the present time,

TAKING INTO ACCOUNT that the Danish Constitution contains provisions which may imply a referendum in Denmark prior to Danish participation in the third stage of Economic and Monetary Union,

HAVE AGREED on the following provisions, which shall be annexed to the Treaty establishing the European Community:

1. The Danish Government shall notify the Council of its position concerning participation in the third stage before the Council makes its assessment under Article 109j(2) of this Treaty.

2. In the event of a notification that Denmark will not participate in the third stage, Denmark shall have an exemption. The effect of the exemption shall be that all Articles and provisions of this Treaty and the Statute of the ESCB referring to a derogation shall be applicable to Denmark.

3. In such case, Denmark shall not be included among the majority of Member States which fulfil the necessary conditions referred to in the second indent of Article 109j(2) and the first indent of Article 109j(3) of this Treaty.

4. As for the abrogation of the exemption, the procedure referred to in Article 109k(2) shall only be initiated at the request of Denmark.

5. In the event of abrogation of the exemption status, the provisions of this Protocol shall cease to apply.

Appendix 3: How the EU takes decisions

MONETARY COMMITTEE

A publicity-shy grouping of national finance ministry and central bank officials, the Committee has an influential role in formulating policy on EMU and the ERM. The Committee typically meets just before regularly scheduled gatherings of the ECOFIN (qv), preparing the groundwork on issues the ministers will eventually decide. In 1996, its work included technical aspects of the stability pact and ERM II. The Committee advises the ECOFIN on whether a government is running an excessive deficit. It convenes whenever any ERM currency needs devaluation or revaluation and decides on applications to join or re-enter the currency grid. Decisions are made by consensus and are usually kept secret from the public. The Committee is due to be replaced under EMU by an Economic and Financial Committee, whose membership has yet to be specified.

EUROPEAN COMMISSION

The EU's executive, the Commission is one of the most important agents in the drive towards a common currency. Its 1995 report outlining how the EU should proceed towards EMU generated considerable progress. The Commission, along with the European Monetary Institute (qv), reports annually to the ECOFIN on the efforts of the EU's 15 nations to meet the Maastricht conditions for monetary union. It makes proposals on other elements of EMU such as the stability pact, the legal framework for the euro, and ERM II, and takes part in evaluating whether countries are running excessive deficits. A Commission member normally takes part in the discussions of the

ECOFIN and EMI Council. Commission representatives attend the Monetary Committee.

EUROPEAN MONETARY INSTITUTE (EMI)

Forerunner to a European Central Bank (ECB) (see Chapter 9), the institution has primary responsibility for developing the ECB's monetary policy tools and, along with the Commission, for annual assessments of member states' readiness for monetary union.

The Maastricht Treaty required the EMI to specify, by the end of 1996, how the European System of Central Banks (ESCB), linking the ECB and national central banks, would operate inside a monetary union. However, this report was unlikely to be finalised until early 1997. The institution is also responsible for developing TARGET (see Chapter 9) and has played a leading role in developing ERM II.

Other areas of EMI concern include preparing EU-wide statistics and foreign exchange policy and planning the production of euro notes and coins. EU central bank governors form the EMI's Council, which meets regularly in Frankfurt. An EMI representative is present at meetings of the Monetary Committee. The EMI will cease to exist once the ECB becomes operational, probably in July 1998.

COUNCIL OF MINISTERS (ECOFIN)

The main legislative body within the EU, the Council is made up of the economy and finance ministers of the 15 member states. With the advice of the Commission, the EMI and the Monetary Committee, the Council makes formal decisions on virtually all aspects of EMU.

Major areas where the Council has influence include:

- Excessive deficits procedure. A qualified majority of the ECOFIN would decide under EMU whether a member state was running too high a budget deficit. The next step, whether fines should be levied, would be decided by a two-thirds majority of the countries within EMU, excluding the country under scrutiny.

- EMU stability pact (see Chapter 1). The ECOFIN was primarily responsible for working out the compromise accepted by EU leaders in December 1996.

- ERM II. The ECOFIN has no formal role because the new arrangements will lie outside the EU's normal legislative process. Like the current ERM, the arrangement will be based on intergovernmental agreement and brought into force by consensus, probably through a political resolution by the European Council (qv) followed by an agreement among central banks on its day-to-day operations.

- Legal framework (see Chapter 9). The ECOFIN is primarily responsible for drafting regulations designed to ensure legal certainty over financial market contracts under EMU.

EUROPEAN COUNCIL

The heads of state or government, who typically meet twice a year, in June and December, for informal discussions, giving them a chance to talk freely. On EMU, they consider legislation proposed by the ECOFIN and usually rubber-stamp it. In early 1998, the heads of state and government will, under a qualified majority, vote on which members qualify for EMU. This decision will follow the ECOFIN's evaluation.

EUROPEAN PARLIAMENT

The parliament has limited powers on EMU matters but must be consulted, under the Maastricht Treaty, on many of the decisions taken.

Appendix 4: Stability and growth pact

Following are key extracts from the EU report outlining the pact aimed at enforcing fiscal discipline under EMU. The extracts are taken from the official summary of the conclusions of the Dublin summit held in December 1996. The Maastricht Treaty articles and protocols referred to in this text can be found in Appendices 1 and 2.

ENSURING BUDGETARY DISCIPLINE IN STAGE THREE OF EMU

18. The treaty imposes on member states in Stage Three of EMU an obligation to avoid excessive deficits. (Reuters note: a footnote to the conclusions says Britain is exempt from this obligation unless it decides to join EMU). Sound government finances ... are an essential condition for sustainable and non-inflationary growth and a high level of employment.

19. To that end, the Council (of finance ministers) proposes to adopt regulations on the strengthening of surveillance and budgetary discipline and on speeding up and clarifying the excessive deficit procedure. These regulations, combined with a European Council Resolution, will constitute a stability and growth pact. The resolution would enshrine the solemn political commitment of the Commission, the Council and the member states to the strict and timely application of the pact. The surveillance procedure and the excessive deficit procedure (except, in particular, sanctions) will be common to all member states. Euro area member states will be obliged to submit stability programmes and will be subject to agreed sanctions for failure to act effectively on excessive deficits. In the surveillance procedure, the other member states

will be obliged to submit convergence programmes only. In the excessive deficit procedure, sanctions cannot be applied to them... .

21. Each member state will commit itself to aim for a medium-term budgetary position of close to balance or in surplus ... .

22. Member states adopting the euro will be required by secondary legislation to present stability programmes, which will specify their medium-term budgetary objectives, together with an adjustment path for the government surplus or deficit ratio and the expected path for the government debt ratio. Furthermore, the programmes will contain the main assumptions about economic developments as well as a sensitivity analysis of the deficit and debt position and explain what is being done to achieve the objective.

23. A separate legislative proposal will be forthcoming from the Commission which will provide for the submission of convergence programmes by the non-euro area member states. The information they will contain, as far as budgetary policy is concerned, will be similar to that of the stability programmes.

24. ... Stability and convergence programmes will be multiannual and will be updated annually ... Member states will make their stability and convergence programmes public.

EARLY WARNING SYSTEM, MONITORING AND SURVEILLANCE

25. The Commission and the Council will study these ... programmes and monitor member states' budgetary performances ... with a view to giving early warning of any significant deterioration which might lead to an excessive deficit. In such cases, the Council will address recommendations to the member state concerned.

EXCESSIVE DEFICIT PROCEDURE

26. Adherence to the objective of sound budgetary positions ... will allow a member state to deal with normal cyclical fluctuations while keeping its government deficit within the three per cent reference value. Nevertheless, to deter excessive deficits and to ensure that, should they occur, they are promptly eliminated, there is a need for detailed provisions for the implementation of the excessive deficit procedure. A Council Regulation will provide for expedit-

ing and clarifying the procedure, in particular by establishing clear definitions and setting deadlines for the various steps. Once it has decided that an excessive deficit persists, and as long as a member state has failed to comply with a decision under Treaty Article 104c(9), the Council will ... impose sanctions on a prescribed scale. The European Council Resolution described in paragraph 37 will provide political guidance on how this procedure can be operated efficiently and speedily.

27. An excess of a government deficit over the three per cent reference value shall be considered exceptional when resulting from an unusual event outside the control of the relevant member state and which has a major impact on the financial position of general government, or when resulting from a severe economic downturn.

28. The Commission will be invited to commit itself in the European Council Resolution (see paragraph 37) to prepare a report whenever the actual or planned government deficit exceeds the three per cent reference value, thereby triggering the procedure under Article 104c(3). The Commission, when preparing such a report, will consider, as a rule, an excess over the reference value resulting from an economic downturn to be exceptional only if there is an annual fall of real GDP of at least two per cent.

29. The Economic and Financial Committee will formulate an opinion on the Commission report within two weeks. The Commission, taking fully into account this opinion and if it considers that an excessive deficit exists, will address an opinion and a recommendation to the Council for a decision. In the event that the Commision considers that a deficit is not excessive, the Commission will be invited to commit itself in the European Council Resolution to present in writing to the Council the reasons for its position. This would give the Council the opportunity to discuss the issue taking account of both the Commission's position and the opinion of the Economic and Financial Committee. The Council could decide, by simple majority, to request the Commission under Article 109d to make a recommendation. The Commission will be invited to commit itself in the European Council Resolution to issue, as a rule, such a recommendation, in response to the Council request.

30. The Council when deciding, according to Article 104c(6) on a Commission recommendation, whether an excessive deficit exists, will in its overall assessment take into account any observations made by the member state showing that an annual fall of real GDP of less than two per cent is nevertheless exceptional in the light of further supporting evidence, in particular

on the abruptness of the downturn or on the accumulated loss of output relative to past trends.

31. Where it decides that an excessive deficit exists, the Council will, at the same time, make recommendations to the Member State concerned 'with a view to bringing that situation to an end within a given period' (Article 104c (7)). These recommendations will accordingly set clear deadlines for: 1) the taking of effective action (within four months), and; 2) the correction of the excessive deficit, which should be completed in the year following its identification unless special circumstances are given. The Council's initial judgement on whether effective action has been taken will be based on publicly-announced decisions of the Government.

32. If a Member State fails to act in compliance with the successive decisions of the Council under paragraphs seven to nine of Article 104c, the Council will, in accordance with paragraph 11 of that Article, impose sanctions including a non-interest bearing deposit. These sanctions would be imposed within ten months of the reporting of the figures notifying the existence of an excessive deficit. An expedited procedure will be used in the case of a deliberately planned deficit which the Council decides is excessive.

33. The excessive deficit procedure will be held in abeyance if a Member State does in fact adopt, through formal government decision, appropriate action in response to a recommendation under Article 104c (7) or a notice issued under article 104c (9). The Commission and Council will monitor the progress of the Member State continuously until the Council decides under 104c (12) that the excessive deficit has been corrected. If the action is not being implemented, or is proving to be inadequate, the procedure will resume immediately. This would lead to sanctions being imposed in accordance with Article 104c (11) within three months of the procedure's resumption.

34. If actual data demonstrate that an excessive deficit has not been corrected within the time limit specified either in the Recommendation under Article 104c (7) or the notice issued under Article 104c (9), the Council will immediately resume the excessive deficit procedure.

STRUCTURE AND SCALE OF SANCTIONS

35. Whenever sanctions are first imposed, a non-interest-bearing deposit should be included. This should be converted into a fine after two years if the

deficit of the government concerned continues to be excessive. When the excessive deficit results from non-compliance with the government deficit reference value, the amount of the deposit or fine will be made up of a fixed component equal to 0.2 per cent of GDP, and a variable component equal to one tenth of the excess of the deficit over the reference value of three per cent of GDP. There will be an upper limit of 0.5 per cent of GDP for the annual amount of deposits. The amount of the sanction will be based on outcomes for the year in which the excessive deficit occurred.

36. Further consideration is being given to the disposition of the interest on deposits and the proceeds of the fines on the proviso that there would be no increase in Community spending.

EUROPEAN COUNCIL RESOLUTION ON THE STABILITY AND GROWTH PACT

37. When using the leeway which secondary legislation necessarily must leave to them, the Council and the Commission may receive guidance from the European Council, through, for example, a European Council Resolution. Such a resolution would give strong political guidance to the Commission, the Council and the member states on the implementation of the procedures. The resolution would invite all parties to implement the treaty and the stability and growth pact regulations strictly. The Commission should express a clear commitment to that effect, which would include an undertaking to prepare a report on the budgetary situation in a country whenever there is a risk of an excessive deficit or the planned or actual government deficit exceeds the reference value.

The Council would be invited to take the decisions necessary for carrying the procedure forward as quickly as practicable. If the Council did not act on a Commission recommendation at any stage in the procedure, the resolution would invite the Council always to state in writing the reasons which justify its decision not to act and to make public the votes cast by each member state. The resolution would also cover political agreements on the implementation of the stability and growth pact. In particular, the resolution would invite the Council always to decide to impose sanctions if a participating member state fails to take the necessary steps to bring the excessive deficit situation to an end as recommended by the Council.

The resolution will contain an undertaking by the member states not to invoke the benefit of the provision in paragraph 30 unless they are in severe recession. In evaluating whether the economic downturn is severe, the member states will as a rule take as a reference-point an annual fall in real GDP of at least 0.75 per cent.

The recitals of the Council regulation would make an explicit reference to the resolution.

Appendix 5: Extracts from the European Monetary Institute's report Progress towards Convergence 1996

Source: ISBN 92–9166–011–6, pp II-XI

EXECUTIVE SUMMARY

... The Report examines both the achievement of a high degree of sustainable convergence and deals with the statutory requirements to be fulfilled for national central banks (NCBs) to become an integral part of the ESCB, with particular emphasis on central bank independence. Overall, the Report concludes that at present a majority of Member States do not fulfil the necessary conditions for the adoption of a single currency ... the present Report highlights the degree of convergence currently achieved ... this year's procedure can by no means pre-empt the assessment to be made in early 1998.

1 Convergence

1.1 Approach taken

... A number of guiding principles are used by the EMI for the application of the convergence criteria ... . 'First, the individual criteria are interpreted and applied in a strict manner. The rationale ... is that the main purpose of the criteria is to ensure that only those Member States which have economic conditions that are conducive to the maintenance of price stability and the viability of the European currency area should participate in it. Second, the convergence criteria constitute a coherent and integrated package and they must all be satisfied; the Treaty lists the criteria on an equal footing and does not suggest a hierarchy. Third, the convergence criteria have to be met on the basis of current data. Fourth, the application of the convergence criteria should be consistent, transparent and simple.'

It is also stressed that compliance with the convergence criteria is essential, not only at a specific point in time, but also on a sustained basis ... .

... Regarding the Treaty provision of membership of the ERM, there is a strong majority position within the EMI Council that the requirement of ERM membership applies. A minority takes the view that exchange rate stability based on sustainable underlying economic fundamentals is more important than the institutional setting within which stability is achieved.

1.2 The state of convergence

... progress in fiscal consolidation has generally been too slow. Most countries have not yet achieved a situation which, in a broader view, might be judged as sustainable in the medium term ... it is emphasised that the improvement of the deficit by measures with a one-off effect does not ensure sustainable consolidation and great attention will have to be paid to the substance and not only to the accounting methods used in measuring both deficits and debts; that consolidation efforts need to be all the more resolute, the higher the initial stock of debt; and that sustainable fiscal consolidation will have to cope with two challenges: first, high and persistent unemployment and, second, those arising from demographic trends.

The criterion on price stability

Over the twelve-month reference period to the end of September 1996, the three best-performing countries in terms of the criterion on price stability were Finland, the Netherlands and Germany ... . These rates have been used to calculate the reference value of 2.6 per cent. Overall ... Belgium, Denmark, Germany, France, Ireland, Luxembourg, the Netherlands, Austria, Finland and Sweden had inflation rates of below the reference value ... crucial elements are that Member States conduct a monetary policy which is strictly geared towards price stability and thereby also conducive to stable exchange rates, that growth in unit labour costs is kept subdued and where necessary reduced, and that fiscal deficits are further reduced.

The criterion on the government budgetary position

... all Member States except Denmark, Ireland and Luxembourg are currently the subject of an EU Council decision that an excessive deficit exists ... . Although debt ratios clearly exceed 60 per cent of GDP also in Denmark and Ireland, account has been taken in the procedure of the progress made in these two countries in reducing the debt ratio.

... For 1996, the most recent Commission data indicate that four countries might have deficit ratios of below three per cent (Denmark, Ireland, Luxembourg and the Netherlands). All other Member States project reductions, which in some cases could be seen as considerable, with the exception of Germany, where a further rise in the deficit ratio is expected.

As regards government debt, in 1995 out of the ten countries with a debt ratio above the reference value of 60 per cent of GDP, only Ireland and Denmark achieved a major reduction, while Belgium, Italy and Sweden also registered some decline. The Commission forecasts for 1996 are that debt reduction in these Member States will continue, albeit at different paces ... the debt ratio is projected to fall slightly in Greece, the Netherlands and Portugal. In contrast, debt ratios are forecast to rise in Germany, Spain, Austria and Finland. In Germany and Finland the debt ratio is expected to exceed the 60 per cent reference value. Three Member States (France, Luxembourg and the United Kingdom) are expected to maintain a debt ratio of below the 60 per cent reference value.

Progress in fiscal consolidation has generally been too slow ... the latest projections for 1996 suggest that further progress has been made ... . However, it is also apparent that this adjustment path needs to be taken further in most countries in a sustainable manner ... the EMI welcomes the undertaking made by all Member States to formalise their sustained efforts towards consolidation in the form of a 'Stability Pact'. Such a pact cannot be a substitute for convincing fiscal consolidation prior to monetary union.

The criterion on exchange rate behaviour

... More recent developments, even though partly related to market expectations about EMU participation, can be seen as an indication of progress in the right direction. To the extent that exchange rates reflect markets' perceptions of overall macroeconomic convergence, this is to be regarded as a positive signal. A consideration of levels of real exchange rates also suggests that recent trends indicate a move towards a more sustainable exchange rate pattern ... .

The interest rate criterion

Over the reference period (October 1995 to September 1996) ten-year government bond yields in the three best-performing countries in terms of price stability ranged between 6.3 per cent and 7.4 per cent. These rates have been used to calculate the reference value of 8.7 per cent.

Eleven countries had rates below the reference value ... . In countries whose rates remain above the reference value, namely Spain, Greece, Italy and Portugal ... differentials still remain wide, which indicates that progress towards overall convergence needs to be strengthened. However, more recently, a general acceleration of the convergence of long-term interest rates has been observed ... .

Other factors

... unit labour costs and other price indices do not provide grounds for reconsidering the judgements regarding the performance of Member States in terms of the price stability criterion; no major current account imbalances are discernible; and progress has been made in terms of the integration of markets. With regard to the integration of markets, indirect taxation and capital income taxation are of particular importance, and there are considerable differences between Member States. Furthermore, while the overall private ECU market contracted further, ECU exchange and interest rate developments since the first quarter of 1996 suggest a decrease in tensions and uncertainties.

1.3 The agenda ahead for adopting the single currency

Confirmation of participating Member States in early 1998

The start of Stage Three of Economic and Monetary Union on 1 January 1999 does not require a majority of the Member States to fulfil the necessary conditions. Rather, in early 1998, the Council ... shall confirm which Member States fulfil the necessary conditions ... . The assessment will be made on the basis of actual data which for public finances will cover the outcome in 1997. At the same time, the essential requirement of achieving a high degree of sustainable convergence has to be fulfilled ... . Decisive and sustained corrective policies of a structural nature are needed in most countries ... . High and persistent unemployment and demographic trends add to this burden ... it is evident that the challenges posed to fiscal policies neither originate from the Maastricht Treaty nor will they ultimately be resolved merely by budgetary improvements over the short term ... . Finally, there is a need to complement such policies by measures which enhance the functioning of market mechanisms, particularly in the labour market ... .

2 Statutory requirements to be fulfilled for NCBs to become an integral part of the ESCB

2.1 Central bank independence

The principle of central bank independence has been elaborated in particular in Article 107 of the Treaty and Article 14.2 of the (ECB) Statute ... . From these Articles, the EMI has deduced that the following features of central bank independence apply to ESCB-related tasks.

As regards institutional independence, the EMI is of the opinion that rights of third parties (eg. government and parliament) to:

— give instructions to NCBs or their decision-making bodies;

— approve, suspend, annul or defer decisions of NCBs;

— censor an NCB's decisions on legal grounds;

— participate in the decision-making bodies of an NCB with a right to vote; or

— be consulted (ex ante) on an NCB's decisions

are incompatible with the Treaty and/or the Statute and, thus, require adaptation.

With respect to personal independence, the EMI is of the opinion that the statutes of NCBs should ensure that:

— governors of NCBs have a minimum term of office of five years;

— a governor of an NCB may not be dismissed for reasons other than those mentioned in Article 14.2 of the Statute (i.e. if he/she no longer fulfils the conditions required for the performance of his/her duties or if he/she has been guilty of serious misconduct);

— other members of the decision-making bodies of NCBs involved in the performance of ESCB-related tasks have the same security of tenure as governors;

— no conflicts of interest will arise between the duties of members of the decision-making bodies of NCBs vis-à-vis their respective NCB (and, additionally, of governors vis-à-vis the ECB) and other functions which members of the decision-making bodies involved in the performance of ESCB-related tasks may perform and which may jeopardise their personal independence ... .

2.2 Integration of NCBs in the ESCB

The full participation of NCBs in the ESCB will necessitate measures in addition to those designed to ensure independence ... . The main areas of attention are those where statutory provisions may form an obstacle to an NCB complying with the requirements of the ESCB or to a governor fulfilling his/her duties as a member of the Governing Council of the ECB, or where statutory provisions do not respect the prerogatives of the ECB.

2.3 Developments since late 1995

In the period between publication of the 1995 Convergence Report and the present Report considerable attention has been paid in the Member States to the need to adapt the statutes of their respective NCBs in order to comply with Treaty and Statute requirements ... . However, the statutes of most NCBs require further adaptations.

Appendix 6: German rulings on EMU

1. THE BUNDESTAG RESOLUTION

Following are excerpts, translated by Reuters, from a resolution passed by the Bundestag, the lower house of the German parliament, in conjunction with its ratification of the Maastricht Treaty on December 2, 1992:

- The German Bundestag welcomes the fact that the creation of an economic and monetary union within the framework of the European Union is planned as a community of stability.

- The German Bundestag takes seriously popular concerns about the introduction of a common European currency. Everything must therefore be done to make these worries baseless. The stability of the currency must be guaranteed in all circumstances.

- The stability criteria must be interpreted narrowly and strictly during the transition to the third phase of the economic and monetary union. The decision to move to the third phase can only be made on the basis of proven stability, of concurrence in fundamental economic data and the proven long-term stability in budget and finance policies of the participating member states.

- The German Bundestag will oppose every attempt to soften the stability criteria agreed in Maastricht. It will ensure the transition to the third phase of the economic and monetary union is strictly oriented to these criteria. The transition to the third phase of the economic and monetary union also requires an assessment by the German Bundestag.

2. THE CONSTITUTIONAL COURT RULING

Following are excerpts, translated by Reuters, from the Federal Constitutional Court's ruling on October 12, 1993 in which it rejects a case against German ratification of the Maastricht Treaty based on the argument that the treaty robs Germany of its national sovereignty:

- The principle of democracy does not prevent Germany joining a supranationally organised community of states. But a precondition of membership is a guarantee that legitimation and influence by the people are secured within the association of states.

- If an association of democratic states takes on sovereign tasks and exercises sovereign powers, it is principally the peoples of the member states who must legitimise this through their national parliaments. Thus democratic legitimacy ensues from the linking of the actions of European organs back to the parliaments of member states. In addition, and increasingly as European nations grow together, democratic legitimacy is conveyed by the European Parliament elected by the citizens of member states.

- It is of decisive importance that the democratic basis of (European) Union should keep pace with integration and that a vital democracy should be maintained as the integration of member states continues.

- If, as is currently the case, the peoples convey democratic legitimacy through their national parliaments, then the democratic principle sets limits on the expansion of the tasks and powers of the European Communities. The German Bundestag must retain tasks and powers of substantial weight.

- The Federal Constitutional Court will consider whether legal acts carried out by European institutions and organs remain within the sovereign rights accorded them or whether they go beyond them.

- In interpreting principles of empowerment through institutions and organs of the (European) Communities, it must be borne in mind that the Union treaty makes a fundamental distinction between the exercise of a limited sovereign right and a change in the treaty. Thus the interpretation (of the treaty) may not have the effect of an expansion of the treaty; such an interpretation of principles of empowerment would not have any binding effect for Germany.

- The Union treaty founds an association of states with the goal of an ever-closer Union of European peoples organised as states, and not a (single) state based on a European people.

- Article F Paragraph 3 of the treaty on European Union does not empower the Union to take for itself the financial or other means which it considers necessary for the fulfilment of its aims.

- With ratification of the Union treaty, Germany is not subordinating itself to an unclear and automatic mechanism towards currency union which it cannot steer. The treaty opens the way to a further, step-by-step integration of the European community of law which depends at every further step either on conditions which the parliament can now foresee or on further approval by the federal government, subject to influence from parliament.

Appendix 7: A guide to finding market information on EMU

Market expectations on EMU can be gauged by comparing the differences between instruments reflecting European currency interest rates in post-EMU years. The closer such rates are to each other, and specifically to the benchmark German market, the more the market prices in a single currency for those countries.

To find the following data on Reuters Terminals, key in the code and hit ENTER (unless otherwise specified).

For specific futures contracts, type the main code, eg FED, followed by a letter denoting the expiry month — H is March, M is June, U is September and Z is December — then the last number of the year. These futures reflect market expectations of three-month interest rates from a set date. For instance, FEDH9 shows prices for three-month mark deposit rates as of contract expiry in March 1999, just after the planned start of EMU. To calculate the implied rate, subtract the price from 100. Thus, a futures price of 95.00 would imply three-month rates of five per cent at contract expiry.

Currency and interest rate swaps SWAP/1
Additional swaps information SWAP/2
EMS currency swaps . . . . EMS1IRS=TRDL
Forward rate agreements FRA/1
All interest rate futures information FUT/IR1
LIFFE Euromark interest rate futures . . . . FED: (then F3)
French franc PIBOR futures . . . . PIB: (then F3)
LIFFE Eurolira interest rates . . . . FEL: (then F3)

General information on futures rates. . . . . FUTURES
Reuters latest polls on EMU expectations EMUPOLL1
Latest news on EMU. . . . . EMU (then F9)

Glossary – EU and market terms

BTP Buoni del Tesoro Poliennali. Italian fixed rate Treasury bonds with varying maturities from five to 30 years. Most of the liquidity is concentrated in the 10-year maturity. Coupons are paid semi-annually.

BIS Bank for International Settlements. A Basle, Switzerland-based institution to promote the cooperation of central banks to provide supplementary facilities for international financial operations. Established in 1930.

Balance of payments Record of one country's net transactions with the rest of the world over a given period, including trade, services, capital movements and unilateral transfers.

Basis point One one-hundredth of a percentage point.

Bear A market player who believes prices will fall and would therefore sell a financial instrument with a view to repurchasing it at a lower price. Opposite to a Bull.

Bond A security under which the issuer contracts to repay the lender a principal amount at a stated date in the future. With the exception of zero-coupon bonds, which are sold at a large discount to their value at maturity, bonds will pay a series of interest payments.

Bonos Spanish government bonds.

Bull A market player who believes prices will rise and would therefore buy a financial instrument with a view to selling it at a higher pirce. Opposite to a Bear.

Bunds (Bundesanleihen) Federal government bonds issued with maturities of up to 30 years (30-year issued beginning 1994). The 10-year Bund is, however, the benchmark for German and European bond markets.

Bretton Woods An agreement signed by 44 nations in 1944 at Bretton Woods, New Hampshire, to effect a post-War international monetary system. From this came the creation of the International Monetary Fund and the World Bank (International Bank for Reconstruction and Development). The system was based on fixed exchange rates, combined with termporary financing facilities to overcome crises. In 1971, the dollar ceased to be convertible into gold and that element of the Bretton Woods system was superseded by an era of floating currencies.

Capital Controls Controls to restrict or completely bar the movement of capital outside a country. Impending capital controls imposed by governmental regulatory authorities can cause investors and fund managers to extract money from one country and send it to another.

Clearing Bank Member bank of a national cheque clearing system. To clear a cheque means to process it through the clearing system so that the payee receives its value.

Commission, European The executive body of the European Union, appointed by national governments, although not to represent them. Also initiates legislation by proposals and recommendations to the Council.

Community, European A previous name for what is now called the European Union (EU), which numbers 15 states. It was originally set up as the European Economic Community under the Treaty of Rome in 1957.

Council The European Council of Ministers, drawn from and representing all EC member states. In conjunction with the European Parliament, which must be consulted on some actions and has powers of veto on others, the Community's law and decision-making body. Acts by unanimity on certain matters, but by qualified (weighted) majority on others.

Convergence The process by which an economic indicator or a market instrument moves towards the level or value of another indicator or instrument. In yield convergence, this means the difference, or spread, between yields narrows. See **De-convergence**.

Convergence trade A trade, frequently made in the bond market, which is undertaken on the view that yields between two debt instruments will converge. Typically, the investor would buy a higher yielding bond and sell a lower yielding bond, taking the position that the yield-differential will shrink whether the overall direction of bond markets is rising or falling.

Core A term applied to countries or currencies which are perceived to be at the centre of the move towards EMU, either politically or economically. Germany has always been included in this group, along with countries such as the Netherlands and Belgium.

Cross trading Trade in two currencies, neither of which is the US dollar.

DTB Deutsche Terminboerse. A German futures and options exchange, based in Frankfurt. It was the first fully electronic exchange to be introduced in Germany.

De-convergence The opposite of convergence. The process by which economic performance or market prices move further apart. See **Convergence**.

Depreciation The decline of a currency or asset in market-trading. A large depreciation, when made against the efforts of a national authority, is sometimes referred to as an effective devaluation.

Derivatives Instruments which derive their value from an underlying market.

Derogation A term which indicates one state is accepted to be unable or unwilling to carry out provisions in an EU matter which another or other states are obliged to carry out.

Devaluation Formal downward adjustment of a currency's official par value or central exchange rate. See **Revaluation**.

ECB The European Central Bank to be set up in Stage Three of the EMU process under the Maastricht Treaty of 1992.

ECOFIN The Council when meeting as economics or finance ministers.

Ecu The European currency unit (Ecu) is a composite currency based on a basket, with each nation's currency weighted according to each country's share in intra-European Union trade, its percentage share of EU gross national product and the relative importance of each country's foreign exchange reserves.EMI. European Monetary Institute. The precursor to the European Central Bank. Located in Frankfurt, it came into existence in January 1994. One of its main tasks is to deal with the practical details of a future European single currency.

EMU Economic and monetary union in Europe.

ERM Exchange Rate Mechanism. A system aimed at limiting movements between some currencies in the European Union. Prior to August 1993, most member currencies were allowed to move by no more than 2.25 per cent, either side of a fixed bilateral central rate against other member currencies. However, a few currencies were allowed to fluctuate by six per cent either side of the central parities. In August 1993, following turmoil on the foreign exchange markets, member currencies were allowed to move by 15 per cent either side of their central rates. The German mark and the Dutch guilder retained a bilateral agreement for a 2.25 per cent band.

ERM II A planned currency grid similar to the ERM, designed to link currencies within EMU to other EU units that are not part of the single currency.

EMS The European Monetary System, which began in 1979, is a system among the member states of the European Union. The chief components are the European currency unit (Ecu) and the ERM. All EU nations are members of the EMS but they do not all belong to the ERM. ERM members can, in times of currency upheaval, leave and then later rejoin the ERM. The EMS was preceded by the Snake. See **Snake**.

ESCB The European System of Central Banks to be set up in Stage Three of EMU. Unlike the ECB, will have no legal identity.

Euro Official name for the future European single currency. The name was agreed at the Madrid Summit in December 1995.

Eurobonds Not to be confused with euro-denominated bonds. Eurobonds are issued in a specific currency outside the currency's domicile. They are not subject to withholding tax and fall outside the jurisdiction of any one country. The Eurobond market is based in London.

European Council The Summit meeting of EC heads of state and government and the president of the Commission. Acts by 'common accord' but has no formal law-making power.

European Union The umbrella term introduced in the Maastricht Treaty to refer to the three-pillar construction in Europe, embracing the Community and two new areas of cooperation – common foreign and security policy and justice and home affairs. Now taking over in common usage to refer to the Community in all its aspects. See **Commission** and **Community**.

Exotics Refers to non-major currencies, which are frequently less liquid than the main units. Many Asian, eastern European and Latin American currencies are often termed exotic currencies.

Forward A contract to buy or sell a security at an agreed price with delivery in the future. It is similar in structure to an exchange-listed **futures** contract.

Fiscal policy Means by which a government influences the economy through its budget, by changes in tax and welfare payments and/or government spending.

Franc fort Literally 'strong franc', this is a term applied both at official and market levels to describe the French government's commitment to a stable currency relationship with the German mark. The pun on Frankfurt is intentional.

Futures Exchange-traded contracts which are firm agreements to deliver or take delivery of a standardised amount of an underlying financial instrument or commodity at a predetermined price. Futures exist in currencies, money market deposits, bonds, shares and commodities. Futures which are for cash settlement only do not take delivery of an underlying instrument. Rather, the investor receives the equivalent value in cash.

G3 The Group of Three. The world's leading three economies, comprising the United States, Germany and Japan.

G7 The Group of Seven industrialised economies. The world's top seven economies, frequently referred to as the world's seven richest nations. It comprises the United States, Germany, Japan, Britain, Canada, France and Italy. It provides a forum for member nations to coordinate monetary and fiscal policies, to form a more stable world economic system.

GDP Gross Domestic Product: a measure of total national output of goods and sevices, valued at market prices. Equivalent to national income arising in the domestic economy. It forms the core part of a country's Gross National Product (GNP).

Gilts British gilt-edged securities. Issued by the British Treasury and sold through the Bank of England. This is one of the oldest government debt markets in the world.

IGC Inter-governmental Conference. A forum for European Union members to decide regional matters.

ISD Investment Services Directive. An EU directive which took effect in 1996 and aims to allow brokers and bourses to operate throughout the EU with virtually the same freedom enjoyed in home markets.

IT Information Technology. A blanket term which refers to various computer and technical issues.

Intervention The market participation of a central bank to influence monetary conditions. It often takes the form of a central bank, either unilaterally or in concert with others, buying or selling a currency to boost or depreciate its value.

LIBOR and LIBID London Interbank Offered Rates and London Interbank Bid Rates. These are the benchmark short-term interest rates in the London money markets.

LIFFE The London International Financial Futures and Options Exchange. Opened in 1982, it is the market for major European futures and options contracts on bonds, short-term interest rates and equities.

Liquidity The depth of the market and its ability to absorb sudden shifts in supply and demand without price distortions.

MATIF Marche a Terme International de France. The Paris financial futures and options exchange opened in 1986. Contracts include futures on three-month French interest rates and the 'notionnel' futures on French government bonds. It also lists contracts on Ecu instruments.

Minimum reserve requirements Funds which banks in a country are required to deposit, often with little or no interest, with a central bank.

Monetary policy An authority's policy on regulating the availability of credit in the economy of a country or region. This incorporates decisions on interest rate, money supply and exchange rate levels.

Money market A wholesale market for the buying and selling of money. Money market paper is predominantly negotiable and traded just like any other product. The market is international as opposed to earlier, insular domestic centres.

Money supply The total stock of money in an economy, according to various definitions, known as M0, M1, M2, M3, M4 and M5. M0 represents the most narrow definition of money. In most cases, it consists solely of notes and coins.

Munis Municipal bonds or notes issued by state and local governments and agencies.

OATs Obligations Assimilables du Tresor. Treasury bonds issued in France with maturities ranging from seven to 30 years, with fixed or floating interest rates. Since 1989, OATs have also been issued in Ecu.

OTC Over the Counter. In financial markets, this refers to agreements or contracts which are not made on an exchange but are made directly between the parties concerned.

Peripheral Countries perceived to be on the periphery of the move towards EMU, either in economic or political terms. The term also can refer to the geographical location of countries in western Europe, and frequently refers to both ideas. Sweden, Italy, Spain, Portugal, whose government bonds are often lumped together as 'high yielders', traditionally have been considered peripheral markets. Opposite of **Core**.

Overweight Holding more assets in a particular category of investment than the proportion set by a standard market index.

PIBOR Paris Interbank Offered Rates. Benchmark French interest rates. The PIBOR contract on the Matif is the futures contract for three-month French interest rates.

Plain vanilla Refers to straight options contracts, which do not include special clauses.

Primary surplus A budget surplus which does not take into account debt servicing costs.

Real economy Refers to the activity in goods and services as opposed to concepts such as money supply and price movements.

Real interest rates An interest rate which takes account of the domestic rate of inflation. It is usually calculated by subtracting the annual rate of consumer price growth from the overall interest rate.

Repo agreement A repo, or repurchase agreement, is an operation consisting of two transactions but treated as one. In the first transaction a dealer sells securities to an investor and in return the investor provides funds to the dealer. The securities from the dealer represent collateral for the loan of the funds. In the second transaction, the dealer repurchases the securities and repays the loan.

Repo rate A simple interest rate calculation to determine how much interest is to be added onto a repo transaction. See **Repo agreement**.

Reserves Official gold and foreign exchange reserves. These are kept to ensure that a government can meet current and near-term claims. They are listed as an asset in a country's balance of payments.

Reserve currency A currency which is internationally accepted and is used by central banks to meet their financial commitments.

Retail Primarily an 'end-user' or commercial market, as opposed to a wholesale market which is for large-scale transactions between institutions. In banking, retail would refer to transactions on behalf of individual accounts.

Revaluation A formal upward adjustment of a currency's official par value or central exchange rate. Opposite of **Devaluation**.

Safe haven Refers to a market or currency to which investors resort during times of political or economic turmoil.

Single market The single European market in goods, services, labour and capital, to be completed in accordance with the Single European Act 1986, which initiated the '1992' programme of EC legislation.

Snake Preceded the European Monetary System. The aim was for member nations' currencies (including non European Community countries) to move together like a snake within a tunnel, when matched against an outside currency like the US dollar. See **EMS**.

Spread The difference between two financial instruments, either in price or yield. See entries **Convergence** and **Convergence Trade**.

Stability pact An agreement, formally agreed in December 1996, where member countries of EMU will adhere to fiscal criteria. The accord includes measures for penalties to be applied when fiscal discipline is violated, but there are provisions for political judgement on whether special circumstances warrant an exemption.

Stage 3 The third and final stage of the Maastricht process of EMU, representing the full establishment of monetary union for states that participate. Due to start on 1 January 1999.

Swaps The exchange of one asset for another. Currency and interest rate swaps are contracts where one party agrees to exchange a stream of interest payments with another party. Often a stream of fixed payments is exchanged for floating payments.

Syndication The process of sharing risk and distribution responsibilities for a large transaction.

Synthetic Refers to a constructed transaction which offers the same market exposure as the instrument it is based on, e.g. a synthetic euro would be a group of currencies which offer the same exposure as the euro (in other words, the currencies that will make it up per their weightings).

TARGET The central settlement (Trans-European Automated Real-time Gross settlement Express Transfer) system to be set up in Stage Three to link national settlement systems operating in euros.

Volatility The amount by which a market or an instrument moves. In options markets, the term 'implied volatility' is a specific measure used for calculating option premiums.

Wholesale The market for large-scale transactions involving major financial institutions.

Yield Percentage return on an investment, usually at annual rate. Native yield calculations in different countries often vary substantially.

Index

References in italic indicate figures or tables